STEEL STRIKE

A case study in industrial relations

•

JEAN HARTLEY
JOHN KELLY
NIGEL NICHOLSON

BOWLING GREEN STATE UNIVERSITY
DISCARDED
LIBRARY

Batsford Academic and Educational Ltd
London

JEROME LIBRARY-BOWLING GREEN STATE UNIVERSITY

©Jean Hartley, John Kelly, Nigel Nicholson 1983
First published 1983

All rights reserved. No part of this publication
may be reproduced, in any form or by any means,
without permission from the Publisher

Typeset by Abettatype Ltd
Thornton Heath
and printed in Great Britain by
Billings Ltd
Worcester
for the publishers
Batsford Academic and Educational Ltd
4 Fitzhardinge Street
London W1H 0AH

ISBN 0 7134 4378 2

Contents

Preface

In December 1979 our preparations were complete for a proposed study of industrial relations in the nationalised steel industry. The research was to be an investigation of industrial relations 'climate' in a number of steelworks; intending to trace over time the developing pattern of management-union relations. For two years since the idea had first been raised, we had been involved in repeated meetings and discussions at the highest level of BSC's management and with the national steel unions, and over the period had carefully evolved the design of a study whose results would be of interest and value to the parties: ourselves, management and unions. The starting date was set for 2 January 1980, but instead what started on this date was the biggest strike in the history of the steel industry, and one of the longest in British industrial relations; a shutdown of the entire public sector industry for three months.

We were aware of the gathering storm some weeks before the onset of the strike, and could only regard it with feelings of helplessness and a fast-vanishing hope that the strike would be averted and our study survive. During the first week of the strike we ruefully assessed the situation. There would be little hope of doing a worthwhile study now, for even if the strike ended rapidly, what could we do that would provide useful information about union-management relations in the aftermath of the strike when the industry was facing vast cuts in capacity? One of us offered the wry comment: 'we should have planned a study of a strike'. At that point it was immediately apparent to us that here was an opportunity for which we were well equipped. We had explored and contributed to the literature on strikes. We had good relationships with and knowledge of the local steel industry. We had the time and resources to immerse ourselves pretty well full time in a study of the strike.

The next day we went to the local strike headquarters at Rotherham and amid the mêlée of pickets, organisers, press, well-wishers and representatives from other organisations, we managed to make contact with one of the local ISTC full-time officials. That was the first of many visits, through which we got to know the strike organisers and they us, and we established a climate of friendship, trust and credibility. It was consequently only a matter of days before we secured the acceptance of our presence as observers to the deliberations of the strike committee. It may be said that we did not figure prominently in their consciousness, having no material bearing upon what primarily concerned them: the prosecution of the strike. Our presence was non-threatening, perhaps sometimes mildly diverting as people to pass the time of day with, but generally irrelevant. Since we sat in unobtrusive positions in meetings and made no contribution to discussions, we rapidly came to feel accepted: taken-for-granted as the furniture and, as observers, as privileged as flies on the wall.

We are grateful for the trust that made this possible, and to which this book is a testament. It is our most sincere wish that any insights we have been able to glean from our observations are of value to the people who assisted us, by helping to explain and understand the events that took over their lives during the first three months of 1980, as well as contributing more generally to a scholarly appreciation of the complexities of strikes.

June 1982   J.H.
                                                                                                        J.K.
                                                                                                        N.N.

List of abbreviations

AUEW	Amalgamated Union of Engineering Workers
BSC	British Steel Corporation
CCC	Central Co-ordinating Committee
CNC	Central Negotiating Committee
CSEU	Confederation of Shipbuilding and Engineering Unions
DSC	Divisional Strike Committee
EC	Executive Council
GMWU	General and Municipal Workers' Union
ISTC	Iron and Steel Trades Confederation
JRC	Joint Representatives Committee
NCCC	National Craftsmen's Co-ordinating Committee
NUB	National Union of Blastfurnacemen
NUR	National Union of Railwaymen
RJC	Rotherham Joint Committee
RSC	Rotherham Strike Committee
SIMA	Steel Industry Management Association
TGWU	Transport and General Workers' Union
TUC	Trades Union Congress
URTU	United Road Transport Union

CHAPTER ONE

Strikes, unions and organisations

This is the story of a strike — the largest strike in post-war history — involving nearly 10,000 workers for a full three calendar months (with 8.8 million days lost, according to Department of Employment figures), and a strike that had a major influence on the future of the steel industry and the industrial relations of the period following it.

Such an event has profound implications from many points of view. Many of these could be seen at the time, reflected in the activities of the media as they analysed and interpreted to make sense of the unfolding pattern of events, and in so doing often tried simultaneously to influence them. What purpose can be served by returning to review the events of the strike now? It is not for the sake of historical completeness, for although in this book we follow a chronological narrative we make no attempt to achieve the historian's God's-eye view or to give a blow-by-blow account of all national and local events. Our view is more partial and particular, looking at the broad framework of events only to help make sense of what was happening in one centre of strike activity, South Yorkshire. Nor is our intent to review and revive the arguments that raged at the time, or to re-evaluate the might-have-beens and should-have-beens of contemporary debate. Our interest is to explain what happened through our having been able to scrutinise it at unusually close quarters, and help the more far-reaching implications of these explanations to emerge.

The contents of this book reflect our unique position as observers and our special interest as applied social scientists. Many academic writings about strikes are from a relatively remote perspective and concentrate on the interactions and bargaining moves of the parties to the dispute. This book belongs to the much rarer tradition of observational studies, where access has been secured to the centres of decision-making and action: in this case the strike committees of the most militant centre of union activity in the dispute. The long duration of the strike meant that our observations were no brief snapshot, but turned out to provide a detailed chronicle of how union structures, motives and actions evolved over time, and in response to certain pressures, events, and processes. As such then, this is a study of union behaviour, but in circumstances that were exceptional and novel for almost all the people concerned.

As in most large scale strikes, the participants were adjusting to the demands of new and unfamiliar roles and pressures, yet ones which any union members may find themselves facing when called to action.

Our orientation is an unusual one in industrial relations scholarship: that of social psychologists committed to transgressing disciplinary boundaries in order to secure a rounded and integrated analysis of social behaviour. Our psychological origins do mean that our recurrent points of reference are the thoughts, feelings and actions of individuals and groups. Throughout this book we shall try to understand people's actions by understanding how they made sense of or interpreted the world around them, yet at the same time we shall try to achieve broader perspectives, in which people's reactions are interpreted through their context of structures, roles, cultures, and changing events. In short, we aim to synthesise structure and agency.

Before we commence our account we shall set the scene, in two ways. First, the remainder of this chapter presents a brief overview of those academic writings which are relevant to our own efforts. These fall into three broad classes of social science writings: i) writings on strikes; their causes, content and effects; ii) the literature on union government and behaviour; and iii) a theoretical corpus on the design and functioning of complex organisations. It is the aim of the analysis we present here to contribute to all three of these literatures. Our second piece of scene-setting is in Chapter 2, which is devoted to giving a simple historical account of the causes of the strike, and the development of the socio-economic climate in which it was initiated.

An overview of the field I: the study of strikes

There is no single integrated body of knowledge about strikes, for in reality there are several literatures on the phenomena which differ a) in their social science orientation — econometric, labour history, sociological, psychological — and b) in their point of interest — causes, processes, and outcomes. We shall not attempt to survey this large literature comprehensively. This has been done elsewhere (Kelly and Nicholson, 1980), and here we shall just draw out some of the main themes.

We can divide the strike causation literature into four approaches focused respectively on organisational environments, industrial relations institutions, collective interests and group consciousness, and employee needs and attitudes. One problem shared by these approaches, despite their many useful insights, is the *meaning* of a strike cause, and the difficulty of determining causes in any given case. The UK Department of Employment's notion of a principal cause is appealing but simplistic since we know that in many strikes a variety of factors could have been categorised as principal causes, depending on how far back in time it is thought useful to dig (cf. Lane and Roberts, 1971; Warner and Low, 1947; Pope, 1942; Marsh, 1967). In some cases longstanding grievances have been categorised as causes; in others the most significant or unusual event immediately preceding the strike would seem to be a candidate; whilst in some cases it appears that the strikers' demands have been defined as principal causes. Some authors have attempted to circumvent potentially hazardous philosophical disputes on the meaning of causation by adopting a distinction between manifest and latent issues (Gouldner, 1954; Kornhauser, 1954; Merton, 1957). Whilst not rejecting the utility of the distinction, it seems to us that the emergence, instigation and progress of a strike is better captured by using a threefold distinction between underlying *issues,* strike *triggers,* and strike *demands.*

Much of the strikes literature has focused on strike causation and therefore leaves us with only a very hazy picture of strike processes: the organisation of the strike has been considered far less interesting than its causation and therefore has been very little studied. There are of course a considerable number of strike 'stories', or narratives which present a wealth of detail on the progress of strikes and their organisation. This detail however is often purely descriptive and partisan, with impressions and anecdotes (often very interesting) abounding in place of hard data and rigorous analysis (Arnison, 1970; Beck, 1974; Dromey and Taylor, 1978; Mathews, 1972). One of the central focuses of our own study — organisational structure and process — is often treated (where it appears) as a rather mundane process of administration and communication, and even though some of these studies have described divisions among the strikers these have not been systematically related to organisational structure and environment, and different modes of striker involvement. Pitt (1978) for instance described the economic and political background to the 1972 miners' strike, and in subsequent chapters outlined the operation of the strike headquarters, the flying pickets, the national negotiations, the effects on the economy and the details of the Enquiry which ended the strike.

A few analytical case studies have been published and it is to these we now turn, starting with the earliest work by Hiller (1928). This book, called simply *The Strike* remains to date one of the best attempts at a processual model of strikes. Hiller subdivided the strike into four broad phases, of mobilisation, preparation, maintenance and demobilisation. Strike maintenance was further subdivided into a set of social processes: maintenance of morale, control of strikebreakers, neutralisation of employer moves and manipulation of public opinion. These processes can also be conceptualised in terms of environments, with the first two constituting actions within the internal environment, and the latter within the external environment of the strike organisation. The possibility opened up by this formulation of a series of strike goals (or sub-goals) is that of conflict between them, and this in turn would present strike leaderships with problems of conflict management and resolution. In considering these issues (which did in fact emerge in the steel strike), the work of Batstone *et al* (1977, 1978) is particularly helpful. Their study of shop steward organisation and its relationship with rank and file trade unionists deployed three major concepts: role conceptions, vocabularies of persuasion, and social networks. Two major types of steward — 'leaders' and 'populists' — were distinguished in terms of their different role conceptions (representative vs.delegate), different vocabularies (trade union principles vs. sectional interests) and differing degrees of integration into the shop steward organisation. Whilst there are problems with the distinctions (cf. Willman, 1980), these ideas are crucial in focusing our attention on what we shall call frames of reference, or the beliefs and values which structure peoples' views and social actions. They also point to the potential significance of differing degrees of social integration of strike activists, an important aspect of the position of the picket marshal, as we shall see.

Gouldner's (1954) classic study of a wildcat strike is often used to illustrate the difference between manifest and latent issues, and to caution against the assumption that strikes are invariably rational disputes over tangible economic interests. Although Gouldner was primarily concerned with strike causation, his study is important for its highlighting of the role of mutual inter-group expectations in the maintenance of social order. Once management set out to break the 'indulgency pattern' of social relations, it reduced the degree of trust developed over a period of years and set in train a power struggle between union and management, and within the union. The role of expectations and trust in the maintenance of social order also emerged in the steel strike both in relations between strike leaders and pickets, and even more sharply in inter-union relations.

Lane and Roberts (1971) also illustrated the complex range of factors which resulted in the Pilkington's strike, and go further than most studies in the detail they provide on the daily operations of the Rank and File Strike Committee — organising pickets, addressing mass meetings, procuring finance — and on the internal division of labour which emerged after approximately five weeks of the strike, far more slowly than in the steel strike. The main strike committee was presented with an agenda and reports by the much smaller negotiating committee, whilst much of the regular daily business was the responsibility of another sub-committee. The study, in common with many others, also reveals the expressed concern of the strike leadership with striker unity and striker morale. Once again though this account offers interesting pointers and suggestions on organisational processes but falls short of a more rigorous analytical account.

Other case studies have also offered glimpses of organisational processes. Karsh (1958) underlines the significance of leadership in the definition of grievances and formulation of demands, particularly with an inexperienced, (and in this case non-unionised) workforce (see also Dromey and Taylor, 1978; Marsh, 1967). Other well-known cases (eg Warner and Low, 1947) are much better on the history of events leading up to the strike than on the dynamics of the strike *per se*.

The existing literature does therefore provide some pointers, and directs our attention to the frames of reference of the strikers, and the social integration of activists into the strike organisation. Beyond this the literature reinforces the importance of organisational structure and processes, and of striker morale, but provides little direct help on how to conceptualise and study these issues. For insights on these matters we must consider theories of organisations, but before doing so we continue within industrial relations by examining the literature on trade unions.

An overview of the field II: the study of unions

As in the literature of strikes there has been a number of highly contrasting approaches to the study of unions. First the rich drama of Britain's long history of trade unions has attracted the interest of many labour historians, concerned to trace the lineage of union traditions, working practices, structural arrangements, and bargaining goals (e.g. Flanders, 1970; Bain, 1970). There have also been more fine-grained examinations of the history of particular unions (e.g. Moran, 1964; Arnot, 1955).

Second, there have been studies of union structure and government in which the emphasis is upon the characteristics of institutional arrangements for policy making and collective action (e.g. Allen, 1954;

Roberts, 1956). These studies take a political science view in which the chief focus is on the formal mechanisms for election, representation and decision-making, rather than informal social process. In similar vein, the Oxford School of British industrial relations has portrayed union internal and external bargaining in formalistic terms as a process of rule-making (e.g. Clegg, 1976).

Third, are studies which have looked more particularly at specific roles and functions within unions, notably union leaders and full-time officers (Clegg *et al*, 1961), and shop stewards (Goodman and Whittingham, 1969). These are essentially descriptive surveys of the work that these officers do and how it reflects the changing pattern of industrial relations. The Donovan Royal Commission on Trade Unions and Employers' Associations was a watershed in this kind of analysis (1968).

Fourth, are behavioural studies of the informal process and functioning of unions, and it is into this tradition that the present study may be located. Behavioural studies have varied widely in scope and focus. Broadly aiming to analyse the nature of the democratic process in trade unions have been comparative case studies like those of Lipset *et al* (1956), Edelstein and Warner (1975), and Hemingway (1978). More focused case studies of individual unions and the relationship between membership opinion, representative action, and leadership behaviour were in vogue in the USA in the 1950s (e.g. Rosen and Rosen, 1955; Seidman *et al*, 1958; Tannenbaum and Kahn, 1958). A resurgence of interest in this approach, deploying more sophisticated theoretical and methodological analytical strategies, is represented in Britain by the recent work of Batstone *et al* (1977) and Nicholson *et al* (1981). The latter book may be referred to as a source of further information about studies of this kind, which it reviews at some length.

From all these treatments in the literature on unions a number of recurrent themes may be distilled. These centre on the problematic status and role of unions under capitalism, for they face a number of challenges in how they go about their internal management and external conduct which do not confront organisations of other types. This does not mean, however, that methods of analysing or theorising about other types of organisation are not applicable to trade unions or to strike organisations.

Broadly, the problems and challenges confronting them are twofold:

1. *Goal orientation.* In capitalist society unions are faced with contradictions thrown up by market forces and their interdependence with management. Where collective bargaining is 'freely' conducted

within a market framework, unions face the dilemma that their members' interests also have common ground with those of the employer, for example, to the extent that wages can be more easily raised when profits are high. Pursuing the economic interests of members to extremes may in practice prove self-destructive. This conflict is evident in the continual debate about wage restraint that has taken place in Britain in post-war years. At the level of the enterprise, this can be seen to extend to the problem of how far unions should seek to secure control of enterprise management, for again, it may be argued that the extreme development of union control in a capitalist economy implies taking over capitalist functions. This can be called the collaboration dilemma, a dilemma between the demands of pragmatism and idealism.

2. *Democracy.* Trade unions are political and ideological institutions in which democratic self-government is an article of faith and a structural imperative. Since the ultimate reference for union action is the interests of union members, the institutions of union government are designed to protect their rights to share in decision-making and the selection of leaders. On the other hand is the need for sufficient integration and unity of purpose to ensure that unions are strong enough to achieve the goals they pursue. In short, there is a need for leadership. The potential for conflict between leadership and democracy is a real one for all unions, driven by contrasting pressures. On the one side are those of oligarchy; the tendency for selective self-qualification for leadership roles, and for power to coalesce around informal elites, formal structures or bureaucratic processes. On the other side are those of participation: the legitimation of leadership by democratic process, the ideology of equal rights and membership sovereignty, and the moral imperative of the positive value of high levels of membership involvement. Following Hemingway (1978), this can be called the democracy dilemma, a dilemma between democracy as an end in itself and as only the means to other ends.

In the public sector the collaboration dilemma is complicated by State ownership or government interest in enterprise management. A common way in which this dilemma is resolved is for unions and management to see their cause as a common one against the policies of central government. The issue of who should have power to make decisions at the level of the enterprise is not, however, resolved by this means, only submerged. In the circumstances of the steel strike the collaboration dilemma was resolved in such general terms by the strikers seeing their common 'enemy' as senior executive management and the government. However, in particular terms the dilemma re-emerged in a number of problematic ways: for example, in relation to other unions, towards the private sector, in relations with the police, and in the granting of dispensations to help strike-bound plants. As our narrative unfolds, these dilemmas of goal orientation recur, and illustrate that even in the circumstances of a strike where the battle lines are firmly drawn, the objectives of union strategy remain fundamentally problematic.

However, this case study also has more to say about the democracy dilemma. Strikes demand increased cohesiveness and at the same time higher levels of membership involvement than in peace-time. The democracy dilemma is thus heightened in a strike, and the longer the strike continues the more problematic it becomes, for success depends upon continued high levels of membership commitment whilst economic and other pressures against continuation mount. All the while it is necessary for leadership to retain control over strategy and tactics for the sake of the power of unity, whilst maintaining the legitimacy of their position through the support of membership. The dilemma is apparent at all levels and historical stages of the steel strike, from the formation of local institutions to prosecute the strike through to the attempt by strike leaders to regulate and control the actions of strikers.

In short, our account aims to contribute to the literature on trade unions by showing how the dilemmas faced by unions in their day to day business are transformed during a strike, and how strike organisations' responses to these transformed dilemmas can evolve as strike issues develop over an extended time period.

An overview of the field III: the study of complex organisations

Unions are complex organisations, but have rarely been studied as such. That is, there have been few attempts to integrate the large literature on union government and action with the equally large literature on how complex organisations function (Mintzberg, 1979). The former literature is to be found within the disciplinary boundary that contains the field of 'Industrial Relations', the latter within the province of 'Management' and 'Organisational Behaviour'. The result has been the almost complete separation of work and ideas bearing on similar problems. Our approach in this book is to attempt to bridge this gap empirically and theoretically, on the premise that organisation theory is potentially superordinate to the ideas that have emerged from the study of unions and strikes. By this we mean that theory building in industrial relations would benefit from more communication with the theoretically rich literature on complex organisations, and that organisation theory would be enriched by encompassing the special problems and issues that emerge from the analysis of union organisations. In particular, the political-ideological foundation of union functioning and the problems of democracy and conflict present a challenge to the theories that have grown from research predominantly geared towards one particular cultural form: private sector business enterprises. This challenge is timely, for it is being increasingly recognised that the features we have identified with union behaviour are present and important in business organisations.

There is insufficient space here to attempt a comprehensive review of organisation theory. Instead, we shall look at two themes that are to be found with varying emphasis in the literature, and which bear upon our purpose here. That is, these are themes which are helpful in supplying frames of reference for the interpretation of the case material in the chapters that follow, and which we shall also use in the final chapter (Chapter 11) to provide an interpretive summary of the book.

Theme 1: Organisations are systems which must manage uncertainty
The classical theorists of organisation took a Weberian approach to them as complex bureaucracies whose functioning was rooted in their structure (see Pugh, 1971). Writings in this tradition were largely preoccupied with finding principles for the design of rules, routines, decisions and authority that would lead to efficient and effective goal attainment. The elusiveness of simple generalisations about this and growing awareness of the complexity of organisational functioning and informal social processes, has led to increasing abstraction and sophistication in functionalist theory.

A key concept in this development has been the notion of *system*. Modern analytical treatments, deriving from roots in the ideas of Weber, Durkheim and Parsons (1949) have used the systems concepts of inputs, outputs and transformation processes to link process with structure (e.g. Katz and Kahn, 1966; 1978), and deployed the notions of integration and differentiation to characterise how activity is co-ordinated and directed toward diverse goals and purposes (e.g. Burns and Stalker, 1961; Galbraith, 1973; March and Simon, 1958).

Systems concepts invite analogies with biological systems, adapting to their environments to stay alive. Systems analyses of organisations similarly use the notion of viability as the ultimate test of performance effectiveness (Beer, 1972). In order to succeed they must balance integration and differentiation by embodying various functions. These have been variously categorised around the following key processes:

Production: the basic transformation of energy and materials;

Maintenance: the servicing and replenishment of production processes;

Regulation:. the control of variability by application of rules and reinforcements;

Intelligence: the use of information to secure a representation of the organisation's environment;

Innovation: the generation of novel responses and adaptive strategies;

Leadership: the formulation of decisions about the deployment of all these processes.

This view of organisational effectiveness is based upon their construal as *open* systems, i.e. having to interact with and survive in an environment that is constantly changing in unpredictable ways. *Uncertainty* is the concept most used to characterise this challenge that faces organisations (Thompson, 1967), and the source of the challenge is twofold: uncertainty in the behaviour of the external environment with which the organisation must transact, and uncertainty in the behaviour of its internal environment, its membership. Viability and performance depend upon how well uncertainty is managed; whether through its being filtered out and neutralised, or by its being successfully predicted and manipulated (Lawrence and Lorsch, 1967).

Although unions engaged in strikes are fundamentally transient organisational forms, this kind of analysis can still be appropriate and insightful. Strikes, as in the present case, can be of long duration, and even in the short run they are frequently known to fail, i.e. crumble through their inability to control, neutralise, or accommodate the uncertainty and hostility of their external and internal environments.

Theme 2: Organisations are cultures which enact their environments
Functionalist theory has proved to be extremely useful for analysing the causes of success and failure in organisations, but has increasingly been criticised for its assumptions and deficiencies (Burrell and Morgan, 1979). Its mechanistic flavour, determinist presumptions, and rationalist portrayal of decisions and behaviour have been challenged by a quite different conception of organisation. This is that organisational behaviour is sustained through shared meanings, collective

definitions, and symbolic behaviours, i.e. organisations are unique cultures (Pettigrew, 1979). Symbols, languages, rituals, myths and mores are imported from wider cultures as well as created within the organisation, and the values and practices of the culture evolve 'organically' over the life-span of the organisation and its membership. More specifically, it has been asserted that organisations should be viewed as *political* cultures (Pfeffer, 1981), in which power relations constitute the structure and content of cultural forms and the transmission of ideologies and values is the process by which those forms are legitimated and sustained, or resisted and changed (Salaman, 1979). The concept of power is closely related to that of authority: indeed a number of writers have used power as an overarching category subsuming under its ambit the idea of authority as a legitimate right to issue instructions and expect compliance (Lukes, 1974; French and Raven, 1959). Where political disputes are conducted in terms of rights to make decisions, we shall use the term 'authority'; otherwise we shall speak of 'power'. This kind of treatment clearly offers considerable room for rapprochement between organisational theory and union research, where the analysis of the 'management of discontent' and other political processes has been well developed in recent years (Batstone *et al,* 1977 and 1978; Nicholson *et al,* 1981).

An important feature of this orientation is that it commits one to a more fluid and dynamic construction of organisational behaviour, focusing on informal processes as more revealing, explanatory and predictive than the formalities of structural design and role requirements. 'Theories of action' (Silverman, 1970) assert that the structures that constrain behaviour are the 'immanent' creations of human action. People's communications with one another are implicit negotiations, or exercises in persuasion and influence to forge agreements about how they will relate to one another in the future, and thus through practice and precedent is the social order continually formed and reformed (Strauss *et al,* 1963; Strauss, 1978). This view can be extended to organisations' external as well as internal transactions. The concept of 'enactment' has been used (Weick, 1969, 1979) to show how organisations do not just passively or reactively confront problems and issues 'delivered' to them by their circumstances, but play a significant role in their construction, by selective perception, definition and action. In decision-making rationalisation more often characterises organisational enactment than rationality. Rather than conforming to the prescribed ideals of problem-solving, problems are defined to fit the range of available or acceptable solutions.

Whilst these two themes represent contrasting traditions with conflicting assumptions, they will be used in the present case as complementary ways of describing organisational behaviour. Theme 1 provides a useful perspective for identifying the causes of variations in the effectiveness of the strike organisation, strategy and tactics. Theme 2 provides keys to understanding how patterns of interaction and decision-making evolved over the course of the strike. Together they offer an interpretive framework that is consistent with more traditional approaches to the study of unions and strikes and helpfully augments their theoretical base. We shall be returning to them in Chapter 11, when we summarise the implications of our study.

CHAPTER TWO

Industrial relations climate and conflict in the steel industry

This book is about *how* the steel strike was run in one of its main centres of union activity, not an empirical analysis of its causes or the quality of union-management relations. Therefore we shall not dwell for long on the causes of the steel strike, which are well documented elsewhere (Upham 1980; 1983; Docherty, 1983). However, it is necessary for the purposes of our case analysis to outline the issues underlying the strike and describe the internal climate of the steel unions, since these are important for understanding the motivation, behaviour and organisation of the strike at local level.

The origins of the steel strike

The causes of the steel strike had deep historical roots and recent historical 'triggers'. The history of the steel industry in many ways is a replica of the changing climate of industrial relations in Britain, in which the profitability of traditional industries has declined and skills have been eroded by technological advance. The industry has been transformed from a profitable and peaceful partnership — in which steelworkers enjoyed the stability and growth engendered by expanding markets, a secure seniority system and a wage determination system that kept them at the top of the industrial earnings league — into a state of crisis in internal relations and external viability (Bowen, 1976).

Two linked influences underlay this transformation: the changing world economy and increasing state intervention in the industry. The first of these two was brought about by the steady growth of steel production in other parts of the world, a growth that gathered pace to overtake the slowing expansion of world markets. Increasing import penetration by technologically advanced foreign giant companies in America, Europe, Japan and, more recently, from Third World producers, could not be resisted by the technologically antiquated and small scale fiefdoms of the British steel barons (Ovenden,

1978). The modernisation and rationalisation of domestic steel production could not forestall the crisis that emerged in the late 70s of world overproduction for stagnating markets, a product of the recession triggered by the dramatic rise in oil prices in 1974. The second influence was linked to the first, insofar as successive governments sought to intervene in the industry to protect and maintain it as a national resource. To compete with overseas giant producers an integrated domestic industry was needed, whilst the merits of private vs. public ownership of this 'commanding height' of the economy became a symbol of conflicting political ideologies. Nationalisation (1949), denationalisation (1953), and partial renationalisation (1967) of the industry were not the only unsettling interventions in its operations, for governments increasingly imposed price controls and restricted investment capital as part of their general management of the economy.

The changes in ownership delayed much needed radical reorganisation and modernisation until the late 60s and early 70s. The 1973 'Ten Year Development Strategy' was an ambitious and optimistic plan for concentrated steel production in a number of technologically advanced coastal sites, envisaging production of 38 million tonnes of steel by 1980. As Table 1 shows this strategy disintegrated with the collapse of the industry's profitability, with steel production in 1981 turning out to be little more than a third of the envisaged figure. The result of the crisis was the 1975 Beswick Plan, a further programme of plant closures, reduced output targets and improved productivity. Political considerations tempered some of the harsher decisions about plant closures but only with the force of delay, and in 1979 such minor flexibility disappeared with the accession to power of a Conservative government committed to a posture of non-intervention in public enterprises. It was within this context of crisis and constraint that in 1979 the Corporation management embarked on the 'empty pockets' bargaining that precipitated the strike.

To understand how this exchange came about, we need to look at the changing climate of union-management relations, and the sources of increasing militancy among a formerly moderate workforce. Technological change was disturbing workplace relations and stimulating increased sectional conflict which especially involved craftsmen, who were growing in number and importance in the new technology of steel production. The steady erosion of steelworkers' position in the wages league (from 3rd to 18th position according to ISTC), changes in working practices, and the gathering pace of plant closures were substituting an anxious militancy for the traditional co-operative mood of steelworkers. At local level, conciliation machinery was breaking down

Table 2.1 Employment and production in the British Steel Corporation 1967-1981

Year	BSC employment[1] (September, iron and steel activities)	Million tonnes[2] crude steel production BSC
1967	217,310	22.1
8	215,750	24.0
9	226,970	24.4
1970	229,940	25.6
1	212,010	21.8
2	203,910	22.9
3	201,420	23.9
4	195,940	19.3
5	191,740	17.2
6	182,600	19.1
7	182,370	17.2
8	167,610	17.3 *
9	161,382	18.3 *
1980	121,290	8.2 *
1981	94,200	13.2 *

1. Source: British Steel Corporation *Statistics for the Corporation*
2. Source: Bryer *et al* (1982); p. 139.
* estimated.

and with increasing frequency 'failures to agree' were being registered in grievance procedure.

Open conflict between unions and management emerged more clearly with each successive plant closure. Potential resistance to closures at Hartlepool, on the Clyde and in South Wales in 1977-8 was mitigated by generous redundancy payments to relatively ageing workforces, but the abrupt handling of closure at Shelton and Bilston in 1978-9 was met with more opposition, though this only achieved the delay of the Bilston closure. Faced with the closure of the profitable Corby works in the East Midlands, the unions mounted their most strategic and co-ordinated struggle against management, though ultimately they lost this battle as they had all its predecessors. During this period the annual wage round toughened significantly — the 1978 bargaining did not reach a settlement until the Spring of 1979.

Thus it was in 1979 that ISTC entered its annual wage round

bargaining with the Corporation in a mood of bitter frustration — at their loss of bargaining power and position over the years, the increasing threat to their membership, and their deteriorating relations with Corporation management. At the same time the newly elected Conservative government was promising a hard line in monetarist economic policy, using cash limits in the public sector to hold down public spending and pay settlements. It was their declared intent not to intervene in collective bargaining or enterprise decision-making taking place within these constraints, whatever the outcome might be in terms of labour conflict. They also had a manifesto commitment to the 'reform' of the unions. Circumstances were thus ripe for a major conflict, and the management supplied the triggers for it with a pay offer of such misjudged tactlessness that some observers were led to suspect that the strike had been engineered by a conspiracy of politicians and managers.

The first of these actions was management's bargaining posture in the brief negotiation that took place, which asserted that cash limits only allowed self-financing pay deals. This meant, said management, that only a 2% increase on basic pay could be achieved through the consolidation of a previous wage agreement. Additional increases in earnings of up to 10% would have to be negotiated in the form of local productivity deals that were entirely self-financing. Such an arrangement in effect told union bosses that they had nothing to bargain for. There would be no centrally negotiated wage rise, and the emphasis in bargaining would shift to local level, where widespread differences among plants could be expected due to variations in local conditions. Such a development would represent a radical shift in the balance of bargaining power within the unions and was seen by the unions as giving management an added ability to divide and rule. Certainly the threatening nature of management's strategy was underlined one month before the strike when they restated their position with the added inclusion of a demand that the Guaranteed Week Agreement be scrapped and that there should be an increase in the amount of sub-contracted labour employed by plants.

The second action that precipitated the strike was the devastating announcement by management during negotiations, of its revised operating target of 15.2 million tonnes and its intention to meet this with a labour force reduced by one third from present levels. Some 50,000 jobs would go through the total closure of Consett works and major labour shedding in plants in South Wales, Scunthorpe and other areas. There was even talk of capacity eventually being reduced to 9 million tonnes.

In the words of Upham (1980), an ISTC Research Officer, 'Tabling these proposals at a time when pay talks were moving towards a strike is now nearly universally recognised as a unique public sector industrial relations blunder. The ISTC was left with no alternative but to break with its tradition of restraint' (p.12). To the union the conflation of these two communications was greeted as nothing less than a declaration of war, to be answered in kind by the calling of a national strike from 2 January 1980. The transformation from a climate of co-operation to one of all-out conflict was complete, and the events of the period following the strike call did nothing except harden the battle lines. Meetings in the early days of the strike between the two sides produced no significant variation in the management offer, no signs of government willingness to intervene and no weakening of union determination. In the latter respect its effect was quite the opposite. Other unions in steel supported the ISTC stance and rank and file steel-workers in the early days of the strike revealed in no uncertain terms the strength of their feelings, adding powerful pressure to the momentum of their leaders.

This was particularly true of South Yorkshire, which turned out to be the most militant area of union activity in the whole of the national strike. One reason was the close proximity of the private and public sectors in the city. As our narrative will describe, this was a spur to some of the most concentrated and eventful picketing of the entire strike. It is also significant that South Yorkshire was rarely mentioned as an area under threat from the economic crisis in steel. The most vulnerable parts of industry were those engaged in basic steel production and derivatives (e.g. bulk steel, tubes, etc) where markets were under greatest pressure from overproduction and where profits were lowest. South Yorkshire is the centre of the special steels industry, producing materials for high technology industries, such as aerospace and hand tools, and the threat to jobs contained in the Corporation's revised plans was thus less direct to the South Yorkshire steel industry than elsewhere. In other areas, like South Wales, the passion of members was moderated by the dead hand of weary fatalism, engendered by their inability to forestall plant closures.

Indeed, it may also be accounted as significant that in 1971, plans to close one of the few 'heavy' steel production plants of South Yorkshire, the River Don Works, were successfully resisted by the action of militant union activists, mainly from the plant's principal union, the AUEW. This success can be seen as having boosted the confidence of the engineering union, already the major force in local union politics, and as providing the rationale for AUEW advisors to have a significant influence over the form of strike organisation in South Yorkshire, even before they themselves became parties to the dispute.

The socio-cultural context of steel has a predominantly conservative influence on industrial relations, through the stabilising effect of long-standing community ties. As in the mining industry, the traditions of these industrial communities have tended to foster a strong proletarian solidaristic consciousness but until recently a low propensity to conflict. The latter can be explained partly by the tradition of regional autonomy, strong in both steel and coal where the shift from private to public ownership did little to change patterns of industrial relations which were primarily shaped by the unique character of local conditions and relationships. But, as we have seen, the climate of local union-management co-operation was shattered from above, by breakdown at national level of bargaining over jobs and pay.

The outcome was the first major stoppage in an industry with a 100 year tradition of union-management agreements, and the commencement of what probably ranks as the biggest strike in the history of British industrial relations, if size is measured by the two dimensions of scale and duration. Nearly 100,000 men and women, most of whom had never been involved in a major strike previously, stopped work for a full three months, from 2 January to 3 April 1980. Perhaps the Corporation underestimated the strength of opposition their bargaining strategy aroused, though their failures to reorient their bargaining position in a conciliatory direction during the early weeks of the strike suggest that they were determined to break established patterns, regardless of opposition. Nonetheless, the scale of the strike, the loss of faith in top management by people in the industry and the general condemnation of their approach to negotiations by the media and in Parliament was damaging to their credibility and led to the replacement of the Chairman of the Corporation later in 1980.

The powerful momentum generated by the strength of feeling of the rank and file and the deep anxiety felt by the union leaderships, was sufficient to maintain solid support for the strike throughout its long duration. The strike ended not because union members lacked the will to fight, but because of the spread of the belief that no further gains were to be had from prolonging the conflict. Despite union picketing efforts, steel was still being transported and used and management's position was almost unchanged. At the same time there was a visible hardening of government monetarist policies, rising unemployment and diminishing expectations created by these policies among industrial workers and their representatives.

We shall anticipate the end of the strike no further here, and will reserve our observations about its aftermath until later (see Chapter 10). Our purpose here is scene-setting, and the remainder of this chapter will be devoted to a description of the parties to the strike: the unions, and in particular the largest of those in steel, the Iron and Steel Trades Confederation.

The steel unions

The steel industry has in common with many others a complex multi-union structure. Annual negotiations have involved no fewer than 18 unions, but of these one has predominated, the ISTC with its 90,000 members (at the time of the strike). The National Union of Blast-furnacemen organised 14,000 workers at the 'heavy end' of steel production in parts of England (though not organising workers in South Yorkshire). Bargaining arrangements have been simplified by the craft unions negotiating collectively through their organisation into the National Craftsmen's Coordinating Committee (NCCC). The other main parties to bargaining are the two general unions, TGWU and GMWU. This structure usually meant that in annual negotiations the settlement secured by the ISTC, as first in sequence, usually committed the other unions to fall into line with similar deals. These negotiations deal exclusively with basic wage minima and differentials, and are customarily without major conflict. Disputes have been more common at local level where crucial details of incentives, manning and conditions are determined.

Apart from running into major conflict the 1979 negotiations also departed from past practice in that ISTC's national leadership was as much directed by as it was controlling the response of its delegation. The annual ISTC/BSC negotiation is a remarkable event, for on the union side up to 100 persons may be legitimately present. Agreements are negotiated by the Central Negotiating Committee (CNC), 70 lay union representatives nominated by Works branches throughout the country (see Figure 2.1). In addition *ex officio* attendance is permitted for the 21 members of the union's sovereign decision-making body, the Executive Council (EC), who are also lay officers elected at local level. Finally the union's General Secretary and his four full-time National Officers may attend. The size of this meeting means that negotiation usually has to take place in the Corporation's cinema underneath its London office. In practice, though, there has been usually only a single chief protagonist on the union side, the General Secretary, Bill Sirs. Negotiations are punctuated by frequent adjournments to allow for informal consultations on the union side, as well as between the sides.

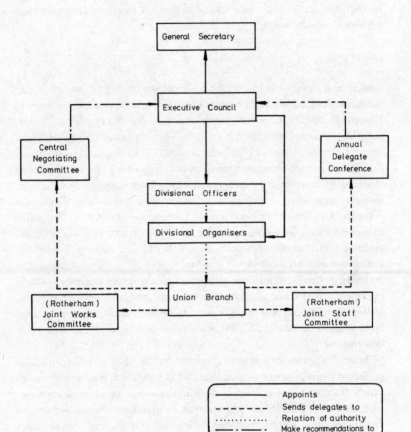

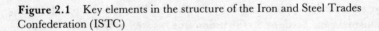

Figure 2.1 Key elements in the structure of the Iron and Steel Trades Confederation (ISTC)

Our informants have told us that in the late 1979 negotiations the General Secretary exercised far less control over the proceedings than usual, and that the lay representatives present were far more vociferous in their participation and demands. At subsequent meetings this pattern was repeated as breakdown followed breakdown.

The negotiating arrangement for ISTC might appear to be unworkably cumbersome, but could be seen to have the merits of reducing the need for intraorganisational bargaining (i.e. within the union) and of helping to confer legitimacy and credibility upon the outcome. It is an arrangement that has the appearance of democracy. However, this judgement cannot be made apart from a wider consideration of the union's self-government, and since this is relevant to our analysis of strike organisation, we shall now examine it.

The balance of power and autonomy in decision making within ISTC reflects the organisation of collective bargaining: there is strong and directive leadership at national level, and a high degree of self-determination at local level. The national union's supreme body is the 21 person EC, which contains a balance of members from the various regions and industrial divisions of the industry. All are elected by the same constituencies that nominate them, though regions and divisions frequently agree to share nominations to secure unopposed election. The EC appoints the General Secretary and other full-time officers for life (except for the figure-head President who is re-elected annually). One-third of the EC retires each year. This system is one that in practice gives the General Secretary considerable power, for if he is able to generate support among a majority of the EC — which under normal circumstances is likely, given his greater experience and expert power — he is unlikely to lose command as the result of a single year's election. Moreover, in addition to his administrative and executive responsibilities for the union machine the General Secretary has much discretion, crucially in his power to call Executive meetings and declare strikes.

Assisting in the day to day running of the union are EC appointed National Officers, of whom there were four at the time of the strike. At regional level are Divisional Officers, each of whom co-ordinates the work of Divisional Organisers (there were five full-time officials in the South Yorkshire and Humberside region).

At local level are the branches. Being an industrial union (organising within a single industry), there is no need for branches to serve the function of lateral integration across disparate industrial subunits, as is the case for the other unions in steel, such as the AUEW and TGWU whose branches bring together workers from often vastly different types of employment. ISTC blue-collar branches are organised at works or plant level, each branch comprising all the production workers of a functional production area (e.g. for a single rolling mill). Clerical and middle management branches have been more recently formed. In size they are usually within the range of 150 to 700, and they elect their own branch officials: Chairman, Branch Secretary, Works Representative and Committee Members. The responsibilities of their offices are not fixed, but generally the Chairman presides, the Secretary is responsible for membership, the Works Representative negotiates, and the Committee Members function as shop stewards in day to day representation and grievance handling, though in practice the senior officers of the branch tend to handle any matters of importance. In Rotherham BSC works there were 35 branches, which would each meet once a month.

In most steel works there are several ISTC branches on a single site and it is common to find them co-ordinated through the institution of Joint Branch Committees. The role of these bodies is advisory and consultative to their constituent branches, and also to liaise with other local unions. The structure of collective bargaining gives considerable autonomy to branches, reinforced by a disputes procedure that encourages settlement at local level. Indeed, until 1979 branches had the authority to agree redundancies locally, a matter since transferred to the EC.

Finally, there is annual conference. In many unions conference is a key countervailing force to the power of the executive and full-time officials. This cannot be said of ISTC, whose annual conference was only instituted in 1976, and had no mandatory or policy functions (powers it has acquired since the strike). Conference operated as a discussion forum, carefully presided over by the National Officers and EC members; in other words without offering a serious challenge to the union's power structure. However, it is significant that in recent years conference increasingly became a vehicle for internal union discontents, witnessing the emergency of a 'Reform Group' canvassing vigorously for greater union democracy in the form of demands for the election of the General Secretary and Divisional Officers, and a shift to regional from trade-based constituencies in EC elections.

We have described how this union organisation has mirrored the two distinct levels of collective bargaining, and how it has favoured conservative leadership and co-operative union-management relations. The rising tensions from eroded status and threats to membership, culminating in the implicit declaration of war in management's 1979 wage offer, transformed this. A moderate membership became angrily militant, and a conciliatory controlling leadership became part of a fighting consensus. However, with the onset of the strike there was more than a change of attitudes. At the functional level there was a complete transformation of organisation and goals. At national level the EC found itself in frequent consultation in order to co-ordinate strike activity — or, to put it more realistically, to keep pace with local activity, for it was at the latter level that the character of the strike was being determined, while the national leadership was mainly engaged in the promotion of the strike cause through the media and through occasional and mostly abortive contacts with management.

CHAPTER THREE

A strike diary

Looking back over the history of the industry, it can be seen that there has been major change, under the guiding hand of economic forces and social movements in British industrial culture generally, and through the changing aspirations and values of trade unionists in steel. The pace of this change quickened dramatically in the late 1970s as pressures mounted to the point where government policy, management decision-making and union frustrations triggered the strike.

We shall now look in closer detail at the immediate period of the strike — before, during and after — so that the local events we portray in our narrative can be set in historical context. This we shall do through a strike diary that provides a timetable of significant events and actions, at both local and national level. These are selected according to two criteria: first, as milestones in the development of the strike, or the aspirations and responses of the union; and second, as keys to understanding the behaviour of the local strikers and their organising committees.

Strike diary

The main events of the strike, both locally and nationally, are included here, and South Yorkshire events are italicised.

1979

September
24 BSC negotiators receive ISTC pay claim and request time to consider.

November
2 ISTC Executive responds to threatened closure of Corby Steel

works with a national overtime ban, suspension of all joint consultation and redundancy negotiation, and a future one-day strike.

December

3 BSC offers to consolidate an existing pay supplement, giving national pay rises of 0-2%, with the possibility of up to 10% in addition from local productivity deals.

6 BSC Chairman announces that the Corporation wishes to cut 52,000 jobs (from the workforce of 160,000).

7 ISTC Executive calls an indefinite national strike to begin on 2 January

16 *Rotherham Joint Committee establishes two works strike committees, and a top-level strike committee (RSC).*

18 *Rotherham Strike Committee (RSC) holds first meeting.*

21 BSC elaborates offer of 2%, plus 3% to buy out Guaranteed Week Agreement, plus up to 10% from local productivity deals.

23 *Rotherham Joint Committee discusses further strike details.*

28 *Divisional Strike Committee (DSC) established.*
BSC makes new offer.
Second RSC meeting. Pickets allocated to geographical cells.

30 *Final pre-strike meeting of the RSC.*

1980

January

2 ISTC and NUB commence strike against BSC.

4 TUC and steel leaders meet BSC to consider revised pay offer of 2% nationally, plus 4% in exchange for Guaranteed Week, plus 6-8% from local productivity deals.
TGWU officially joins strike.

7 ISTC General Secretary Bill Sirs proposes a pay settlement of 8% nationally, plus 5% from local deals. BSC offers 8% (nationally) and 4% (locally) only for three months.
8 GMWU officially joins the strike.
First arrests of pickets in Rotherham/Sheffield. By this time the RSC, and other strike committees, had coined the slogan '20% — no strings' to summarise their pay demand, and their rejection of productivity deals tied to the annual pay settlement. Several strike committees, particularly the RSC, had despatched flying pickets throughout the country — to ports, steel stockholders, private steel producers, and steel users — in order to stop 'all steel movement'.

9 Wales TUC calls a General Strike for 21 January in protest at plant closures and redundancies. *RSC leaders meet CSEU shop stewards.* NCCC officially joins the strike.

14 Wales TUC postpones General Strike until March.
Central Coordinating Committee established. RSC discussion of private steel sector.

16 ISTC Executive Council decides to call out private sector steel workers from 27 January.

17 BSC announces plans for new round of job losses in the South Wales steel plants.
GMWU and NUB join the Divisional Strike Committee.

18 House of Commons debate on the Steel Strike.

19 ISTC and NUB leaders (Bill Sirs and Hector Smith) meet Secretary of State for Industry, Sir Keith Joseph, to discuss the government's attitude to further subsidy to BSC.

21 Bill Sirs and Hector Smith meet the Prime Minister. Sir Keith Joseph rejects union demand that a portion of the £450 million allocated by the EEC for steel restructuring should be used to fund the annual pay increase. *Demonstration and rally of several thousand steel strikers and supporters in Sheffield. Flying pickets despatched in large numbers to private steel plants in Blackburn and Manchester.*

23 *ISTC members of the RSC begin criticising the Central Coordinating Committee. NCCC joins the Divisional Strike Committee.*

24 National Union of Railwaymen's (NUR) Executive decides to stop all movement of steel from 27 January.
By this stage the local CSEU has agreed to black all steel crossing ISTC picket lines.

25 16 private steel firms are refused an injunction in the High Court to restrain ISTC from calling its private sector members out on strike.

26 Lord Denning, in the Appeal Court, reverses the High Court ruling and grants an injunction against ISTC to the private sector firms.
ISTC EC, acting on legal advice, decides to comply with the injunction, but appeal to the House of Lords.
ISTC pickets on plants covered by the injunction are replaced in South Yorkshire by pickets from other unions.

27 Craft union leaders meet BSC for separate pay negotiations. Private sector ISTC workers join the strike.

28 One day strike and demonstration in South Wales is addressed by Bill Sirs.
CCC organises mass picket at GKN, Leeds.

29 *Private sector ISTC joins the Divisional Strike Committee, but drops out after three weeks.*

31 *Mass picket at Templeborough Rolling Mill (TRM).*

February

1 House of Lords overturns Denning judgement.
TUC meets government to discuss the strike.

4 Private sector rejoins the strike. *Hadfields threatens to withhold tax to compensate for private sector strike effects.*

6 *Unions withdraw safety cover at some plants.*

7 Mass picket in Birmingham broken up by Special Patrol Group.
Last effective meeting of Central Coordinating Committee.
New round of national talks collapses in acrimony: no change in basic offer revealed after raised expectations.
Return to work proposals first discussed at RSC.

10 *Hadfields strikers vote to return to work.*
Mass picket at Barrets organised by DSC.

11 NCCC offered 14.4% total settlement.
Preliminary meetings (early-mid February) to establish a National Strike Committee.

12 *Mass picket at Hadfields.*

13 *3 more South Yorkshire private steel plants return to work.*
TGWU reject 14.4%. Divisional Strike Committee endorses vote of 'no confidence' in Sirs, ISTC General Secretary, moved by the RSC.

14 NCCC delegates reject 14.4% offer. *The major mass picket at Hadfields, with 22 arrests. Hadfields come out on strike again.*
RSC demands that local management withdraw its recognition from SIMA.

15 *Local CSEU supplies list of picketing targets to RSC.*

19 It is revealed that the Government are actively looking for a replacement for Corporation Chairman, Charles Villiers.

20 Government publish draft code on picketing. *Unsuccessful mass picket at Sheerness. Coaches from Sheffield and Rotherham.*

22 *RSC organise a picket of SIMA members.*
Welsh miners' strike in support of steelworkers is called off.
ISTC and NUB leaders propose 15% (national) + 15% (local) pay deal to BSC.

23 *Fire guts South Yorkshire ISTC strike headquarters.*

24 *Hadfields decide to return to work, along with 4 other major local private sector firms.*

24 BSC decides to independently ballot workforce on whether they want to be balloted on the 14.4% offer.
ISTC states that it will instruct its members to boycott the ballot.
Private steel firm Firth Brown returns to work.

25 Major meeting of the unofficial National Strike Committee.

27 *Mass picket of Templeborough Rolling Mill.*

28 More than 3,000 ISTC private sector workers have now resumed work.

Late February *RSC begins to concentrate on cutting off raw materials supplies to steel firms.*

March

3 *RSC establishes sub-committee to draw up list of blacked haulage firms.*
BSC Chief Executive Bob Scholey sees EEC about possible financial aid. *DSC calls for union credentials of private steel sector ISTC officials to be withdrawn by the EC.*

4 *After local discussions, BSC ballot papers publicly burned in Sheffield.*

5 Solidarity is asserted in a national meeting of all the main steel unions. They announce a joint negotiating framework for eventual settlement, consisting of a 14% (national) plus 5% (local) demand.

9 TUC anti-government demonstration in London of 50,000 with a large steelworkers' contingent, *including several coaches from Rotherham.*

10 BSC's ballot produces conflicting results with a majority of voters (but a minority of those eligible to vote) voting for a ballot on BSC's pay offer.
National negotiations begin again but after eleven hours no settlement has been reached.
CSEU (South Yorkshire) instructs local engineering workers not to cross ISTC picket lines, as a result of which local engineering firms rapidly start to close down.

11 TGWU finally issues an instruction to its members not to cross ISTC picket lines. Mass pickets in South Wales.
BSC offers a total settlement of 14.4% including productivity deals.

12 *RSC sends telegram to EC urging them to hold out for '20% — no strings' and declaring morale was never higher.*

13 National negotiations break down again.
Mass picket at Hadfields.

14 *CSEU (South Yorkshire) instructs its members to return to work, ostensibly because of its opposition to the 13 March mass picket at Hadfields.*

17 British Rail workers are ordered by the High Court to release steel blockaded in one of their depots.
RSC begins again to discuss the return to work.

18 Unions are divided on whether to accept conciliation: ISTC is opposed, TGWU in favour.

20 Conflicting claims about strike impact: CBI says production is only down by 4%.
RSC decides to pay £5 per week to local pickets.

21 BSC say ballot papers ready for distribution.

23 Liverpool dockers vote to strike. *RSC (with DSC support) urges Bill Sirs not to co-operate with the proposed Committee of Enquiry because of the prospect of a national dock strike.*

24 Employment Secretary James Prior sets up Committee of Inquiry. The terms of reference cover pay only. AUEW says it will abide by the results.

25 TGWU refuses to make dock strike national and official.

27 *Whole RSC meeting on the return to work.*

29 Committee of Inquiry (3 man team) meets.

31 Committee of Inquiry reports. Recommends a 15.5% increase overall (11% on basic rates and 4.5% through local deals).
Recommendation hotly debated at DSC.

April
1 Executive Council of ISTC recommends return to work.

2 *Final RSC meeting.*
Mass meetings in South Yorkshire accept settlement.

3 Strike ends.

South Yorkshire out on strike after management disciplines a worker for refusing to unload a blacked lorry.

CHAPTER FOUR

Strike preparations

Introduction

The strike call was issued by the Executive Council of ISTC on 7 December 1979, and in the few weeks which elapsed before the start of the strike on 2 January 1980 an extremely complex organisation emerged in order to prosecute the strike locally. The present chapter describes the bases on which this organisation was constructed, and in particular, draws attention to several features of the organisation which subsequently gave rise to a number of unintended consequences.

At a surface level, it would be easy to think the strike organisation (see Figure 4.1) had been consciously designed in order to perform a number of essential tasks, and meet a number of pressing needs. Each element in the strike organisation can be traced to a decision reached at a particular meeting, either of the Rotherham Joint Works Committee (see below), of the nascent Rotherham Strike Committee (RSC) or of the small elite of leading officers of these bodies. In practice organisational structure often evolves in a much more *ad hoc* way, and within certain constraints. The local strike organisation was no exception, for although the organisational structure emerged fairly rapidly, it did so initially within the parameters of existing trade union structures, as the EC had advised:

> Divisional officers would call for meetings of the joint Committees to discuss strategy, picketing etc at local level. (ISTC EC Minutes, 7 Dec, 1979)

Strike committees

An unusually well-attended meeting of Rotherham Joint Committee (81 delegates compared with the usual 30 or so) took place on 16 December to receive reports from the local CNC and EC members on the state of negotiations, and to begin preparations for the strike. As indicated already, the strike was widely seen at this stage, at least by local activists, as inevitable, and a range of questions was raised by delegates

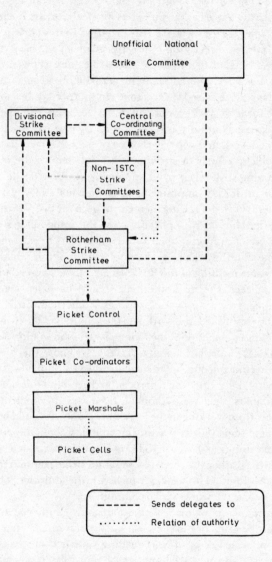

Figure 4.1   Organisation in the 1980 steel strike, Rotherham and area

uncertain how to act in this new situation: should they retain some safety cover on struck plants? should they give dispensations to allow firms to continue working? how should they encourage participation of the private as well as the public sector steel workers in the strike? and who was eligible for social security benefits? In short discussion covered all the parties directly or indirectly involved in the strike, and the resources needed to prosecute the strike, and showed considerable evidence of foresight and planning across a broad spectrum of issues. One major issue raised several times in this period, but to little effect, was the surge in BSC production in the weeks leading up to the strike. This increased output was based largely on extra overtime and higher manning levels, and was clearly part of the BSC, steel users' and steel stockholders' efforts to stockpile steel and reduce the impact of the forthcoming strike. It proved impossible however for delegates at the Rotherham Joint Committee to agree on a feasible way of preventing their members from raising their earnings in the pre-Christmas period, despite its long-term implications for the impending strike (indeed some were encouraging their branch members to earn more through overtime, not fully realising the implications of this advice).

The same meeting of the RJC (16 December) agreed to the suggestion that each site in Rotherham should have its own area strike committee, whilst an overall, top-tier Rotherham Strike Committee would be established to co-ordinate the activities of the twin committees and organise, in addition, the flying pickets who would operate outside the strikers' immediate vicinity. As far as we know, there was no debate at this meeting on alternative structures. In addition it was local (rather than flying) picketing which preoccupied people at this stage because of the numbers that were thought necessary to prevent non-ISTC members from working in the local BSC plants. It would be misleading however to suggest there was any inevitability about the structure of the strike organisation, because ISTC in Scunthorpe created very different structures. Rather than create a separate strike committee, it adapted its works Joint Committee, which for the duration of the strike, functioned as the works strike committee.

What *was* common to the Rotherham and Scunthorpe strike committees was the influence in these early days of a small elite, or dominant coalition, consisting of the leading officers of the joint works committees and a small number of non-ISTC union leaders who enjoyed (for varying reasons) high status in the workplace union. These elites almost certainly predated the strike preparations: in Rotherham, the leadership of the Rotherham Joint Committee (RJC) had only recently passed into the hands of a group of younger, more militant activists. This group was able to continue its influence within the strike organisation, in part because the absence of any formal rules or procedures governing ISTC strike committees allowed them to do so, and because they were supported by one of the local full-time officials (also part of the informal elite), who was to become the 'strike co-ordinator'. In contrast, the Scunthorpe decision to use as a strike committee an existing body with a definite constitution and tradition meant that the elite exercised its influence formally (rather than informally), through one of the sub-committees of the strike committee (the 'main sub-committee') which included the local full-time official among its seven members.

The composition of the newly created RSC changed rapidly in these early days (mid-December) as one would expect in view of its broad objective (organisation of the strike), and the absence of any agreed rules regulating membership. Six leading members of the RJC — the informal elite — were elected to form the RSC on 16 December, but two days later the inaugural meeting of the RSC was attended by 13 branch officials (indicating the permeability of its boundaries), and the meeting itself decided to expand its membership further with the addition of branch officers from the under-represented finishing end of steel production. The desire to ensure a wide base of representation from the various stages of steel production may be seen as evidence of a concern to establish the legitimacy of the RSC, understandable in terms of the committee's novelty (see Chapter 7). It also testifies to the continuing influence of trade union structure: the RJC was open to delegates from all the works' ISTC branches, covering all stages of steel making, as well as a wide range of grades of worker (blue and white-collar), although in practice it was dominated (numerically and otherwise) by manual workers.

The first meeting of the RSC on 18 December endorsed the two-tier strike committee structure, and continued detailed preparations for the strike begun by the RJC. Decisions were taken, for instance, to circulate the TUC code on picketing (1979) and to invite a speaker from the Claimants' Union to address the RSC on social security. Longer-term decisions were also taken, such as the one to book Sheffield City Hall for a rally on 21 January, taken at the second RSC meeting on 28 December, though it is unclear whether this was thought of as a post-strike victory rally, or a mid-term morale boost.

It is worth emphasising the distinctive character and speed of emergence of the Rotherham strike organisation. In the Sheffield steel works, less than ten miles away, and part of the same large conurbation, there was *no* pre-strike structure comparable to that in Rotherham, and the earliest activities of the Sheffield strike committee were conducted (in January) from a caravan parked outside a public telephone box which served as the committee's main channel of rapid communication. Indeed after three weeks of the strike there was no properly-functioning strike committee contracting strikers and organising meetings. One of the explanations for this difference is that the Rotherham activists believed there *would* be a strike and that it was necessary to organise for it. This organisation was initiated through their functioning Joint Committee, a structure practically absent from the Sheffield works.

Extensions of the strike organisation

The strike organisation had hitherto followed the contours of the trade union structure at works level, but the local would-be strike leaders increasingly came to believe there was a need for co-ordination between the different works, partly because (at least in Rotherham) their intention to despatch flying pickets to other regions might clash with the activities of other strike committees.

The next tier in the union structure above the works is the Division. But this is an electoral unit, i.e. a full-time officer's territorial unit: there were no Divisional union structures as such. Tentative links between works' strike committees began to emerge through very informal meetings (within the boundaries of South Yorkshire and Humberside Division of ISTC) between members of the Rotherham elite and union leaders in Sheffield, Stocksbridge and later, Scunthorpe. As a result of these private meetings, held over drinks between Christmas and the New Year, and including the wives of the activists who were present, it was agreed to establish a Divisional Strike Committee (DSC) ostensibly to co-ordinate picketing between the different areas, and to provide a forum for information exchange. This seemed, on the face of it, a sensible and understandable development, but it was one which was to lead to several unintended consequences not least because of the ambiguity of the term 'co-ordination'.

It was unclear at this stage whether this co-ordinating body was to exercise *authority over* the works' strike committees, or was simply to liaise between them (see Chapter 8). The membership of the DSC also departed from the strike co-ordinator's intention, as individuals were brought on for particular reasons: one member was added because he controlled fund-raising; another was brought on because of his membership of the CNC. The accumulative result of these particular decisions was a substantial change in the size and nature of the DSC. One immediate consequence of the creation of the DSC was a change in the status of the RSC. Five senior members of the RSC (senior also in terms of their union positions) were 'elected' by the RSC to sit on the DSC: the overlapping membership of the two committees would presumably have facilitated liaison between the committees, as intended with the creation of the latter. As it turned out, attendance at the daily meetings of two strike committees (in addition to other strike duties) very quickly proved to be too onerous for these five overlapping members, and with the agreement of the RSC four of them sat only on the DSC. This decision, taken like many others to resolve an immediate problem, also had an unintended consequence in that it dramatically reduced links between the RSC and the DSC, and facilitated the emergence of different outlooks among the members of the two committees.

Another consequence arising from the creation of the DSC, though one of lesser import, was the disappearance of the two site strike committees 'below' the RSC, although one of the them continued as a picket headquarters with a number of cells being directed and organised from there.

The importance assigned by the RSC leadership to the private sector steelworkers also resulted in meetings, during the first week of the strike, with local engineering shop stewards and, a few days later, to the creation of the multi-union Central Coordinating Committee. The CCC comprised two delegates from each of the ISTC, NCCC, TGWU and GMWU, although other strikers and supporters attended some of its meetings. In early February a few of the more active regions sent members to a small, informal meeting which established an unofficial National Strike Committee (NSC) for purposes, initially, of information exchange and 'co-ordination'.

Picket recruitment

Officers of the two largest staff branches, with a combined membership of 1,200, were surprised at the strong support for the strike, and similar sentiments were expressed by officers of several large and influential manual branches, as well as by the EC member, who addressed some of the December branch meetings. Branch meetings were used by some branch committees to recruit volunteers for picketing. Other branches simply collected signatures or displayed recruiting notices at the workplace, and, as one would expect, the response to these requests varied enormously. A small number of manual branches reported positive responses from 80-90% of members, whilst some of the clerical and technical branches reported similar rates of *non*-volunteering.

Some officers had to resort to skilful persuasion to elicit a positive response, particularly where workers agreed to volunteer only on condition that others would do likewise. However, some branch officials were hampered by their lack of a clear view of the requirements of picketing.

The picture which emerges both from interviews and the post-strike questionnaire is that the recruitment of pickets was far easier among manual workers, but that age constituted a barrier for some. Amongst clerical workers, where union traditions are of more recent origin, it was younger, politically committed union activists who tended to be involved in picketing (see also Chapter 5).

Organisation of the picket cells

Lists of picket volunteers were forwarded to the Rotherham Joint Committee throughout December and passed to the RSC. Before the final pre-strike meeting of the RJC the lists of picket volunteers from the branches were re-divided to form small groups or *picket cells,* composed of people living in the same area. The rationale for this decision, according to the principal organisers of the cells (later, Picket Control), was to facilitate the transport of groups of pickets to the same picketing target, and also to reduce the costs of picket travel. The cell system was copied from the National Union of Mineworkers whose local officials the ISTC leaders met once or twice around the start of the strike. Cells varied in size from 25 to 50, with the average size at the start of the strike being 30. By 1 January 28 cells had been created. A number of branches were reluctant to have their members organised across branch lines, and vestiges of branch cells were still being re-allocated into geographical cells in mid-January. (One branch, in fact, maintained a number of cells under its own control for the entire duration of the strike).

Each cell was assigned a leader, or *picket marshal,* whose responsibility it was to organise the members of his cell. The marshals were told of their selection only a day or two before the strike was due to start. It is unclear to us how the marshals were selected (we were given several different accounts), beyond the fact that they were seen to possess undefined 'leadership qualities'. We were variously told that the marshals were mainly branch committee members, or that they were foremen (they were certainly all men), and the marshals themselves could offer no precise account of their own selection. If we compare the union positions of the RSC and the picket marshals, we find that the RSC was composed of the 'first line' senior union activists, whilst the

marshals consisted of a 'second line' of less senior officials as well as a
periphery of non-officer branch activists, a fact which underlines the
parallelism between the hierarchy of the strike organisation and that of
the union.

Table 4.1   Union offices held by the RSC and by a sample of picket
marshals

	Branch Secretaries	Chairmen or Vice-Chairmen	Works Represent-atives	Other Committee Members	Non-Office Holders
Core Rotherham Strike Committee (ISTC members) (N = 19)	10	3	6	0	0
ISTC Picket marshals (N = 20)	0	3	1	8	8

In late December, *picket co-ordinators* were appointed by the RSC and
each one was assigned 5-6 picket cells. On 30 and 31 December the
co-ordinators visited their marshals, informed them of their nomination
by the RSC and asked if they were agreeable. Though some were surprised, none refused, and each marshal was handed a list of the names,
addresses and telephone number of his cell members. Many marshals
felt they had to visit their members that same night though the strike
was not due to start until 6.00 a.m. on 2 January. They were told the
name and address of the plant which they had to picket on the first
day, and some were informed of the shift systems worked by their
'target'. Many marshals were given complete discretion however about
the deployment of their resources (although some were advised to adopt
four hour shifts), and this naturally resulted in considerable variation
between cells (see Chapter 5). The clear majority of local cells were
allocated private sector steel producers, stockholders and users, an
indication of the centrality of the private steel sector within the local
ISTC's picketing strategy.

It is important to emphasise the *distinctiveness* of the Rotherham
picket organisation, and the fact that it reflected a degree of *choice* by the

pre-strike leaders. Picket cells created by the NCCC following their entry into the strike on 9 January were all organised on a 24-hour continuous shift system, with each shift working eight hours, with little discretion allowed to marshals. The marshals themselves were shop stewards and the cells were organised mainly along existing branch lines. Another method was adopted at Stocksbridge, Sheffield and Scunthorpe where steelworkers were organised on a general roster: pickets volunteered on a day-to-day basis for picket lines at the strike headquarters, and were despatched in picket groups from the same office, but were not organised in permanent cells.

All the marshals held full cell meetings within a few days in order to explain to their members how they were to be organised. These meetings however discussed the fine detail of shift systems rather than picketing itself. Some marshals later created a further level in the strike organisation hierarchy by appointing a leader on each shift with whom the marshal would liaise. The shift leaders (also known as deputies, team or group leaders) were responsible for picketing in the absence of the marshal. In other word marshals enjoyed a considerable degree of autonomy from the onset of the strike, a fact which was to influence their relations with the RSC in the later stages of the strike. It should also be noted that some pickets were organised *outside* the cell system, on a roster of flying pickets, although before the strike began this was only a small proportion of all picket volunteers.

Relations with ISTC nationally and with other steel unions

Although the responsibility for the details of strike organisation had been devolved to Divisional level, this did not mean that ISTC Head Office was without influence or that local strike committees did not interact with it. On the contrary Head Office had considerable power: through its control (initially) of finance; through having the sole authority to instruct private sector workers to come out on strike alongside the public sector workers; and through its control of the Divisional Officers who were under instructions to send daily reports to Head Office. It was the RSC which on 18 December instructed the local EC members to raise these first two issues at the next EC meeting, and press for an increased financial allocation for Rotherham and for the swift entry of the private sector steelworkers into the strike, both of which instructions presaged future poor relations between the RSC and the Executive of the ISTC, and also indicated the considerable importance attached by the RSC to private sector participation in the strike. The RSC was also in dispute with the EC for its decision to transfer a popular local ISTC organiser out of the Division on 31 December — the eve of the strike. .

Despite the importance attached by the RSC to the support of the private steelworkers, as shown in their plans to attend a private sector joint committee shortly before Christmas, there was no suggestion that they be invited onto the RSC.

The boundary for RSC membership seemed to be set by the limits of the BSC works since other unions which organised in Rotherham works — TGWU, NCCC, GMWU, URTU — were invited to send delegates to the RSC even before their *official* entry into the strike. The rationale for the numbers of other union delegates on the RSC is unclear: there were two members of URTU, one TGWU, one GMWU and two NCCC, a distribution which was certainly not a function of their membership distribution in Rotherham works (URTU had only 100 or so members in Rotherham works). Some had been invited to join the RSC on the basis of personal, work-based contacts: both the GMWU representative and one of the URTU representatives were known personally to the RSC chairman, Sam B.[1] Certainly the numbers of the non-ISTC members on the RSC — they were always in a minority — clearly reflected ISTC's ambivalence towards other unions in the strike. On the one hand the ISTC leaders of the RSC perceived a need to co-operate closely with the other steel unions; on the other hand, they also wished to retain in the strike their position as the dominant and largest single union in the steel industry.

It is also worth noting, finally, the influence of the environment on the structure of the strike organisation, shown most clearly in the appointment of a local press officer. Presumably the perceived hostility of the striker's environment (which would include the organisations of the media) suggested the importance of centralising control of links with the media through the agency of a single press officer.

Concluding remarks

It should be said, firstly, that the complexity of the local strike organisation was actually quite remarkable in view of the lack of strike experience among its leaders, and this lack of tradition served to open up the organisational structure to a number of influences.

One influence on the design of the strike organisation was the existing trade union structure of ISTC: the site works and divisional levels of the union constituted the corresponding levels of the strike organisation. Beyond the works level however, there existed no divisional union *structures* as such, and it was here that new links between works committees were created. Such links were not without problems since the absence of divisional union structures meant there were no established principles to regulate relations between bodies at this level. Equally, below works level, pickets were recruited through union branches, but organised (by ISTC in Rotherham) in geographical cells. The union structures were far from being determinate however, and there did exist both environmental influence and organisational choice. It cannot be emphasised too strongly that it was an organisational choice by the Rotherham steelworkers to create *new* bodies to prosecute the strike (albeit, ones led principally by the local union leadership), whereas Scunthorpe steelworkers adapted their existing works joint committee.

The explanation of this difference may rest with the *distribution of power* in the pre-strike union organisation. The Rotherham ISTC branches enjoyed considerable independence from their local full-time officials, the officials (with one exception) playing virtually no role in the strike, but continuing with their regular union duties. By contrast the Scunthorpe Strike Committee's 'main sub-committee' which actually ran the strike locally included the local official among its members, and because of his conception of his role would have found it difficult to do otherwise. The cell system of pickets at Rotherham therefore seems to have reflected a stronger workplace branch organisation, evidenced, for instance, in the supply of pickets, as compared with the open-roster system at Scunthorpe in which the branches played little or no role.

Several features of the strike organisation were also to generate unintended consequences. Picket marshals exercised considerable discretion in the detailed organisation of their picket cells, a fact which was to contribute to some differentiation within the strike organisation. The piecemeal creation of Divisional links intended to achieve co-ordination between works strike committees would also turn out to be problematic, according to whether co-ordination was seen by local strike leaders as an administrative or a political process.

NOTES
1. All names (apart from those of a few national figures) are pseudonyms.

CHAPTER FIVE

On the picket lines

In this and the subsequent chapter we take a close look at picketing and the evolution of picket organisation. The previous chapter described the creation and emergence of the strike organisation with the hierarchy of coordinators, marshals and pickets below the RSC. In this chapter we focus on the inter- and intra-group processes which gradually modified the organisation's structures and range of activities on the picket lines, beginning with a short account of the ways strikers learned to picket.

The chapter focuses in particular on the stabilisation of intergroup relations, and the cohesion of picket cells. Both processes proceeded unevenly over time and thereby resulted in an organisation that was considerably more complex and differentiated than its original 'design'. We shall explain these processes by referring to the different experiences and conceptions of picketing within the strike organisation. The following chapter (Chapter 6) examines the consequences of these inter- and intra-group processes within the context of the larger strike organisation.

Who were the pickets?

The characteristics of picket volunteers were fairly complex, and the 535 post-strike questionnaire respondents have been divided into manual, clerical and supervisory groups because the factors associated with picketing involvement were different for each group. Indeed occupational group was one of the most important factors: 94% of manual respondents had picketed compared with 70% of supervisors and 51% of clerical workers, and this seems to be a reasonably accurate ratio even if the absolute values are less representative of the body of strikers. Age was also an important influence for manual and clerical workers: for manual workers, pickets averaged 38 years, whilst non-pickets had an average age of 50. Likewise, clerical pickets averaged 33 years and their non-active colleagues 38 years. Another characteristic distinguishing manual pickets and non-pickets was their expectation, on 2 January, of the final strike settlement, with the pickets showing an average expected wage increase of 15.5% compared with 13% for their non-picketing fellows. Expectations of strike outcome were unrelated to the involvement of the two other groups.

Finally, manual pickets showed higher levels of union involvement before the strike, and went to more strike meetings than their non-picketing counterparts. Political interest and left wing political views were associated with picketing *only* for the clerical workers. So too were attendance at pre-strike union branch meetings and length of union membership (despite the fact that clerical pickets were, on average, younger than their non-picketing colleagues). Age did *not* discriminate between supervisory pickets and non-pickets. The pickets expected the strike to last significantly longer than non-pickets (7½ vs 4½ weeks), but no other difference was found among the supervisory strikers. Interestingly, views of the quality of departmental management and of pre-strike industrial relations bore no relation to picketing.

Learning how to picket

Pickets arrived at the gates of their assigned plants in the early hours of 2 January. Seventy-five per cent were on strike for the first time in their lives, and even those with strike experience had rarely picketed. Most arrived on that cold morning at plants of private steel producers and stockholders whose names might have been familiar, but which were otherwise completely unknown. In almost all cases there had been no contact established with the trade unions inside the target plants, and understandably the pickets encountered some hostility from incoming workers. Some of the multi-cell picket lines at the bigger plants were 'supervised' by police. Other steelworkers were picketing BSC plants, in order to prevent the members of other unions, who were not yet involved in the strike, from going to work. As one marshal said, pickets were unsure whether to stand and shout, to try and argue peacefully or to hurl objects at lorries attempting to cross their lines. The BSC picket lines were respected by members of the NCCC, TGWU and GMWU although one NCCC member, later to join the RSC, described those first picket lines as 'chaotic', with groups of men massed around the BSC gates without clear organisation or leadership, and uncertain about how to behave.

In theory, pickets should have received copies of the TUC code on picketing and a document on picketing legislation which the RSC had requested a Divisional Organiser to draft and circulate on 18 December, but we saw no copies of the former, and very few of the latter. One week later it was also agreed that the RSC would circulate a document of their own on strike tactics, including picketing, through the union branches. But in the absence of a single or coherent role model, strikers learned about picketing from a variety of sources, formal and informal, verbal and written. Some marshals reported that their members were briefed on the first day of the strike by local full-time officials; others learned from flying pickets despatched from the nearby Stocksbridge steel works who had been on strike throughout December because of a local dispute; others learned about picketing from non-ISTC unionists. One NCCC member described how he spent several hours on 2 January explaining to novice pickets how to stop lorries and argue with their drivers. In the early days pickets were unsure of their legal rights and even unsure of the activities which constituted picketing. These factors generated, and in some cases combined with, a lack of confidence in approaching potential violators of picket lines. Pickets developed various arguments to persuade drivers not to cross their lines: they justified their strike demands, appealed to union solidarity, described their harsh plight without income and/or threatened drivers with blacking once the strike was over. Some cells developed a stable internal division of labour, in which one picket would act as spokesman in interactions with drivers attempting to cross picket lines, whilst the others stood behind in support.

The key problems facing many pickets however, were firstly, that a section of their own members, in the private sector, was still working, and this made it difficult to convince other trade unionists to make sacrifices. Secondly, TGWU members had received only a *request*, not an *instruction*, to respect picket lines, a fact that caused considerable debate and some tension among the strikers.

The uncertainty of picketing activity was compounded in those early days by considerable confusion at the level of the RSC about the most appropriate targets for picketing. Of the 20 cell marshals whom we interviewed after the strike, nine had their cells redirected within the first three days, and only two remained on the same target from 2 January. Seven cells were moved by the end of the first day, and three of those were redirected *twice* on the first day of the strike. This rapid redirection of picket cells was an indication of both the strength and weakness of the strike organisation in the first few days of the strike. Many firms when faced with a steel picket, immediately contacted the strike office in Rotherham to apply for a dispensation to continue

normal working. If a dispensation was granted, as quite a number
were, then cells would be relocated. Alternatively, agreements were
reached between pickets and the unions inside the plants to black
defined categories of steel, which meant that plants continued to
produce steel but then stockpiled it in their yards. Occasionally joint
union-management deputations reached agreement either with the
DSC or with local pickets, though more often it was the former. The fact
that dispensations were granted at all, and that they were often granted
by the DSC without consulting local pickets, caused considerable
resentment. Within a few weeks the initial flood of dispensations
reduced to a trickle, causing fewer problems on the picket lines.

Redirection of cells also reflected the rather haphazard nature of
target selection. Targets for picketing were culled from a variety of
sources, including the strikers' own (very limited) personal knowledge,
as well as other unions. Indeed on one occasion the RSC even used the
Yellow Pages of the telephone directory in search of new picketing
targets (cf. Pitt, 1978 who reported a similar diversity of information
sources in the 1972 British miners' strike). Understandably therefore
mistakes were made in the early days of the strike, as the RSC's
knowledge of the private sector was patchy. This was epitomised in the
notable case of the picket cell despatched to a 'local steel stockholder'
only to discover the plant in question was a flour mill!

Flying pickets
Rather less confusion characterised the small (5% of pre-strike volunteers) but growing number of flying pickets, who were mainly despatched to East and South coast ports from 2 January. Some were on short
stays of less than 24 hours, whilst others, such as the South coast
pickets, were away for up to two weeks. The other main targets for
flying pickets were steel stockholders and private steel producers,
especially in the West Midlands, the ports and, later in the strike, steel
users such as engineering components and vehicles plants. There is
little reason to suppose that the experience of these early flying pickets
was significantly different from that of their local counterparts. The
numbers of pickets at any one target were, at this stage, comparable,
and the plants even less familiar than the South Yorkshire locations
assigned to local pickets. Presumably volunteers for flying picketing
may have differed in their personal attributes from 'local' pickets but
we simply have no information on this for the early stages of the strike.

Inter- and intra-group processes and picket activity

. . . ANARCHY HAS WON
. . . One thousand two hundred pickets . . . frightened the workforce back on strike. As Mr 'Dan' Norton, chairman of Hadfields put it: 'Intimidation and anarchy has won a total victory.' *(Daily Express,* 15 February 1980).

This quotation perhaps summarises a popular conception of picketing: it is a violent activity involving large numbers of strikers endeavouring to coerce other people, and it is probably illegal, undoubtedly illegitimate and definitely dramatic. There is some truth in *some* of these characterisations, but the experiences of many local pickets were often quite different. Even after a few weeks, marshals were saying that picketing was becoming 'just the same routine', and pickets were suffering 'boredom' and 'tedium'. On an eight-hour shift, even during daytime, pickets might be faced with as few as three or four lorries, whose drivers they recognised, and whose behaviour they could predict. The remainder of their shift was spent sitting inside a shelter (often it was cold or snowing) waiting for the next lorry, reading the newspaper, listening to the radio, chatting to fellow pickets, or just watching passers-by. But the day-time staff at least had some 'business', however routine: on the late afternoon, or night shifts, pickets were likely to be seated outside a closed and deserted plant, guarding the gates just in case the firm should try to move steel in or out. During the daytime, the waiting was punctuated with activity: at night it seemed endless. When it is recalled that some pickets worked five or six shifts per week, and many did at least three, it can readily be seen that for many of the local pickets, drama, violence, massed confrontations, and heated arguments with furious lorry drivers were events they watched on television, or read about in their papers as they sat quietly whiling away the time.

How can we account for the discrepancy between the image and this reality of picketing? The answer to this question lies in a series of changes in the task and the environments of pickets which had the effect of reducing uncertainty. The early days of the strike were characterised by a high degree of uncertainty in the external physical environment of pickets (because of repeated redirection of picket cells); there was uncertainty emanating from the task of picketing itself because of the inexperience of the majority of strikers, from the *external* social environment of picket cells as the composition and activities of other groups continually changed, and finally from the *internal* social environment of the picket cells as pickets transferred between cells. In the first few weeks of the strike, these sources of uncertainty gradually abated as the environment and the task of picketing were stabilised.

How this stabilisation took place can be dealt with briefly. Seventeen of the 20 cell marshals interviewed reported all their moves within the first two weeks of the strike, and thereafter they remained on the same targets until the end of the strike. Most of the local pickets therefore soon arrived at what was to be their location for the remainder of the strike. But the most striking manifestation of the stabilisation of the physical environment was the proliferation of the pickets' shelters. These makeshift but elaborate constructions were built from scraps of wood, tarpaulin, plastic sheeting, corrugated metal and anything else donated by their owners or which could be 'removed' from them without risk. Many contained the usual braziers as well as an extraordinary range of furnishings: chairs, sofas, tables, radios, and in some cases, even television sets powered by car batteries. So attached did pickets become to these shelters that one marshal cited the police destruction of his cell's shelter as a blow to their morale.

A similar process could be discerned with respect to the picket's task. The uneven distribution of formal instructions or briefing was corrected within the first week of January by the circulation of an RSC leaflet on picketing (although the extent of distribution is unknown). This informed pickets how to approach drivers, suggesting they should transmit details of the strike and ask them to contact their own branch secretary if they were union members. If necessary they were to be threatened with blacking after the strike. The leaflet conveyed the view that neither the law nor the police were to be relied upon and that only 'numbers and determination are effective'. Finally it gave instructions on what should be done in case of arrest, and the telephone numbers of the ISTC solicitors.

Inter-group relations

The most fascinating and undoubtedly the most significant area of stabilisation was in the realm of inter-group relations, where the stabilising process extended to embrace the formal enemies of the strikers, and relations with the police provided its clearest illustration. Several marshals felt that on balance the local police had behaved quite reasonably, and that some had even been 'helpful'. One marshal severely castigated the violence of the SPG and proceeded to contrast them with the local police who had even flagged down approaching lorries to allow the pickets to speak with their drivers. Other marshals described their relations with the local police as being 'quite good' and even 'friendly'. Some cells and shifts developed a joking relationship with their formal antagonists; others extended the hospitality of their elaborate shelters to the police. The closest relationship with local police was developed by one cell whose assigned constable reported for duty before the picket shift began, and who helpfully lit the brazier before the pickets had arrived. It might reasonably be objected that this is only one, and indeed, an unusual example of a close relationship between pickets and police, but as we shall see in the next chapter it was an example which exerted a powerful influence on the RSC. The official South Yorkshire police report on the steel strike made a similar point about police-picket relations when it noted that

> . . . the majority of the time there was no confrontation between the police and pickets and relationships were extremely good. (p.11).

In the famous Pilkingtons strike in 1970 its chroniclers observed that

> Relationships with the police and the Pilkington security men seemed to have been amicable when things were quiet: they talked and drank tea with the pickets. (Lane and Roberts, 1971, p.171).

Such relationships arose primarily because of the repeated interactions between groups performing essentially similar tasks, although they were also a function of police tactics. The Chief Constable of South Yorkshire arranged a meeting with the local strike leaders shortly before the strike began to explain the laws on picketing and the way his forces would handle picket lines, and this contact was maintained throughout the strike. Several marshals reported that police attitudes changed significantly after the most violent mass picket, on 14 February, a fact which also points to the tactical nature of such close relationships.

The behaviour of lorry drivers became more predictable to pickets in the first few weeks of the strike, as they became able to assess the likelihood of stopping particular drivers. Many of the local plants were regularly serviced by a relatively small number of drivers and within a matter of weeks many cells knew which drivers or firms would cross the picket lines and which would respect them and turn back. As one marshal said 'people stop bothering when they see the same lorries'. According to the marshals, very few drivers changed their behaviour following their initial decision on whether or not to cross the lines. Even new drivers displayed recognisable signs of their intentions to the perceptive picket. Several marshals noted that drivers intending to cross their picket line would either accelerate shortly before reaching it, or if they did stop, would engage the pickets in protracted arguments before finally moving into the picketed plant. And as drivers respecting picket lines were increasingly laid off, the proportion of 'cowboys' prepared to cross them correspondingly increased. Once the behaviour of drivers was perceived as inevitable, several marshals reported the development of not unfriendly relations with 'scab' lorry drivers who regularly crossed picket lines. The pickets in a few cells got onto first-name terms with some of these drivers despite the mutual knowledge that the driver would cross the picket line and weaken the strike.

Relationships with workers inside some of the picketed plants showed similar tendencies at work. One cell came very near to closing down a private steel producer, which would have resulted in the complete lay-off of the workforce. Despite this the cell enjoyed a 'very good' relationship with the non-striking ISTC convenor of the plant, and workers there even contributed a levy to support their striking colleagues.

Another marshal recalled that his cell had been transferred from its first target after the firm's director had issued a written undertaking not to bring in new supplies of scrap metal. The RSC indicated their trust in this Director by accepting his undertaking. Another marshal observed that his cell felt 'no animosity to the management' inside their plant as they were, after all, only 'doing their job whilst the pickets were likewise doing theirs'.

Stabilisation of inter-group relations was not confined to local picket sites, but also occurred at flying picket locations. The number of pickets at Dover was eventually cut back by the RSC (in February) as it was felt pickets were attracted there by the material benefits (free or subsidised food, drink and accommodation, courtesy of the Kent NUM) and were failing to pursue a sufficiently aggressive policy towards local drivers, employers and police.

On these picket lines therefore, the formal antagonisms between pickets, police, lorry drivers and workers inside the picketed plants were accommodated into stable sets of relationships based on shared expectations and norms. Each of the parties came to accept the legitimacy of the others' activities provided they were conducted on the basis of the norms or rules which had arisen on the lines, and which entailed a certain 'model' of picketing. Within this model, picketing was definitely non-violent; it rarely involved displays of force; it stayed within the law; and its principal instrument was peaceful persuasion. As one marshal graphically stated, his cell's target and the picketing required was 'a pension number'. Not least of the problems facing pickets in such settings was that of boredom brought about by prolonged periods of inactivity interspersed with picketing whose outcome was often entirely predictable.

Intra-group processes

The stabilisation of the physical environment, of the picketing task, and of inter-group relations on some of the picket lines were social processes which interacted with a number of intra-group processes. Firstly the *internal* social environment of picket cells stabilised as strikers selected themselves into and out of various cells, and the frequency of movement in and out of cells appears to have diminished within approximately two weeks of the strike's inception. Almost every marshal reported a small initial loss of members, varying from one to seven and averaging four (out of 30). The reasons, reported by almost all, were a combination of boredom with the routine of local picketing coupled with the attractions of flying picketing: the excitement and/or the payment of £1 per day for living expenses. Almost all of those who switched to flying pickets were young, single workers who were therefore ineligible for supplementary benefit. Local pickets by contrast received no payment, with the exception of those who incurred petrol costs in driving to and from their picket lines. There was also movement into and out of local cells by workers who preferred to picket with their friends than with a cell where they knew few, if any, people. But many pickets not only remained in the same cell, they also remained in the same shift team of five to six pickets with whom they therefore spent the overwhelming majority of their time. Most of these fellow pickets belonged to other union branches and were only casually acquainted at the start of the strike: the picket marshals, for instance, knew on average only five or six of their cell members at the beginning of the strike, and three knew none at all.

The existence of small, isolated, stable groups with few prior friendship bonds working in a potentially or actually hostile environment provides fertile conditions for the growth of group cohesion. What evidence is there that such cohesion actually developed? And since cohesion is one element within the concept of morale (the others being individual satisfaction and goal commitment), what was the state of pickets' morale?

Firstly, several marshals reported the growth of friendships within their groups, some of which persisted after the strike. Indeed many interviewees reported a considerable increase in inter-group co-operation at work after the strike. Among flying pickets, one marshal noted that his cell had become like a 'small community'. Secondly, some of the marshals reported feelings of mutual obligation as a factor which inhibited 'absenteeism', as they termed it. One marshal said his cell required little control as the shift teams were 'self-regulating'. In other words the identification of pickets with their shift team developed to the point where they were reluctant to let down their fellow strikers by taking time off, and the weekly hours worked by pickets were therefore remarkably constant, averaging 23.7 in January, 23.0 in February and 22.6 in March (see Appendix 2). To a large degree the stability of reported hours can be attributed to the cell structure with its regular shifts and shift teams. Picketing hours which were multiples of five, six and eight were reported by approximately 85% of pickets in each of the three months of the strike.

Absenteeism is exceptionally difficult to assess even in the fairly orderly strike organisation at Rotherham. RSC reports were unreliable until near the end of the strike because the committee lacked systematic information on numbers of pickets and shift systems. The marshals' reports are open to question because of their vested interest in presenting an account of a well-managed cell (cf. Berman, 1974 on group-loyalty). All we can do here is report the more systematic data from the marshals, with some qualifications where possible. Only two marshals were unable to answer a question on absence, and 13 of the remainder reported some, whilst five (three of whom were flying picket marshals) claimed there was none at all. These differences were not related to frequency of contact between marshals and pickets. Marshals either worked with a single shift and met the other teams at the start and finish of their own shift, or visited the picket lines in the middle of each of the shifts being worked. Four marshals said (not surprisingly) that absenteeism was concentrated on the most tedious and unsocial shifts, i.e. nights and weekends, a fact apparent to the RSC as early as 14 January. Another report, from Picket Control, found that an impromptu visit to a number of local plants late at night revealed that many of them were not covered by pickets (who presumably had absented themselves). Although weekend and night working was sometimes a cause of difficulty, three other marshals allowed absence at weekends. One indeed argued that it was 'impossible to expect people to turn out every day'. In cells of approximately 30 pickets however, marshals who quantified absence tended to say it was only between one and four individuals who were 'a problem'.

Loss of pickets is another possible indicator of cell cohesion. In interviews eleven marshals reported a net increase in cell size during the strike, five reported a decrease and two witnessed no change. Of our questionnaire respondents, 109 did not picket in March, an increase of 21 over the corresponding January figure. Such figures should be treated with caution: people who dropped out of local picket cells did not necessarily drop out of strike activity.

A number of marshals actually sought to encourage pickets to identify with their shift teams by assigning each team a number or other distinctive label. A similar degree of identification was evident at the level of whole cells, particularly in those which were differentiated from other cells by their performance of a distinctive function. After a few weeks of local picketing, cell 11 volunteered *en masse* for flying picketing. Its marshal sought to maintain the morale of his members by promoting the reputation of the cell. He regularly composed poems about its exploits, which were read out *en route* to picketing targets, and he heightened its attraction to members by telling them there was a waiting list of those anxious to join its ranks. Other cells participated in the flourishing enterprise of badge production and cell members displayed their symbols of group membership: B—.'s Battalion, G—.'s Gorillas, Oxford Brigade, R—.'s Battalion.

Turning to other aspects of morale, 15 marshals said morale (individual feelings of satisfaction) was generally good, three said it was not so good, and three said it varied or was hard to tell. Marshals cited a variety of influences on local picket morale, but the most frequently cited (by 11 marshals) was *national* events. Often these were reports of disappointment or anger at decisions of the General Secretary and EC, or of a failure in negotiation, and this evidence is consistent with that of pickets' demands for information, which showed a strong bias towards national events and developments. Inequities in payments or shifts were cited by half of the marshals as a cause of frustration and dissatisfaction, especially after the mass pickets in February, and eight of these 10 marshals were in charge of local cells (see next chapter). The position of the private sector featured in the comments of six marshals, with some pointing to the morale-boosting effects of mass picketing, whilst others cited the return to work of the private sector, and the granting of dispensations by the RSC, as negative influences on morale. There were variations in morale over time and five marshals reported a mid-strike trough, between the sixth and tenth weeks, when national negotiations were making no progress, and when the RSC organised a series of mass pickets partly in order to boost what it correctly perceived as a decline in morale. Seven marshals reported an end-of-strike trough either in anticipation of or in response to the final settlement. Interestingly only six marshals suggested that the daily experiences of picketing were closely tied to morale, four of whom considered that the lack of efficacy of their cell had a depressing effect on their members.

The unevenness of stabilisation of the picket organisation

Over the first few weeks of the strike the physical environment and the social composition of the picket cells both *stabilised,* i.e. they became less salient sources of uncertainty for pickets. The internal life of the picket cells was regularised as pickets worked in small, cohesive and stable groups on a stable system of shifts. This internal stabilisation both influenced and was influenced by stabilisation of inter-group relations. *In part* some of these inter- and intra-group processes may be seen as responses to uncertainty as pickets and strike leaders adjusted their organisation to a changing and uncertain social environment, and indeed tried to reduce uncertainty. These processes were certainly not the result of *decisions* taken by groups within the strike organisation, but nor were they simply the inevitable changes wrought by a hostile and turbulent environment. The degree of stabilisation described thus far was not inevitable, but contingent, because it did not occur uniformly across the whole picket organisation. Some cells displayed evidence of extensive stabilisation, whilst others showed only sporadic or limited stabilisation of inter-group relations. Before offering an explanation of this variation in picket organisation, we need first to document the picket situations which showed only limited stabilisation.

Limited stabilisation: local pickets

The clearest examples of target plants in this category were Hadfields, Templeborough Rolling Mill (TRM) and Arthur Lee, two of which were the scene of mass pickets in February and March. Relations with the police were variable, but certainly the degree of co-operation and friendliness attained elsewhere was reported less frequently here. The police presence at these targets was often considerable. At one stage police on Arthur Lee, one of only six local targets where any arrests were made, outnumbered pickets by 5:1 and there were large numbers also at Hadfields and TRM. It is important to stress that police behaviour varied between individuals and over time. One marshal reported that the aggressiveness of picketing permitted by the police varied with the particular officers on duty. Other marshals reported considerable differences between the behaviour of the local police, who *could* sometimes be friendly, and those from outside the region, who were considered far more aggressive. Police on these targets also sought quite actively to regulate picket numbers and produced a variety of 'interpretations' of the law in so doing. Pickets at Laycock and Osborn were informed that picket numbers could legally not exceed six; a cell on Firth Brown's was informed that they were entitled to a maximum of two pickets per union, in response to which the 12 ISTC pickets promptly 'joined' a variety of unions to retain their picket line. Such petty harassment contrasts sharply with the easy-going or friendly relations established under conditions of considerable stabilisation.

Relations with the *employers* at TRM and Hadfields were often hostile and the Chairman of Hadfields, Derek Norton, acquired considerable notoriety for his forthright verbal attacks on the pickets. The private sector steel members of ISTC employed in Hadfields were led by Andy M., who was intensely distrusted by the RSC and other strike leaders, though the attitudes of the pickets were less clear. Finally, the absence of stable sets of relationships was signified by violence, in which each party deliberately sought to achieve its objectives by using force against one or more of its antagonists. Indeed, over 90% of the arrests made by South Yorkshire police were at Hadfields and TRM and these were not occasioned solely by the RSC inspired mass pickets of 12, 14 and 27 February and in March (see below). Arrests of pickets at Hadfields and TRM began on 8 January, over one month before the first mass picket, and further arrests were made on 9, 10 and 31 January, and 1, 11 and 19 February.

Picketing at these and other locations did not then display extensive stabilisation. There was little clear evidence of mutual adjustment of expectations and norms to regulate behaviour. Instead, each of the parties continually sought to impose its own norms in order to achieve its objectives, and the absence of mutual adjustment is indicated most clearly by mass picketing, on the one hand, and police arrests on the other. These observations apply with even greater force to the institution of flying pickets.

Limited stabilisation: flying pickets

The stabilisation of picketing roles or locations would appear, almost by definition, to be incompatible with the use of 'flying squads' of pickets, some of which moved rapidly around the country from one target to another and sought to shut down plants by the use of force and/or numbers. In some areas (e.g. Dover), elements of extensive stabilisation did emerge, but the more conventional flying pickets operated very differently. Flying pickets were organised daily from 2 January and consisted of two groups of workers. On the one hand there were local cells or fragments of cells which had transferred to flying picketing (six of the 20 cells covered in our marshals' interviews fell into this category). On the other hand there were individual members of cells who were 'off-duty', and individuals unaffiliated to any local cell. The numbers of pickets varied considerably but on average two coaches with 80 pickets were despatched daily (Monday-Friday) from Rotherham between January and March.

No clear organisational structure emerged until the 'fiasco' at Walkers of Blackburn (22 January), a big steel stockholder in Rotherham. The mass flying picket at Walkers was met by a superbly organised and sizeable police contingent and its efforts that day were entirely fruitless. In response to this, one of the marshals made the first attempt to draft an organisational structure and a set of operating procedures for flying pickets. They were highly militaristic and were adopted almost wholesale by the RSC (see Chapter 8). It is possible that one effect of grouping flying pickets into units of 25, each under the charge of a marshal, was to increase the cohesion of such units and of the flying picket 'squads' as a whole. Certainly a high degree of cohesion emerged within the cells engaged in permanent flying picketing but it is difficult to say much about the attitudes of individual flying pickets who operated outside the cell structure.

The normal pattern of flying picketing was to descend on a plant and rapidly establish picket lines and a local picket control responsible for all necessary arrangements. The picket lines were maintained for up to approximately eight hours, and drivers attempting to cross these lines were met by considerable displays of force. Clearly then opportunities to develop stable sets of relations with drivers, police, employers and workers inside the picketed plants almost never arose owing to the suddenness, brevity and forcefulness of the picketing. Relationships between these parties and the flying pickets were often extremely hostile. The hostility was generated and reinforced by the behaviour of the parties towards each other, and also by their internal organisation. The flying pickets came to be organised on a quasi-military basis and it is conceivable (though we have no evidence of this) that such organisation itself promoted or was conducive to attitudes of marked inter-group hostility, an argument derived from social psychological theory (cf. Tajfel, 1978).

The most extreme cases of hostility and physical violence occurred in Birmingham (and not, in fact, on the local mass pickets). Birmingham had the second largest concentration of steel stockholders in the UK and it obviously figured from the start of the strike as a major picketing target. The reaction of local drivers was, in some cases, extremely hostile, and South Yorkshire pickets reported threats of violence issued by drivers wielding spanners and other heavy implements. At a 'closed' meeting (i.e. ourselves and other observers excluded) on the 24 January the RSC heard a presentation from a member of the Committee on the impossibility of conducting normal, peaceful picketing in

Birmingham, and accepted the case for the use of 'special' tactics, to defend their own pickets as well as to prevent steel movement. These tactics certainly included sabotage, and members of these special squads were carefully selected for their physical strength and their willingness to use violence.

Variations in picketing as different 'negotiated orders'

These differing degrees of stabilisation can be understood as different systems of order constructed on the basis of different sets of rules or norms. On the strikers' side most had no prior strike experience, and at the outset of the strike there was considerable confusion among pickets as to the nature and limits of their role. The police, as already observed, presented *different* rules to different groups of pickets and, judging by the official police report on the strike (South Yorkshire Police, 1980), sought to pursue an overall goal of maintaining control (even at the price of tolerating minor breaches of law) which was sufficiently vague to permit different interpretations. In the absence of any environmental features which *compelled* participants to adopt a particular form of organisation, we have here the preconditions (lack of consensus, competing goals) necessary for the participants to construct and negotiate their own social orders on the picket lines.

The questions which then arise are: what were the norms and rules on which these orders were negotiated? and why did they vary *between* situations? To answer the first question we examine the conceptions of picketing prevalent throughout the lower levels of the strike organisation, in order both to establish the activities and norms that were common to all pickets, and those which differentiated some pickets from others. In examining these norms we are concerned in particular, given the uncertain legality and legitimacy of picketing, with the ways in which pickets distinguished legitimate and illegitimate behaviour, in other words with the *boundary of legitimacy*.

The variety of negotiated orders

The precise relationship between people's experiences and their conceptions of picketing is difficult to determine, but the movement of individuals out of local and into flying picketing (and in some cases, in the opposite direction) can be interpreted as an attempt to correct a mismatch between the two by self-selection.

There is certainly evidence to suggest that the process of stabilisation found among some of the local picketing sites was associated with particular conceptions of picketing. One marshal stated that his cell members did not like mass picketing, as they were 'respectable pickets'. And he explained his cell's lack of success with its allocated target by noting that picketing could only have been effective if his members had been prepared to break the law — which they were not. Another marshal, again an older worker, also made clear that his pickets wanted to remain 'within the law' and 'to be legal'. It was in these, and a few other local cells, that violence and mass picketing became issues, and these picket marshals variously reported their members as feeling frightened, or disapproving of the perceived violence, and reluctant to disrupt their established picketing routines (see below). These strikers were not therefore committed to *any* forms of picketing that were required to achieve their objectives: the end did *not* justify all of the means available. Their boundary of legitimate picketing was set by at least two factors: on the one hand *legality* and on the other *non-violence*. But limited commitment among some of the strikers operated not only with respect to the *form* of picketing but also to its *duration*, a fact that emerged in questions to marshals about picket morale.

Despite substantial variations in the reported efficacy of picketing (see below) most marshals said that pickets were none the less reasonably satisfied with their picketing duties. What exactly did satisfaction mean in this context? For those strongly in favour only of peaceful picketing, it referred to the fact that they had been assigned a particular responsibility and were entitled to feel satisfied when their responsibility was discharged as effectively as possible. Several marshals spoke, in this context, of pickets 'doing their bit', of 'doing their stint'; others more directly observed they were 'there to do a job', or 'had a job to do', and one even remarked that after some weeks picketing was not unlike 'going to work every day'. What comes across from these comments is an implicit recognition and acceptance of the strike organisation's division of labour: some have the 'job' of picketing, whilst others have the 'jobs' of administration, decision-making, etc.

Even more telling was the response by some of these (and other) cells to an RSC allocation of additional pickets. Periodically the RSC redirected a few picket cells, usually onto strategically important plants in order to increase the effectiveness of picketing. In two of these cases marshals used the additional resources to *reduce* the length of shifts or weekly hours worked by individual pickets. In at least two more cells marshals allowed pickets the option of not working weekends, despite their knowledge of the RSC's concern with 'absenteeism' at weekends and nights. In terms of the analysis of extensive stabilisation we can see that marshals provided with additional resources and an instruction to 'beef up' their picketing confront a dilemma. To comply with the request might increase picketing efficacy, but it would also disrupt the stable relations built up between pickets, drivers, police and employers and within picket groups. By reducing the hours of each picket, and leaving the strength of picket lines unchanged, the allocation of extra resources was thereby accommodated without generating disruption. This example also points up the ambiguous position of the picket marshals: on the one hand they worked closely with their cell members but on the other they were 'representatives' of the RSC. Indeed their position is not unlike that of a 'foreman' facing conflicting pressures from above and below.

A final strand of evidence consistent with the conception of picketing described so far comes from the information sought by pickets. In five cells, marshals reported that pickets were predominantly interested in national events, that is to say, in the negotiations between unions and the Corporation. In a further seven cells, pickets sought information on strike pay, payment of supplementary benefit, union branch meetings and the RSC in addition to details of national events. In only three cells did marshals report that pickets were *primarily* interested in local issues, or matters of immediate self-interest, such as strike pay. In other words, whilst the RSC (see Chapter 8) was predominantly concerned with picketing, the pickets, judged by their information demands, were far more concerned with national negotiations: only *one* of the marshals reported requests for information on other cells' picketing. It is also interesting to note that whilst the majority of these respondents described official trade union sources as 'very' or 'fairly' reliable sources of information (75%), as many as 36% described the mass media in similar terms.

This pattern of information demand *could* reflect the fact that pickets learned about other cells from workmates, but had no informal sources of information on negotiations. It could, alternatively, reflect an instrumental attitude towards picketing, in which it is seen simply as a means to an end. Such an instrumental view is compatible with the perception of picketing as a 'job' and with satisfaction based on 'doing one's bit' to further the strike (cf. Berman, 1974 who found similar degrees of limited commitment in a revolutionary, military organisation).

On the picket lines which witnessed the most far-reaching stabilisation of inter-group relations we find then a set of norms compatible with this process. Picketing is an activity circumscribed by a boundary composed of peacefulness and legality, and by instrumentalism, the latter evidenced in a perception of picketing as a 'job' or obligation. Such norms were also compatible with those of the police, anxious to maintain control.

Yet this was by no means the only set of norms which arose on the picket lines. Three marshals reported that their cells' picketing became 'more aggressive', 'more ruthless', and 'tougher' as the strike wore on through its first few weeks. Picket tactics shifted as the strike progressed, and as the RSC marshals and pickets judged such changes to be necessary. In these cells marshals did not report respect for the law (either in general, or as embodied in the police) to be an insurmountable constraint on their picketing. Two marshals who appreciated the necessity to 'step up' picketing simply noted that police cover on their targets was variable and that it was possible 'to cause aggravation' in their absence. In the same vein another criticised sabotage of lorries not because it was wrong but because it provoked a police backlash. Several marshals reported that mass picketing at Hadfields boosted picket morale considerably, and one proudly told how his members returned to the later mass pickets despite the arrests of some of them on the first mass picket. Descriptions of picketing as a 'job' with definite boundaries were rarely produced: indeed one marshal said that he and his cell were 'prepared to work any hours' in order to win the strike.

Finally, there existed among a small section of strikers a distinct readiness to use force. Force could mean either mass picketing, or actual physical violence, but such views were voiced more often on and around the RSC than in the lower ranks of the strike organisation, a fact evidenced in the enthusiasm and frequency with which the RSC debated the deployment of the mass picket in the second month of the strike (see Chapters 6,8). In this conception of picketing the activity was regulated less by legal norms than by calculations of self-interest and opportunism. Not surprisingly these norms·were more frequently articulated by marshals on plants with more arrests and higher levels of police manning. It should be stressed that the patterns of norms described here were by no means discrete and exclusive, but that there was overlap. For example, one of the marshals reporting that his cell engaged in more aggressive picketing in the absence of police, also described relations with the police as generally 'good'. Another marshal, whose members were described to us as 'respectable pickets', hostile to mass picketing and unwilling to increase picketing effectiveness by breaking the law, was presented with a dilemma by the Denning injunction. The marshal's cell was located at Arthur Lees, one of the firms from which ISTC had to remove pickets following the injunction granted to 16 private sector steel firms. Rather than obey 'the law', the cell initially passed themselves off as non-ISTC members, before being redirected by the RSC. This example shows the complexity both of terms such as 'the law' and of pickets' attitudes.

Determinants of variation

What then were the situational factors associated with variations in stabilisation of inter-group relations? The key factors appear to have been, firstly, the *strategic importance* of the picketing target as perceived by the parties in the strike, and secondly, the variability in the *tactics* of the parties. The local firms which were the site of the most arrests were TRM, Hadfields and Arthur Lees, whilst elsewhere it was the West Midlands conurbation, and the Sheerness plant in the south of England. The three local plants are amongst the largest private sector steel producers and employers in the Rotherham area and were therefore seen by the RSC as posing the greatest threat to the strike. The West Midlands area has the largest concentration of steel stockholders in the UK as well as a steel plant part-owned by BSC. Sheerness, finally, was the largest private steel producer in the UK outside South Yorkshire and the West Midlands. The strategic importance of these plants lay both in their production and/or distribution of steel, and in the fact that continued working by their ISTC employees was a potent source of inter-union discontent (see Chapter 9).

Secondly, such plants were singled out by the RSC for mass picketing throughout January and February, a mode of picketing which certainly strained stabilised inter-group relations though it did not necessarily disrupt them irreversibly. The mass picket can be taken as evidence of a high motivation to win on the part of the strikers, and a similar level of motivation was evident in the police opposition. Indeed the mass picket may also be seen as a tactic deployed by the strikers to assert their concept of order on the picket lines against that of the police in a situation where no accommodation seemed possible. By contrast more peaceful picketing was found either on the smaller steel plants, or on the larger plants where pickets had 'accepted', and accommodated to, an unfavourable situation.

CHAPTER SIX

Controlling pickets: problems of authority and militancy

In this chapter we examine the integration of strikers into the strike organisation. By integration we mean both the successful co-ordination of activities, through organisational networks, between groups of strikers required to co-operate with each other in pursuit of organisational objectives; and the acceptance by strikers of the objectives and methods of the strike, and the authority of the strike leadership.

There are several grounds for thinking that the integration of active strikers into the strike organisation would have been relatively unproblematic. Firstly, the strike organisation was established to promote their immediate economic interest in securing a wage increase commensurate with the cost of living; secondly, active participation in the strike was, for the most part voluntary; thirdly, the organisation structure looked, on paper, like an efficient, well-designed bureaucracy within which people's roles were fairly clear; fourth, *most* of the strikers would be performing a similar task, viz. picketing, which means that the organisation would manifest a relatively low degree of differentiation; fifth, the internal flow of information between activists and leaders was regular and extensive; and finally the strikers were operating in a hostile environment, a condition conducive to intra-group cohesion. Surely therefore integration would be unlikely to constitute a problem for the strike leadership?

In fact, for reasons identified in the previous chapter, the strike organisation was rather more complex than the above picture suggests, not least because of the uneven process of stabilisation of intra- and inter-group relations and the growth of cohesion within the picket cells. Certain cells cohered around norms which were, as we shall see, at variance with those promulgated by the RSC. Furthermore it was not at all obvious that the strike organisation was a bureaucracy, with power and authority flowing from the top downwards: the marshals' influence over their pickets gave them a potential power resource, magnified by their key liaison role between pickets and the RSC; and the voluntary status of the pickets also raises a question about the basis on which they came to accept the authority of the RSC, and whether indeed the strike organisation *did* function as a bureaucracy. The voluntary status of pickets, the fluidity of organisational boundaries and the absence of any obvious sanctions available to the RSC would suggest severe limits on the possibility of striker integration through bureaucratic procedure.

In the present chapter therefore we begin by examining the formal organisational structure created to integrate and control strikers. At the same time it will also be necessary to examine the *informal* structure which evolved alongside, that is, the networks of contacts which predated the strike or developed in the course of it. This dissection of a seemingly neat and simple, though actually 'messy' organisation forms an essential backcloth to the ensuing account of the RSC's picketing strategy and its perception of the strike organisation. The adoption of the 'mass picket' as a key tactic in the second month of the strike revealed some startling discrepancies between the actual evolution of the strike organisation and the RSC's perceptions of the organisation, generating a number of unintended behavioural consequences.

Formal and informal mechanisms of integration

One of the greatest dangers facing any strike is open division among the strikers over the means and/or the ends of the strike. One of the reasons for such division may be that some of the strikers succumb to hostile propaganda; consequently, strike 'handbooks' place considerable emphasis on the maintenance of unity through regular flows of information between strike leaders and rank-and-file (e.g. Johnston, 1975).

Branch meetings

Most of the ISTC union branches met weekly during the strike, and some of them combined to hold regular mass meetings attracting up to 500 strikers. The mass meetings, and some of the branch meetings, were attended by members of the RSC and by Rotherham's delegates on the Executive Council. Reports would be given to the meeting on the state of negotiations, the latest offer by BSC and the union objections to it, as well as other matters discussed at the 11 EC meetings held during the strike (they are normally held *once* in three months — see Chapter 9). A member of the RSC would give a report on picketing, and details would be given of any special requests, such as a forthcoming mass picket or a demonstration or rally. Sometimes there would be a morale-boosting speech by the strike co-ordinator. Finally, there would be questions from the floor, which varied from detailed queries about pickets on a particular plant through to general questions about strike or even post-strike strategy, e.g. how would non-pickets be punished for their inactivity? The formal mechanism devised to facilitate more detailed co-ordination of pickets was twofold: first there were weekly meetings between the picket marshals and members of the picket control and RSC; second, there was a permanent strike administration, Picket Control.

Marshals' meetings

Picket marshals' meetings were held weekly throughout the strike at the strike headquarters. They were attended by a large majority of marshals, and were chaired and introduced by leading members of the RSC and Picket Control. The format of the meetings varied, but usually included reports from Picket Control on picketing targets and morale, or changes in tactics; reports from individual marshals on their own situations: and discussions between the marshals and strike leaders on a variety of strike issues.

The marshals' assessments of these meetings varied considerably: whilst 11 found them useful, six did not. Almost half of the marshals valued the meetings for the instructions and information they exchanged with the strike leaders, but the other half found most benefit in their discussions with fellow marshals. The meetings certainly *did* transmit instructions to the marshals, e.g. to adopt eight-hour picket shifts, and to submit lists of their cell members to Picket Control. Yet these and other instructions were ignored by some of the marshals, who were far from being compliant subordinates within a conventional authority structure, and who exercised discretion in respect of RSC instructions. But it would be wrong to focus purely on the formal means of co-ordination because both the RSC and the marshals used channels other than the regular weekly meeting. In February, the RSC sought to mobilise pickets directly by simply phoning marshals and directing them to specified targets (see below). The marshals, for their part, did not rely solely, or in some cases to *any* significant extent, on the meetings as a source of information, because many had personal contacts with members of the RSC and DSC, and they visited the strike office, on average, three to four times each week. Not surprisingly, those who made fewer informal visits were *more* likely to find the formal, marshals' meetings useful.

The important feature of picketing related to use of informal networks in the strike organisation was the degree of *stabilisation* of inter-group relations on the picket lines. The six marshals in the most stabilised settings visited the strike office on average only twice each week, whereas their counterparts in less stabilised settings, or on flying picketing called between four and five times weekly. This reduced contact between marshals in stabilised settings and the RSC and Picket Control was reinforced by an active withholding of information on the part of some of those marshals. One said, 'Once we were organised, I didn't bother the strike committee with our problems', whilst another 'left Picket Control alone, as they had enough to do'. In other words these marshals had their 'job' to do (as did the RSC) and they simply got on with it.

Picket Control

Picket Control was housed in the strike headquarters and was a focal point of activity. One section (covered by up to three strikers) handled telephone calls (seven days per week, 24 hours per day) requesting or providing information, as well as personal calls either from outside, or from strike leaders working nearby; another section was in charge of picket cells, regularly updating lists of cell members and their locations, redirecting cells in the light of RSC decisions and debates, merging cells depleted by loss of members, and generally endeavouring to introduce some order into the potentially chaotic ebb and flow of large numbers of novice strikers. Surrounded by charts, maps and lists they contrasted with the fitting austerity of the financial section which occupied a bare table for the payment of petrol and other expenses. Most, though not all, of these strike administrators were white collar workers: technical and supervisory staff (all belonging to ISTC), by contrast with the manual worker dominance in picketing. Information was scrupulously recorded: details of all incoming telephone calls were logged in a book recording the identity of the caller, the topic, date and time.

In theory, information received by Picket Control was passed up to the RSC and processed by the Committee; any decisions issuing from their discussion were relayed back to Picket Control for transmission to marshals, and/or relayed directly at the marshals' meetings. But Picket Control was not simply an information channel, and its members not only received enquiries from marshals, but also took decisions, extending on some occasions to the redirection of picket cells. It is surprising, in view of its obvious prominence, that no members of Picket Control occupied a place on the RSC in their own right, but this situation changed after four weeks of the strike when one of the picket cell organisers from Picket Control (a staff branch secretary) began regularly attending the RSC, and was joined over the next few weeks by several of his co-workers.

The initial absence of Picket Control from the RSC arose from the fact that the Committee was organised on the basis of works constituencies, not strike functions, and its gradual rise onto the Committee in early February is easily explicable since it coincided with a series of crucial discussions on the RSC about picketing morale and effectiveness. These discussions took place within the context of an organisation which superficially appeared to be fairly simple, with a short hierarchy, clear lines of authority and a high degree of consensus on the activities pursued by the organisation. But the discussion of integration through the marshals' meetings, through informal contacts and through Picket Control highlights two very important features of the strike organisation. The first is that the organisation was understood as a clear authority structure by some of the marshals, but not by all. The second is that the formal organisation (embracing all the marshals), existed alongside an informal organisation which embraced only some of them. The flying picket marshals, compared with their local co-workers, were more closely linked with and more reliant on information from Picket Control. In other words, picket marshals were *differentially* integrated into the strike organisation, a fact which became apparent to the RSC only with its organisation of mass picketing half-way through the strike.

The RSC and local pickets: stabilisation as organisation decay

Between mid-January and mid-February, all the aspects of stabilisation described in the previous chapter were raised and discussed at the RSC: absenteeism in some cells and the growth of friendly relations between pickets and their protagonists — drivers and police. But where we analysed a set of processes through which conflicts were accommodated, the RSC perceived only processes of organisational decay. On the 22 January there was a long discussion about some of the symptoms of this decay. Some local pickets did not always turn out for their shift; the whole cell system was growing in an unco-ordinated way, as evidenced in the tremendous variability of picketing hours between cells; and some cells were working only a few hours each week. The last point was underlined in the fourth week of the strike when ISTC cells had to be replaced by NCCC cells whilst the Denning injunction was in force. A difficulty emerged because the NCCC cells all worked eight hour shifts whilst some ISTC cells worked only four hours. On the 1 February it was noted in relation to a flying picket at Stockport that picket numbers were diminishing. An explicit discussion of 'morale' was held for the first time only at its meeting on 4 February. Some of the local cells, it was noted, were becoming demoralised and 'were not doing much', although in some cases this was because their firms had closed anyway. On the same afternoon, RSC delegates on the DSC argued that there was a need to escalate action in the dispute, and later in the meeting it was agreed that a 'psychological victory' was required at Hadfields, the largest private producer in the area, where steel was once again on the move.

By early February, the RSC had identified several problems within the organisation. Behavioural commitment was thought to be weak, uneven and/or declining; whilst a subsidiary problem of morale had begun to emerge. By morale the RSC normally meant subjective feelings, of despondency, or elation, rather than goal commitment or cohesion (see Chapter 5 above). Furthermore, morale and picketing behaviour were thought to be intimately related: aggressive picketing was both an effect and a cause of high morale, whilst its absence signified and promoted low morale. These problems were attributed to a lack of control or authority within the organisation at the level of the picket cell. The point was made repeatedly throughout the strike that cells were organised on geographical rather than branch lines (although there were a few branch cells in ISTC, and some branch cells were created in mid February) and this prevented the marshals from 'putting pressure on people', or 'controlling them' since most of the picket cell members were unknown to the marshals at the start of the strike (see Chapter 4).

In other words the organisational structure was not conducive to the RSC's control since it failed to exploit the authority enjoyed by branch officers over their union branch members. Furthermore the RSC did recognise that in the last analysis the pickets were *'volunteers'* not *'conscripts'*. They could therefore refuse to accept RSC or marshal's directions, leave the organisation, and cease to be active. By contrast the NCCC cells were organised on the basis of union branches; the picket marshals were stewards who enjoyed the support of their members; and members had been *instructed* not *requested* to picket. Hence the problems of authority and control perceived by ISTC were a specific feature of their own strike organisation. Theoretically, the problem with the picket organisation viewed from above was that it was limited in its capacity to function as a bureaucracy: power and authority were *not* concentrated in higher positions; roles were not always clear; and 'subordinates' did not always conform to leadership (i.e. RSC) expectations, a fact which emerged when the RSC first responded to its various problems.

It did so by breaking up and dispersing a number of cells with declining membership (at the end of January) to form 'cell 24', which was given a roving commission to tour local picket lines and 'beef up' or 'motivate' the poor picketing behaviour of some of the local cells. This was to be done by descending on the local picket line and, for a few hours, setting an example of the hard, aggressive picketing preferred by the RSC which would, hopefully, then be emulated. Local cells apparently did not respond well to the tacit suggestion they were in need of reform, quite apart from their disinclination to engage in the sort of picketing offered by 'cell 24'. But there was little subsequent discussion on the RSC about the effectiveness of this cell, and no attempt to evaluate its activities, and the assumptions about morale and behaviour on which they rested. The RSC's own conceptions of picketing were thus shielded from critical feedback, but they were to be tested, and other features of the strike organisation sharply revealed (differences in 'the negotiated orders' of picket lines; uneven integration of marshals into the strike organisation; ambiguity among marshals over the authority structure) when the RSC adopted mass picketing as a *central* and not just an occasional element in its strike strategy. This change in strategy was precipitated by the dramatic change in the position of private sector steel workers in the fifth and sixth weeks of the strike.

Mass pickets
The problem of the private sector
The private steel sector (see Chapter 4 above) was discussed fully at a joint ISTC/NUB Executive meeting on 16 January where it was agreed that private steel workers would be called out on strike from Sunday, 27 January in support of the public sector pay claim. On 26 January an injunction was granted in the Appeal Court, restraining ISTC from calling out on strike its private sector members in 16 firms, but it was subsequently overturned in the House of Lords. Before the House of Lords ruling the RSC declared that it would continue to picket three of the 16 firms named in the injunction with plants in the South Yorkshire area, but would use NCCC cells instead of ISTC cells as the former had not been cited in the injunction and were not therefore subject to legal restraint. After the House of Lords ruling it was confidently anticipated that the private sector would quickly rejoin the strike. Optimism was increased by the scheduled national joint negotiating meeting on 8 February (between ISTC, NUB and BSC), because there was some expectation that a new, and more acceptable offer would be made by BSC. Finally, the Strike Co-ordinator had reported to the RSC on 5 February the possibility of 'a major breakthrough' in Birmingham, one of the centres of private steel making and stockholding. This was because on Thursday, 7 February, there was to be a mass picket at the

Castle Bromwich plant of British Leyland. It appeared to many on the RSC that the strike was about to enter a new phase, with a significant shift in the balance of forces in favour of the strikers.

By 10 February all these hopes were shattered as the strike suffered three setbacks within a matter of days. The mass picket at Castle Bromwich was met and defeated by an unprecedented display of SPG (police) force; on 8 February negotiations with BSC broke up after 20 minutes amid recriminations and charges of deception; and on Sunday, 10 February, workers at Hadfields voted to return to work the next morning, in a decision which the NCCC members of the RSC had worried about as early as 6 February. From the outset the private sector's commitment to the strike was questionable (partly because of their separate bargaining structures), and several private sector delegates had spoken against their involvement at the ISTC Executive meeting which called them out. The mood at the RSC meeting on 11 February was understandably one of depression, and in this respect mirrored the reports by picket marshals of the influence of national events on morale, and of mid-strike trough in morale between the sixth and tenth weeks (around 4-24 February). It was in this context, of a series of setbacks, that discussions on mass picketing took on new significance.

The February offensive

It is difficult to determine precisely when a picket becomes a mass picket and when a mass picket becomes a demonstration. It is even difficult to distinguish them precisely by their different modes of operation: whilst it may appear that a mass picket substitutes force of numbers for verbal persuasion, the actual differences and similarities can be more complex. A picket at TRM on 27 February was a mass picket, in terms of numbers (there were 150 pickets on one gate) but its leaders sought to persuade the plant's union leaders of the justice of their case. Only when these talks failed were lorries physically prevented from moving. On the other hand, local, small picket groups would also obstruct lorries and threaten drivers, as well as using verbal persuasion, and so the term mass picket will be reserved for a large demonstration designed to blockade a plant and obstruct the flow of people and/or materials (a definition which makes the mass picket a rare event, see Marsh and Gillies, 1981).

Although the RSC organised a series of mass pickets in February, the tactic was by no means a product solely of a crisis in the strike. The RSC Chairman referred to the use of mass pickets at Hadfields in the second week of the strike, although at that stage they were comparatively small.

A mass picket was organised by the local inter-union Central Co-ordinating Committee on 21 and 22 January but its organisation was heavily criticised at the RSC the following day. This was not a criticism of mass pickets *per se* since the RSC had decided only the previous day to increase the number of flying pickets and organise daily trips to selected targets which would be shut down with mass pickets (and this operation did in fact begin on 25 January). But mass picketing was by no means *unanimously* supported, as a discussion on 24 January indicated. Faced with considerable opposition and outright hostility from Birmingham private steelworkers, the RSC engaged in a long debate on the relative merits of surprise mass pickets and preliminary negotiations with the non-striking workers. It emerged that ISTC was considerably more enthusiastic about mass pickets than other unions, but the RSC organised only one local mass picket between mid-January and mid-February. The issue was not discussed at any RSC meetings between 25 January and 6 February, although it was raised at the DSC, which organised a mass picket in Leeds on 28 January.

By Monday, 11 February the strike had suffered the setbacks described above and a mass picket seemed to the RSC the only recourse if Hadfields' employees were to be prevented from working. The strategic and symbolic significance of a return to work by Hadfields in particular and the private sector in general made the present situation 'very depressing' and it was argued on the RSC that an effective mass picket was imperative. Of all the local private sector steel plants, Hadfields was easily the biggest in terms of production and employment. It was therefore seen as a 'pace setter' by the RSC: strike support from Hadfields would facilitate their winning support from the rest of the private sector. Conversely, a return to work by Hadfields could be used by other private steelworkers to justify their own imminent desertion of the strike.

The first Hadfields mass picket duly took place on 12 February with an estimated 350 pickets on Hadfields' gates at 6.00 a.m. rising to approximately 620 as the day progressed. As the workers arrived for the early shift at about 7.00 a.m. there was a series of surges by the pickets to break through the police cordons and physically obstruct the road leading to one of the main entrances into Hadfields. The police responded with arrests of 64 pickets: some were unfortunate enough to be within reach of the police; others were verbally conspicuous; others seemed to be simply snatched from the crowd almost at random. Nevertheless, Hadfields remained open, as it did the following day when another ten arrests were made as 300 strikers picketed the plant. On the same day (13 February) the RSC praised the previous day's picket on the grounds that it had raised morale, although some members had reservations about the tactics used on the picket. Morale featured more prominently in the discussion of how to deploy the several hundred pickets currently at Hadfields. On the one hand it was argued that leaving people there would raise morale because Hadfields was about to close and pickets would want to be there to see the closure, and feel that it was *their* victory. Equally, moving pickets away for the afternoon before the next day's mass picket, was defended on grounds that it would raise morale by reducing the tedium of local picketing. Although other arguments were added, picket morale had now become the key criterion in considering strike strategy, and Hadfields in turn was a key factor in morale. It was 'the big target'.

On 14 February, the sixth week of the strike, the biggest mass picket took place. It was this picket above all others which featured prominently in media reports, partly because of its size, and partly because it actually succeeded in closing Hadfields. An estimated 2,000 pickets had gathered around the main entrance to the plant by 6.00 a.m. and police were there on a similar scale. Faced with this display of force and strength of feeling, the Hadfields' workers, who had entered the plant, voted to come out again on strike alongside their public sector fellow-workers. The strikers' victory came to be known (and celebrated) locally as the 'St Valentine's Day's Massacre'.

The RSC's experience of mass picketing underlined the utility of the tactic: with the closure of Hadfields on 14 February, many reports reached the RSC from marshals and rank-and-file pickets, of increased morale (and three of our picket marshals reported likewise). But these reports co-existed with continuing scepticism on the RSC about the commitment to 'hard picketing' of some of the local cells. A suggestion was made at the RSC on 15 February that more cells should be deployed on local plants which had remained open despite the picket lines. Arguing against this proposal, the RSC Chairman caustically observed that the local cells would simply accommodate the additional forces by working 'shorter shifts and doing less work'. None the less, it was agreed in the interests of morale, to circulate to local cells a list of plants shut by picketing. The same meeting resolved to 'keep up the Hadfields momentum' in particular by participating in the nationally-organised mass picket of another large private steel producer, Sheerness Steel, in Kent. The pickets arriving at Sheerness on the 20 February were greeted by local people and the Sheerness workers with considerable hostility: they were refused service at shops and bars; tightly controlled, away from the steel plant, by well drilled police; and made no impact on steel production or the steel workers in Sheerness.

Furthermore, there were complaints by pickets about the lack of organisation at Sheerness, and the long hours of inactivity which resulted.

The high expectation of success (with its implications for the strike's effectiveness and for strikers' morale) contributed to a profound demoralisation on the RSC in the days after the Sheerness picket, and these feelings were reinforced by continued reports of stabilisation of inter-group relations on local picket lines. Reports and discussions of picket morale continued on the RSC throughout February: the subject was raised extensively again on the 25, 27 and 29 of that month (the eighth week of the strike), and was a clear sign of the failures of local and mass picketing, coupled with the absence of any clear alternative. Indicative of the heightened priority asigned to morale in respect of strike tactics was the final mass picket, at Hadfields, on 13 March (week ten). The RSC discussion made it clear there was no expectation of shutting the plant: the aim rather was 'to boost' the morale of local pickets. Indeed some RSC members referred to the event as a demonstration, not a picket. But the failures of mass picketing did not simply generate a predictable concern with picket morale on the part of the RSC, they also generated a number of unintended consequences connected with the ambiguity of the authority structure of the strike organisation, and with differences between strikers in conceptions of picketing. The two main consequences (which were themselves connected) were resistance by some local pickets to mass picketing, and complaints by local pickets about inequities in rewards.

Mass picketing and the authority structure of the strike organisation

The February offensive against the private sector, spearheaded by mass picketing, had brought the RSC to the second major turning point in the strike. The use of mass picketing rested on a series of assumptions about the Rotherham strike organisation and about strike strategy which were only partially valid. The RSC assumed that it could exercise authority over the marshals and that the marshals in turn would instruct their cell members. Whilst these assumptions were satisfied by a section of the picket cells and marshals, in other areas they were not. Hundreds of local pickets did report for mass pickets, as instructed by the RSC, and many marshals did pass on RSC instructions on this and other occasions. Even amongst the marshals whose conception of picketing was most distant from that of the RSC, there was still considerable loyalty. One marshal in charge of a stabilised target kept his cell there for weeks although no steel was moving because the RSC had not instructed him to do otherwise (nor, to be fair, had he passed on much information to Picket Control, as he said they 'had enough to do'). But we have already seen that there was no consensus amongst picket marshals on the limits of the authority structure of the strike organisation, and such limits to the authority of both the RSC and the marshals began to emerge most clearly in the preparations for mass picketing.

Although a mass picket at Hadfields had been discussed as early as 4 February on the DSC, and raised at the RSC from 6 February, it was not finally decided upon until Sunday, 10/Monday, 11 February by the local strike leaders and the RSC respectively. Hadfields was the first item on the agenda on 11 February and it was made clear by the Secretary that it had to be 'attacked . . . even if this means disrupting the cells'. The organisation of a mass picket, it was generally agreed, must have priority over all other local targets. Although the RSC had by this stage recognised many of the signs of stabilisation among local picketing, it was left to Picket Control to articulate some of the implications of stabilisation. They noted at the outset that 'there would be a lot of argument about doing it, especially about taking people off other places. Pickets wouldn't want to leave.' But the points were ignored. When it was announced later by the Secretary that cells were to report to Hadfields at 5.00 a.m., Picket Control asked what would happen if people refused, but this forewarning of the problems of power and authority was likewise ignored. Later in the meeting, one ISTC member of the RSC did return to this problem by arguing picket marshals had no authority over their pickets, as they were unable to mobilise union discipline, whilst others were simply 'all for the easy life', and might not comply with instructions.

The relevance of the arguments was graphically brought home to the RSC when its meeting on the day before the 14 February mass picket was interrupted by an indignant marshal. He had just heard about the mass picket from Picket Control, which was mobilising cells directly without going through a marshals' meeting, because of the shortage of time. The RSC, in other words, was acting *as if* it had the authority to redirect people as appropriate. Whilst agreeing that Hadfields was 'the big target', he protested that his cell was 'just getting on top' of their target and said he would not pull his men off. Faced with this assertion of cell autonomy and of marshals' power, the RSC backed down, and simply asked for cell members who were off duty that morning, although the marshal insisted even then he would *ask* them and not tell them. What was the reaction in other cells to the mass picket? We have little direct information from flying picket cells, which were diverted for the day, but it would seem reasonable to infer that they would have supported a mode of picketing that was in several respects similar to their own. The two marshals who spontaneously praised the mass pickets (for their morale boosting effects) were both in charge of local cells whose picketing had barely stabilised. Conversely, of the five marshals who were hostile or critical towards mass pickets, three were in charge of stabilised picket cells (though it is difficult to attach significance to such small numbers). Their objections to mass picketing (and those of their cell members) reflected their conception of picketing described earlier.

They complained about the violence, saying they were peaceful pickets; or referred to the illegality evidenced in the numbers of arrests and charges, which offended their respect for the law; or they said that they simply didn't want to move because they were settled on their local target.

For these strikers, mass picketing was beyond the *boundary of legitimacy,* and therefore the authority of the RSC did not hold sway. They had placed themselves at the disposal of the RSC and of the cell marshal but their commitment to the strike was not unlimited. Their behaviour as strikers was not simply a result of their position in an authority structure which they unconditionally accepted. Rather it was regulated by norms which they had 'brought into' the strike and/or which had arisen as part of a negotiated order on the picket lines. Indeed even in the heart of the strike organisation there was resistance to authority. It was reported at the RSC in mid-February that cell 24, created in January as a 'flying squad' to 'motivate' flagging pickets, was only working a morning shift, was 'unwilling to be *told* where to go', and was in fact 'difficult to get hold of'.

Of equal significance was the authority structure *within* the picket cells. The marshal who refused to *tell* his pickets to report to Hadfields was not alone in his view that pickets were volunteers, not conscripts. At least two of his fellow marshals in stabilised picket cells also reported limits on their authority. One said you 'can't expect people out every day' and made weekend picketing optional (thereby undermining the RSC's authority), whilst another felt 'you can't bully people', and just had to accept what they were willing to offer. These perceptions of limits to marshal authority were also found among cell leaders in less stabilised settings, who said there was nothing they could do if pickets were absent, since the activity was voluntary in any case, and no sanctions were available. (Conversely, two more marshals even went so far as to threaten absentee pickets with job loss and other sanctions after the strike, and one flying picket marshal reported no problems at all in 'telling people to do things').

Not all of the marshals then acted as part of a bureaucracy and transmitted the authority and influence of the RSC down to their cell members. A few resisted or evaded the authority of the RSC and shielded their members from its influence (cf. Berman, 1974). Where members identified with their cell and its activity such marshals often enjoyed the consent of their cell members in exercising their discretion. In short, the strike organisation was caught in a tension between bureaucracy (where authority flows downwards) and democracy (where authority rests with the rank and file members). At times the organisation functioned as a bureaucracy, at other times the authority of the RSC was contested by the volunteer pickets.

Yet so long as the strikers retained a *moral* involvement in the strike organisation, that is, members and 'leaders' shared and pursued the same goals and norms of conduct, these contradictions need not have been productive of discontent. Mass picketing however, had a second effect on the strike organisation (in addition to its exposure of the authority structure and its ambiguities), directly connected with the basis of strikers' involvement, to which we now turn.

Mass picketing and striker involvement

The overwhelming majority of pickets volunteered for the activity without any expectation of economic reward, as it had been made clear at the outset (certainly to ISTC members) that there would be no strike pay. Some, it is true, subsequently transferred to flying picketing *in order* to obtain 'expenses' that did not attach to local picketing, but these were a very small minority of the active strikers. In Etzioni's (1961) terms the dominant mode of involvement in the strike organisation was moral, not calculative. Mass picketing, however, gave considerable impetus to the development of a more calculative form of involvement among pickets, and to more calculative and coercive modes of control by the RSC, in particular, because disparities in picket 'payments' were clearly revealed.

Payment of expenses to pickets was unco-ordinated for three reasons: first, works strike committees were autonomous and free to decide on their own levels of expenses. Secondly, finance was raised both locally and nationally, although national funds were distributed equally to different areas. Since different areas had mobilised very different numbers of pickets, the national funds available for individual pickets varied inversely with the number of pickets available. Hence the large number of Rotherham pickets were each paid very little (if anything) whilst the smaller number of Scunthorpe pickets received more. Thirdly, other unions in the strike gave strike pay to their members: GMWU and URTU members received 'official' strike pay; NCCC members received a combination of funds raised at public meetings, money levied from AUEW members and (eventually) official strike pay; all TGWU members received strike pay (but pickets received it before non-pickets), on production of a card bearing per week at least three of the stamps issued daily on picket lines (a system which broke down shortly before the end of the strike, but which ensured for a time a high turnout of pickets). Local ISTC pickets received reimbursement only for petrol expenses, if they were incurred; ISTC flying pickets received £1 per day 'expenses', a sum which was raised several times, reaching £3.50 per day by mid-February.

Although local pickets might 'work' as much as the flying pickets the logic and justice of differential payment was widely accepted. This acceptance might have been eroded simply by the growth of serious financial difficulties, reported 'very often' by 24% of strikers in January, by 35% in February and 49% in March. But the decisive factor in undermining the system was the mass pickets themselves which brought together not only pickets from different parts of the country, but local and flying pickets from Rotherham. For the local mass pickets, flying pickets were 'diverted' to the targets (e.g. Hadfields) but despite its proximity, still received £1 expenses. Local pickets who travelled as far to reach the same target, received nothing, and pickets travelling in from other areas received between £2 and £5 for the day. In other words on the same picket line it was possible to find at least three different rates of 'pay'. These discrepancies were discussed at length among local pickets and were a major source of discontent. Only three of 20 marshals interviewed said that payment was not a problem, whilst 13 said it definitely was. In every case it was the differences in payment between local and flying pickets or between regions which provoked feelings of inequity. There was a predictable difference between modes of picketing in the perception of inequity as a problem: flying picket marshals indicated their members were generally satisfied and attributed 'the problem' to local pickets. One flying picket marshal did report an increase in numbers and a drop in absenteeism when expenses were raised (though the duration of these effects is unknown).

Pay inequity had first been raised in the RSC on 28 January, shortly after Flying Picket Control had been wound up and flying pickets were being organised by the RSC Secretary. On his initiative the issue was discussed but there was no support for payment as local pickets were not demanding it, and it could not be withdrawn from flying pickets without loss. It is a measure of the perceived unimportance of the issue, (whose re-emergence was inspired by the mass pickets) that it was not discussed on the RSC (or the DSC) for another three weeks. In the aftermath of Sheerness, the fact that Welsh pickets received £8.50 for the day (whilst Rotherham pickets received £3.50), was cited as a 'problem' (21 February). In this context, where low morale was frequently described or referred to, it was agreed that picket expenses should be investigated, although the rationale was not clearly spelled out. The following day (26 February) a report was made to the RSC of payment in Scotland where higher rates were offered for shift work as an *incentive*. There were continuing reports at the RSC of low morale throughout the eighth week of the strike, and one criterion in the refusal of dispensations was the damaging effect they would have on picket morale. The RSC eventually harmonised petrol allowances between unions (27 February) and agreed a new daily flying picket rate of £2.50 provided the daily trip was for 12 hours or more, but continued the practice of paying no expenses to local pickets, as it would prove too expensive. Nevertheless, morale continued to be discussed throughout the next three weeks, although only sporadically. A mass picket was proposed on 6 March at the DSC and at the RSC on 10 March, in order to boost morale, and took place at Hadfields on 13 March. Reports came in occasionally to the RSC of elements of stabilisation: poor attendance by local pickets was reported in the tenth week of the strike (10-14 March); as was resistance to changing targets, hostility to cell 24, and friendliness with police.

Eventually, it was announced at a picket marshals' meeting on 20 March that local pickets would receive payment from the following week at the rate of £5 for a minimum 32 hour week, although the decision was only announced to the RSC on 21 March, the day *after* it had been announced to the picket marshals. What was discussed and accepted at the DSC was a proposal to gear provision of hardship monies to picketing as an *incentive* for those who drew on the hardship fund, but contributed little to the strike. But the introduction of local picketing pay was only in part an incentive to encourage *continued* attendance by existing pickets. The RSC Secretary suggested that *new* pickets reporting for duty should *not* receive the money, thereby indicating that the money (in his, influential view) was not so much an *incentive* for future behaviour as a *reward* for past behaviour, and this was accepted by the RSC. What did these discussions of payment signify about relations between the RSC and pickets?

Mass picketing and RSC control of pickets

Prior to the mass picketing offensive, the RSC sought to control the behaviour of pickets mainly through the formal channels of the strike organisation. It did occasionally discuss the problems of local picketing and the desirability of reconstructing picket cells on the basis of union branches, primarily reflecting a desire to extend the moral, or normative control thought to be inherent in trade unionism at the workplace. These discussions were also marked by a distinct undertone of coercive control, in which it was implied that picket marshals in branch-based cells could more effectively discipline cell members who failed to meet their requirements.

The period of mass picketing generated two major changes in RSC efforts to control pickets: firstly, it witnessed the development of an instrumental, or calculative mode of control, evidenced in the changes in picketing pay discussed above; secondly, it gave an impetus to the development of coercive control of non-picketers. The latter issue emerged from a number of mass meetings in February and was discussed at length on the RSC on February 28. It was suggested *inter alia* that non-pickets might be deprived in the future of overtime working, or prevented from taking voluntary redundancy, but it was noted that rule 43 of the ISTC gave any disciplined member the right of appeal to the EC, which was thought to be opposed to punitive action of that sort. On the 28 February the DSC agreed that the EC should be urged to withdraw the credentials of ISTC officials who had crossed picket lines (a decision which would affect mainly private-sector officials), and there was considerable support locally for the EC decision of 25 February to expel the whole Sheerness membership for refusal to support the strike. Some wanted further action: at a mass meeting in Rotherham on 27 February there were rank-and-file calls for sanctions against those who were on strike but did not picket. Finally, at the RSC post-mortem on Sheerness on 21 February, there was strong support for a morale-boosting exercise aimed not against the private sector, but against the non-TUC union SIMA, most of whose members had worked throughout the strike. SIMA had been an occasional target of picketing in the first few weeks of the strike, and a frequent target of abuse. In March the discussion which began on conditions for return to work included *inter alia* an insistence that any meeting or committee attended by SIMA would be boycotted. These discussions signified a considerable shift in the RSC attitude towards an insistence on punishing those who threatened the strike, as part of a 'campaign' of punitive militancy.

The growth of punitive militancy was precipitated by the failure of mass picketing and was made possible by the strategic hiatus into which the RSC fell at the end of February and the beginning of March. Indeed, once picketing pay had been resolved on 29 February, there was only one discussion of pickets on the RSC in the next two weeks, and that resulted in a curtailment of pickets at Dover as part of a retrenchment back into South Yorkshire. But the growth of punitive militancy was not simply a response to organisational failure, a useful diversion in lieu of any alternative strategy. It also represented an attempt by the RSC to retain its moral authority with the active strikers who were pressing for sanctions against their inactive fellows. Had the RSC failed to discuss coercive control of inactive strikers, it might well have been faced with a revolt by activists and a challenge to its authority more serious than anything presented by the opponents of mass picketing. In other words the elaboration of both instrumental and coercive modes of control was inextricably linked with the maintenance of moral authority, or normative control, by the RSC, and they cannot be analysed apart from one another.

In the third and final month of the strike, the steel strikers became increasingly dependent for victory on other groups of workers (see Chapters 7-9). The corollary of this dependence was a reduced concern for the efficacy of local picketing, which was rarely discussed throughout March. Indeed it may be that the RSC accepted, however pragmatically and reluctantly, the stabilisation of local picketing and its own inability to influence this process.

CHAPTER SEVEN

The Rotherham Strike Committee: leadership and legitimacy

In this and the following chapter, we focus more directly on the Rotherham Strike Committee (RSC) itself. When it was established, in December, it had been charged by the RJC with the responsibility for running the local strike organisation. Its purpose was to establish activities to prosecute the strike and to co-ordinate or control those activities. Although the RSC was, within the first month of the strike, embedded in a cluster of committees in South Yorkshire, there was a strong commitment to local autonomy, as we shall see, and this gave the RSC considerable discretion in the way that the local organisation functioned. In this chapter, we start by examining the composition and activities of the RSC, and the frames of reference of the RSC members. In the following chapter we turn to examine how the RSC functioned, by focusing on the debates and decision-making, both within the committee and between the RSC and other South Yorkshire strike bodies.

The RSC procedures

A daily meeting of a strike committee is commonly viewed, in labour movement tradition, as an essential component of a large or long strike. This point had been emphasised by the experienced strikers amongst the Yorkshire miners when the RJC members had met them at the pre-strike planning meeting. Encouraged by the Strike Co-ordinator, the RSC arranged to meet regularly around 9 a.m. each weekday morning at the strike office, in the regional ISTC office in Rotherham. They met in whatever large room was available at the time of their meeting: there was an implicit agreement in the RSC that their meetings were not necessarily more important than other claims on room space, such as picket briefings or meetings of other strike bodies such as the DSC. Meeting length varied from an hour to a whole morning, with issues being discussed without any attempts at guillotining the debate. This was in contrast to the more stringent time constraints imposed on DSC discussions, where meetings were limited by the chair to a pre-determined length. The commitment to meet daily was broken only by the large scale involvement of the RSC members in the mass pickets of Hadfields and Sheerness (14 and 20 February). At weekends, the RSC was replaced by the RJC meetings, which took place every Sunday morning during the strike, although RJC meetings were used to obtain wider legitimacy and support for RSC decisions and actions rather than to take over the functioning of the RSC.

The RSC possessed certain features of formal structure. There were only two formal roles: a Chairman, Sam B., who ran the meeting and set an informal agenda where this was needed, and a Secretary who noted down details of decisions or information which needed to be relayed. The Chairman was, in fact, the newly appointed Chairman of the RJC, indicating the overlap between trade union and strike structures. In his occasional absence, the chair would be assumed by another member of the RSC. Although not always the same person, the acting Chairman would be an ISTC official, emphasising the ISTC control of the RSC. (The final meeting of the RSC was actually chaired by an NCCC official, with Sam B. present, but the circumstances of that will be related in Chapter 10.) The secretary of the RSC, Fred T., was a senior branch secretary. In his absence, no-one assumed that role.

The lack of role differentiation was associated with the fact that the formal features of the RSC were limited. Unlike many trade union organisations and in fact in contrast to the DSC, there were no minutes nor any formal record kept of the proceedings. Each person jotted down whatever information he wanted, or needed, for liaison meetings or for branch and mass meetings. An agenda, set by the Chairman, was not always used or was interrupted. Its absence occurred particularly later in the strike when events became more predictable and responses more routinised. Where used, the agenda consisted simply of the Chairman's verbal presentation of items. An alternative procedure, which the RSC began increasingly to use, was the routine of reporting back. This occurred after the agenda items and consisted of a brief information report being given by each RSC member in turn, going round the room, generally commencing with the Secretary. The report back was usually brief — less than five minutes — and frequently elicited no reply from other RSC members. The report-back system meant that, within the RSC, there was a flexibility about information exposure, since each member could participate on each occasion and thus any subject felt to be important could be raised and, if seen likewise by other members of the group, could be discussed. Although mainly uncontroversial — the transmission of simple factual data about picketing targets, for example — occasionally report-backs would generate more extended discussion. Report-backs became more evident as the strike progressed and the pattern of the strike became more predictable; there was less pressure to devote attention to urgent, unanticipated demands on RSC time. This is reflected in the length of RSC meetings. During January, their average (mean) length was 2 ¼ hours. In February, they lasted for an average of 1 ¾ hours and in March there was a further reduction to 1 ½ hours.

In the RSC discussions, the Chairman was only rarely obliged to exercise his formal powers of control, being able to rely on the fact that RSC members were experienced and disciplined trade unionists. Where discussion began to grow heated, the RSC members were generally able to control and moderate their contributions, and so interruptions were rare. The formal procedure of voting was only occasionally used, where it was restricted to ISTC branch officials, indicating again the predominance of ISTC on the RSC.

Membership of the RSC

We now turn to examine the people who attended the RSC. Who were the steel workers who daily discussed the activities of the local strike organisation? Perhaps inevitably in a temporary organisation, and particularly one which had had little time to establish clear rules and roles, personalities were important in shaping the preoccupations of the RSC and more widely of the South Yorkshire strike organisation. However, it is important that not too much emphasis is laid upon leadership, for this should not obscure the significant influence of structure on the use of information, decisions and evaluations by the strike committee.

Membership of the RSC had originally been determined by election at a December RJC meeting (see Chapter 4), where six leading RJC branch officials had been chosen. Yet by the time the RSC met, two days later, there were actually 13 in attendance, indicating that membership criteria were flexible since nearly half the RSC at that stage had not been formally elected but rather co-opted. However, they were all 'first-line' union officials — Secretaries, Chairmen or Works Representatives (see Table 4.1 on p. 39). Non-ISTC members joined the RSC in the first two weeks, as representatives of other striking unions. RSC membership continued to increase steadily throughout the strike. Attendance by individual members varied considerably: some were at almost every meeting; others were only occasionally present at part of a meeting. The varied levels of time commitment, combined with differences in primary identification, suggest that it is useful to make a distinction between the core and periphery of the RSC.

The Core of the RSC

Here, the core is defined as consisting of individuals who attended for more than three meetings and who stayed for the duration of the sessions. Importantly, they perceived their primary contribution to the strike as occurring through the RSC rather than any other strike body. The RSC representatives from non-ISTC unions did not precisely fit this criterion of core since they were faced with a dual and sometimes conflicting loyalty between the RSC and their own strike committees. However, they were regarded as central members of the RSC and often expressed identification with the aims and values of the RSC. The core of the RSC consisted entirely of Rotherham branch officials.

There was a gradual numerical increase in core members over time. During January average attendance was 13-14. In February, membership had risen to 15, although a greater increase is evident in the week between the mass pickets of Hadfields and Sheerness (14 and 20 February) where numbers were up to 17. In March, core membership remained at 17. The tendency to an increased size arose from two sources of new members. First, when an RSC member was unable to attend for a period of several days, due to other strike obligations, he might send a deputy from his branch, another official who might, if enthusiastic, continue to attend. Secondly, new members joined where they were responsible for a particular strike function or possessed particular contacts which had become important to the RSC as the strike progressed, although significantly the initiative for attendance came from the new member not the RSC. The most outstanding example concerned Picket Control. As the behaviour and morale of local pickets became of increasing concern to the RSC, there was a corresponding increase in attendance by Picket Control. In the first month there had only been one RSC member from Picket Control, and no-one for the week he was on nightshift. From around 11 February there was always one and sometimes up to three members of Picket Control at RSC meetings, and from 10 March there were usually four, including the controller of picket finance. Their increased attendance was their own decision not that of the RSC, which had been indifferent to the lack of systematic contact with pickets in the early weeks. They increasingly attended as local picketing stabilised, with less urgent work for them to do and as the RSC discussions were of direct concern to them.

Another example was the regular attendance by a bus marshal from 5

March. He attended RSC meetings on all the days when he was not out at 6 a.m. leading his team of flying pickets. As with Picket Control, this was not a result of co-option by the RSC but rather the individual's own wish to attend, which was acceded to by the RSC.

The presence or absence of core attenders occasioned no surprise, comment, explanation or apology. Unlike more formal trade union committees there were no expectations that all members would attend. It was accepted that individuals had the responsibility to make their own decisions on attendance, based on the competing demands for their attention. There was only one exception to this when at the RSC meeting of 25 February, characterised by low morale and pessimism, the Chairman and another prominent RSC member were challenged in their attempt to leave to go to a meeting in Sheffield. On the strength of feeling of the meeting they stayed and delegated the task to two other RSC members.

The periphery of the RSC

There were a number of irregular or temporary attenders, who constituted the periphery. These were strikers who only came for a few meetings, sometimes for only part of a meeting. They saw themselves as having a legitimate presence at the RSC, although their primary identification was elsewhere, based in other committees or in a picketing group. They attended RSC meetings to make unsolicited contributions to the running of the strike, by presenting ideas, suggestions or information.

The principal peripheral attenders were core members of the Divisional Strike Committee (DSC), from the Rotherham area. They had high status due to their participation in ISTC affairs at national level. They included the two EC members, the Worker Director and the Strike Co-ordinator. Their attendance at RSC meetings generally occurred where they had been called on to debrief on national events, or where they wanted a response or commitment from the RSC for certain courses of action. Where information about EC meetings was wanted by the RSC, the meeting would often commence with an outline from an EC member followed by a discussion. Often the EC members would leave after their contribution, in order to attend to other strike duties. The Strike Co-ordinator's presence at parts of meetings signified that there would be a request for pickets to be deployed at a certain location or in a particular way. Other South Yorkshire DSC members were also part of the RSC periphery.

Often the DSC members wished to attend RSC meetings on particular issues. Consequently, the numbers attending the RSC waxed and waned according to the perceived topicality or relevance of the issues under discussion. While one might anticipate that this overlap would increase where there was conflict or tension between the two strike bodies, in fact the increase occurred when the external environment was particularly hostile. The largest meeting occurred in the temporary premises just after the fire (26 RSC members present in total). Attendance also increased in the last two weeks of the strike, with numbers (total) over 20.

The peripheral attenders described above were well known around the strike office, with recognised strike roles and duties, and their attendance at RSC meetings was never questioned. (There was only one exception to this, when Eddie H. tried on 19 March to resume the Secretaryship of the RSC as a protest against an RSC decision, but even here the protest was against his assumption of the role not his presence.)

By contrast, another type of peripheral attender can be identified; those who were unsure of their rights and who *asked* to attend the RSC. Often their contributions were either timid or hedged by remarks indicating that they intended to criticise the RSC in a way which should be taken as benevolent not destructive. Such peripheral attenders were invariably ISTC members, though not necessarily branch officials. The RSC would grant the right to attend, though would often determine the length of time the person stayed. In this category came the 6 bus marshals, who, on 5 March, demanded to see the RSC, charging them with being out of touch with picket marshals and suggesting means of changing the situation. On 13 February, a picket marshal interrupted the RSC to express his cell's objection to a mass picket. Other such peripheral attenders were the representatives, on separate occasions, from the Sheffield and Scunthorpe strike committees and the attendance, on a single isolated occasion, of a senior branch official from a private Sheffield firm. In total, there were between one and three peripheral members at about two-thirds of all the RSC meetings.

The peripheral members must be distinguished from *visitors* to the RSC, who had been asked by the RSC to attend part of a meeting in order to provide certain specific information or who as non-strikers volunteered it. There was no sense, on either side, of their being members: the expectation was clearly that the visitors should provide information but not advance opinions or contribute to the discussion unless a particular query was directed at them.

The significance of the membership

Unlike many committees in industrial and trade union organisations, and in contrast to the DSC, the RSC had relatively permeable boundaries between membership and non-membership. This was evident in the gradual numerical increase in members over time. New members were never questioned by the RSC or asked to furnish a reason for their presence. Their right to be there was accepted. This 'open government' was evident, for example, in the case of the 6 bus marshals, or in the case of a flying picket marshal from Dover who complained strongly about the RSC decision to replace the picket and who took up nearly an hour in the 5 March meeting explaining his case. The view that anyone could contribute to the proceedings was, in fact, explicitly stated on the occasion of the 6 bus marshals' visit when the RSC Secretary, Fred T., said that 'it is always open to people to come in [here] to add their own comments'.

However, while the expressed policy was essentially open, in reality it is important to recognise that ideological barriers prevented some rank and file strikers from attempting to articulate their views at the RSC. While new members could attend on the basis of their interest in the strike proceedings, an underlying criterion for acceptability was an ideological congruence between the new members and the RSC. New members were similar in their degree of militancy, their beliefs about the main protagonists in the strike, and their views about the most effective means of prosecuting the strike. For example, new core members were flying rather than local cell marshals, and the peripheral members were more predominantly drawn from the former category. This accords with the information already noted that the less stabilised picket groups held ideas about picketing more congruent with those of the RSC than the more stabilised picket groups (Chapter 5). A further indication of the prevalence of ideological influences on the RSC concerns the two RSC members who dropped out of the RSC, the only members to do so. They were two older staff branch officials who became engaged in administering the hardship fund, and giving social security advice. On 26 February they claimed that the pressures of work meant that they had to cease attending the RSC and concentrate on their welfare duties instead. Given their more conservative outlook their reason for leaving can also be interpreted as an acceptance of their lack of congruent views with the rest of the RSC.

Ideological or value-normative influences were also important, perhaps, in the uneven representation of Rotherham branches on the RSC. Some branches were over-represented (sometimes with three branch officials present), while others had no-one on the RSC. Conspicuously absent were representatives from a number of staff branches, traditionally less militant groups. Certain manual branches and the private sector ISTC branches also failed to be represented on the RSC.

The theoretical openness of the RSC though served a number of important functions for the organisation. Firstly, it was a means by which the RSC's authority could be legitimated. The acceptance of suggestions, opinions and criticisms may have crucially contributed to the authority and respect accorded to them from strikers in the field of operations, by reinforcing the democratic ethos of their leadership role. Secondly, openness also helped to diffuse responsibility for decisions and actions. This was particularly important where decisions were not only serious in their own right for the strike but also had major implications for the resumption of work. As the leading institution of the strike the RSC was well aware that rank and file strikers could hold them responsible, once the strike was over, for any poor decisions. The appearance of democracy helped the RSC feel able to make serious decisions while also generating greater commitment to those decisions from the rank and file. Thirdly, the apparent openness of the RSC may have given members greater confidence in their own views and militancy. It may have helped them to maintain a militant perspective by giving them the impression that they were sampling, and taking into account, a wide range of opinions from the rank and file. Finally, openness can be seen to have been an important means of neutralising criticism by letting critics feel that their views had been listened to and weighed up, even though in some cases the RSC did little more than defend themselves against criticism.

The distinction between the core and the periphery of the RSC, combined with its permeable boundaries of membership and its norms of values and beliefs, underline the view that the RSC was more a political than a purely bureaucratic organisation. Strikers attended the RSC to represent the interests of certain groups within the strike organisation rather than because they had a particular strike role (with the exception, perhaps, of members of Picket Control). Thus although the RSC had been planned as a small group of eight members, at times it swelled to a gathering of more than 25. The RSC's acceptance of newcomers reinforces the idea that commitment was a more important asset than skills or experience, underlining the essentially political nature of the organisation. As a consequence of its political basis, it was relatively cut off from certain sources, for its members could sometimes not provide much needed information, attending as they did on the basis of enthusiasm rather than their particular skills or knowledge.

Briefly, we should note the potential information loss occurring as a result of who was *not* included in RSC membership. Although, of course, there was informal contact between strikers outside Committee meetings, the information avoided or missed within the RSC had consequences for attitudes and behaviour in the RSC and for what were regarded as legitimate topics for discussion. The RSC had minimal formal contact with the two CNC representatives, except in the last two weeks of the strike. Consequently, bargaining was not a major item of interest for the RSC as a whole, being raised only intermittently and briefly by the non-ISTC representatives (since three of the five were engaged in national negotiations or the associated lay delegate conferences of their unions). However, being an ISTC-dominated committee, relatively little attention was paid to these comments. The absence of any ISTC strikers on the RSC concerned with the national negotiations, already evident, meant that the separation between bargaining and strike activity increased. Additionally, the RSC had little contact with the full-time officials. Direct contact with the Strike Co-ordinator was limited and at only one RSC meeting did another Divisional Organiser attend. (By contrast, there were up to three Divisional Organisers at most DSC meetings.) The RSC, then, had little sustained contact with the national level and hence less of a sense of 'the wider perspective' than might otherwise have been the case. This meant that the RSC had fewer constraints on their behaviour and perspectives, particularly concerning the legality of their decisions, thus further encouraging their militant attitude.

A further informational loss concerned the private sector. Although officially on strike for several weeks, private sector branch officials only attended the RSC once. It cannot be argued that the RSC were unprepared for their entry into the dispute, since the RJC had resolved, at its first strike preparation meeting, to encourage them into the strike. It appears that the RSC never seriously considered a collaborative approach, despite exhortations by the NCCC members on the RSC to do so. The RSC was not unusual in South Yorkshire or in the country in this respect. However, the relative isolation fostered and maintained the cultivation of separate group identities for each.

Activities of the strike organisation

The RSC had been established to generate and control activities prosecuting the strike locally. Yet what were the activities which the RSC felt responsible for? Figure 7.1 indicates the activities which the

RSC, at some stage, discussed at its meetings although emphasis on each changed as the strike progressed. Certain activities, or parts of them, were delegated to sub-committees or individuals, while some others were run through shared responsibility with other committees. Here we briefly describe the activities which occupied the RSC in order to give an indication of their scope and complexity.

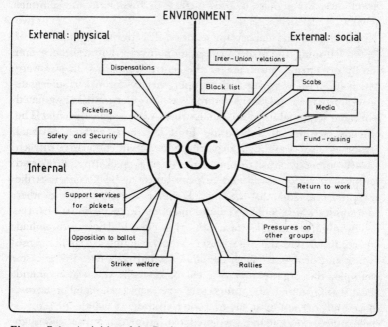

Figure 7.1   Activities of the Rotherham Strike Committee

We found it conceptually useful to divide the environment, which the RSC was attempting to manage, into external and internal components, further subdividing the external environment into the physical and the social. The physical external environment concerned objects and places, for example the selection of picket targets and the granting of dispensations. All activities here were directed towards applying pressure to the opponent (BSC management and government). The external social environment consisted of relations with influential groups and parties not on strike. Activities in this category include discouraging scabs and handling the media. The internal environment consisted of the membership of the strike organisation, itself a source of uncertainty which required control if integration was to be achieved. To make these distinctions we have located the organisational boundary (problematic though it is), as being around the Rotherham strike organisation, since this was our focus. The three types of environment have been chosen for their conceptual value in broad terms, rather than their empirical validity, which is more doubtful given that an activity may have consequences for more than one area even where primarily located in one. For example, constructing the blacklist was important in attempting to prevent lorry drivers crossing picket lines, although it was also central to discussions about the return to work.

Immediately noticeable is the scope of the activities of interest to the RSC. Running the strike organisation involved much more than simply organising resources for the central concern with picketing. Much attention was given to the support services for pickets such as the provision of food and fuel. Attention was also given to striker welfare in a broader sense: advising on social security claims, liaising with DHSS officials, setting up a hardship fund for those without financial resources. As well as the strike participants, activities had to be directed towards other groups: to opponents through picketing, threatened removal of safety cover and dispensations, as well as to potential sympathisers, such as the media, other unions and the wider community which could be helpful in giving financial donations.

The initial organisation of activities however, had been rudimentary and confused, with the strike leaders simply reacting to a small range of events and problems which demanded rapid response. Initially, for example, the organisation of local picket cells was rather chaotic because information about picketing targets and cell membership was inaccurate or non-existent; as picket volunteers wandered into the strike office, they had to be assigned to groups. Also, on occasions, the strike office became crowded with private sector employers and trade unionists who wanted dispensations, and several RSC meetings were disrupted by such requests. Within ten days, however, the RSC members were better able to plan and control activities, as familiarity with the environments increased predictability. The development of procedures for organising flying pickets, the paying of picketing expenses and the establishment of picket marshals' meetings helped in this respect. Also, fund-raising was organised and rules agreed in the DSC as to how funds should be distributed so that duplication of effort by different groups was lessened. Certain strike activists became known for their involvement in administering particular strike activities, so that queries and problems could be directed to them, thus reducing the information flow within the organisation, which had previously been suffering from overload. Rules, roles and procedures were a major contribution to the stabilisation of the organisation and its attempted control over its environments. Success in this respect is indicated by the shortening of RSC meeting length over time.

Additionally, the strike organisation introduced a greater degree of discipline in order to regulate contacts with the external social environment. For example, contact with the media was soon restricted due to the rapid realisation that they were more complex than the strikers had originally thought, certainly not simply a means of recording, word for word, messages to the public. In the first couple of weeks anyone who happened to be near a telephone would talk to the press when the telephone rang and the printed version, sometimes misinterpreted, turned out not to be always in the best interests of the strikers. The DSC appointed a press officer who thereafter controlled contacts with the press, radio and television, via daily press conferences, and arranged the phone-in and television appearances of particular members of the RSC and DSC. Similarly, stricter controls were introduced about dispensations. At first dispensations had been authorised by the signature of any RSC member and this had quickly resulted in a large number of forged dispensation forms (since pickets were unclear who was on the strike committee or what the signatures should look like). Within a week or so, a procedure for handling dispensation requests was established, whereby only the signature of the RSC Secretary and that of a DSC member were valid. (Later, the procedure was modified again.)

As the strike organisation stabilised and the environment became more predictable, the RSC was able to turn its attention from immediate pressing demands to extending and improving the range of its activities. For example, the picketing support services had originally consisted of the supplying of expenses for flying picketing, but within a short space of time more extensive supports were arranged, such as the provision of soup and sandwiches to night shift and flying pickets, and the distribution of coke to local cells for their braziers. The attention paid to rallies went beyond the initial Sheffield rally on 21 January to include a further one in Rotherham as well as the organisation of other morale-boosting and fund-raising activities such as a folk concert.

However, there were still unanticipated demands on the strike organisation. For example, as arrests on the picket line became more frequent (the South Yorkshire police made 159 arrests) court appearances became another novel dimension of being a picket. Pickets were unsure about, and sometimes intimidated by, police and court procedures, and their confidence was further undermined by the fact that they faced these alone. At one of its March meetings, the RSC decided that advice and moral support in the courtroom should be available and delegated an RSC member to attend the courts, whenever possible.

The announcement by BSC that it would hold a national employee ballot about a ballot also generated some oppositional activity by RSC. They agreed that it was important to discredit the ballot although they felt the method adopted by Scunthorpe of printing extra ballot forms (to show how easily results could be manufactured) was too risky. No alternative proposals were put forward however, although on 3 March a multi-union body, led by the NCCC, held a mass meeting in the City Hall, Sheffield, and followed this with a ceremonial burning of ballot papers outside some BSC offices.

Some activities were modified as circumstances changed. Adjustments to picketing organisation, targets and remuneration have already been noted. The hardship fund was modified after a suggestion that a food voucher system, by arrangement with local supermarkets, would be preferable to distributing cash (21 March). Although briefly adopted, the RSC soon learnt of the humiliation and embarrassment caused to shopping strikers and the change was abandoned. Although the RSC then discussed whether hardship payments should be made conditional on picketing service, the proposal was abandoned as lacking in compassion.

Occasionally RSC members were able to make use of extra-union affiliations and roles. For example, during the strike, there was a short dispute between the local education authority and schoolteachers which resulted in the stopping of the school-meals service. Action by two RSC members, in their capacity of school governors, persuaded the teachers to resume meals supervision so that the strikers' children would not be deprived of this benefit, free to children of social security claimants (discussed at RSC on 19 February). Town councillors on the RSC were able to attend council meetings pleading leniency for strikers who were finding it increasingly difficult to pay rates and council house rents (22 February).

A number of activities were designed to achieve more than one aim. For example the occasional picketing of local BSC offices, where staff were still working, applied pressure to local management, as well as stimulating afresh flagging media attention to the strike. Other activities were in danger of pursuing one strike goal at the expense of another. For example, dispensation requests were particularly problematic where the RSC wished to condemn the use of scab labour while upholding the traditional union stance of preserving the jobs of young people on apprentice and other training schemes.

Information and activity

The description of the RSC's activities or those for which they were responsible indicates that the purpose of the RSC was primarily to integrate the activities of a large number of groups within the strike organisation. Information handling is an important process in integration and the RSC was a major mechanism for processing information. This helped it to gain control over the environment by reducing uncertainty. Yet, for an organisation operating in an external environment which included groups hostile to its aims and very existence, information had a particularly double-edged significance. While information flow was essential for co-ordination, and also in order to maintain the commitment of the strikers, there was also a need to conceal information from groups who might use it to the strikers' disadvantage. We have already noted the more cautious and disciplined contact with the media within a couple of weeks of the start of the strike. Contacts with the police over flying and mass pickets also aroused greater caution in the way in which information was handled. Picket Control reported very early on that their phone lines were being tapped, and claimed to have proved this by sending out a false message over the phone about a planned picket. Apparently, the police had turned up at the appropriate destination and time, although no pickets were in evidence. However, the event which probably most strongly fostered the desire for secrecy was the arson attack on the ISTC strike headquarters, which demonstrated the existence in unidentifiable quarters of considerable hostility towards the strikers. After their relocation to disused council offices, there was much stricter control over access to the strike office. Whereas in the old building, access had been unrestricted, now there were strikers permanently on guard, limiting access to those known to the strike activists inside. In addition, a 24-hour watch by a police van outside the new office was a continual reminder that there were hostile interests from whom the strikers needed protection. Also from the date of the arson attack, the RSC meeting room was kept locked while the RSC was in session, which had a side effect of increasing the separation between the RSC and the rest of the strike organisation.

An illustrative RSC meeting: 6 February

To provide a flavour of the manner and content of RSC meetings, we present a description of one meeting. It has not been chosen as typical: in a situation as complex and changeable as a strike the notion of typicality is unhelpful.

The meeting room was the basement of the union headquarters. As the committee members wandered in remarks were exchanged about the latest developments. Some talked with interest of the latest moves in proposing to withdraw safety cover while others were preoccupied with the 'new' pay offer just announced. The meeting was of average size for that time — 16 strikers and additionally an ISTC branch official from Scunthorpe and, for part of the time, one of the EC members.

The Chairman called the meeting to order around 9.15. Although it was customary for the Chairman to present a short agenda to the meeting of pressing items, on this occasion the two extra GMWU officials who had to attend another strike meeting half an hour later started the proceedings.

One GMWU member wanted to comment on the latest decision about withdrawing safety cover. He said that a letter had been sent from their own strike committee to the RSC pointing out that ISTC had no authority to withdraw safety cover and that the action was strongly disapproved of. The Chairman indicated that the decision had come from Central Co-ordinating Committee not the RSC and that all four unions (including GMWU) had made the decision. He added that the decision had been taken primarily to gain media attention and that this had been achieved even though only boilermen had been withdrawn so far. Having made their point, the GMWU members left.

The Secretary then raised an item: had the DSC given a definition of finished steel? (a definition which was a source of friction with the local CSEU). The question was partly to highlight the problem for the RSC generally, since the Secretary was in fairly close touch with the DSC in any case. The Chairman replied that no definition had been provided yet although he added that the DSC 'didn't discuss a great deal yesterday' so he had 'nothing to report from that meeting'.

Joe S., an older, experienced and sometimes cautious member of the NCCC pointed out that steel was 'pouring out' of Hadfields, due, according to TGWU and URTU drivers, to a dispensation from the local engineering unions confederation (CSEU). The TGWU member commented that the incident illustrated the problem of steel movement definition since Hadfields and the CSEU were claiming that as it was between 2 sites of the same plant it did not count. There was a short discussion of how the steel movement could be prevented by picketing — perhaps a mass picket? The Chairman suggested that getting transport union members to black the steel might be more effective.

Tony L., the other NCCC member, gave his report. He urged the need to lay contingency plans, such as preparing a mass picket for the possible return of Hadfields, which seemed certain after their announcement of a return to work on Monday, whether or not the strike had finished. The Chairman confidently commented that on Monday, Hadfields were only having branch meetings, and in any case 'only a couple of branches' wanted to go back to work and that 'the TV reports should not be believed'. The TGWU member added that Hadfields might not be the only company wanting to go back to work but the Secretary disagreed strongly. The matter was dropped.

An ISTC member reported that meals were still being served to SIMA members at the works sports and social club, which caused general laughter (since considerable attempts had already been made to terminate this). The Chairman curbed the discussion, saying that the matter should be dropped until the AGM of the club, and that it was no longer a matter for the strike committee.

The EC member came in to let the RSC know that TGWU officials had given a dispensation to lorries at the BSC chemical works of Stanton and Staveley. He was worried that this might undo efforts to persuade TGWU officials in Birmingham to give crucial support. He left immediately to sort this out, and the TGWU member of RSC accompanied him.

The GMWU member reported on his flying picket trip the previous days to Lincolnshire, which had been 'dispiriting for all' participants since the workforce had drifted back to work later. He also said he was not sure who was in charge of that picketing trip, although no-one attempted to clarify this for him. Joe S. brought up another item about the flying picket to Birmingham. The NCCC had organised their own bus for the trip, subject to the approval of the Central Co-ordinating Committee, but it was unclear whether the venture was for 24 or 48 hours. Tony L., the other NCCC member, wanted to know who was the 'link man' for the expedition. No-one was sure and the Chairman suggested getting clarification on all details from the Strike Co-ordinator.

Other members gave detailed comments about firms which had closed or were about to close, details of where lorries were still getting through, queries about stand-by pickets. Overall, a lot of information was exchanged about steel leakage and how it could be dammed up. A member of Picket Control quietly announced that they were holding a picket marshals' meeting that afternoon.

There being no more matters raised, the meeting ended two hours after its start, and members drifted off, to go to other meetings, to meet people to give them new information or to have a cup of coffee and a talk with pickets and strikers rushing in and out of the strike office.

RSC member's frames of reference

As observers, we noted consistencies in the outlook, values and beliefs of the RSC members. These systems of thought, particularly in terms of RSC identity, can be described as frames of reference. In a strike, where behaviour is potentially highly variable and where the environment is uncertain, frames of reference have strong behavioural implications. The systematic network of beliefs can be important in legitimating, supporting and explaining action which has occurred or is about to take place. The influence of frames of reference was particularly important in two areas of RSC functioning: firstly, in RSC decision-making and secondly, in inter-union relations.

The RSC's self-image had a number of connected elements. First, in common with all the strikers nationally, they had a strong view of themselves as *victims*. They felt victimised by the BSC and the hostile intentions of management were linked with those of the Conservative Government. They felt the steel unions were being made into sacrificial lambs for the trade union movement. Hostility from private sector employers also added to the sense of being victims, given the recession in steel. The strikers felt they had had no choice but to strike.

Although the RSC perceived themselves as victims, this did not denote weakness or passivity. On the contrary the RSC saw themselves as *strong and powerful*. Their sense of strength derived largely from their wide-ranging picketing activities, both locally and in flying groups, and was endorsed by other local strike groups. The media had also quickly sized up Rotherham as a force to be reckoned with in the picketing arena, reporting it as one of the most vigorous and militant strike areas.

Consistent with this, the RSC members viewed themselves as *leading the strike*, by initiating new structures and proposals for action, sometimes when other strike committees were only struggling into existence. Rotherham established the slogan '20% — and no strings' and, with Corby, the unofficial National Strike Committee, as well as a variety of picketing tactics and targets.

Great value was placed on being *autonomous* from the central organisation in London. In part this derived from traditional union branch freedom from central control but was also fed by hostility to national ISTC initiatives. The RSC members perceived themselves as ready and capable of separate independent action without requiring central office permission.

Finally, the RSC saw themselves as *committed* to their original position on the dual objectives of bringing the private sector into the dispute and maintaining adherence to the full wage claim. By contrast, the RSC viewed some other areas, and some other committees' support for the strike as precarious or less hard-line.

These aspects of the RSC's self-image, forming a systematic framework, were important influences on the behaviour of the RSC. We now briefly outline some of the consequences of these images. For example the sense of being victimised gave the RSC a moral certitude about the strike and their actions in promoting it, and an almost crusading sense of purpose. The fight by the steel workers was not just for themselves but for the whole of the trade union movement, giving them a sense of urgency in their fight. This was valuable in legitimating action, particularly the more violent aspects of picketing. The moral justification of fighting on behalf of other trade unionists may also have raised their expectations about the degree of support and help they would receive from other unions.

The sense of crusade combined with the sense of strength or power gave the RSC an undaunted optimism. Set-backs were seen to be only temporary or else when expectations of particular support were dashed, hope was relocated to a different agent. Although the optimism was sometimes misplaced, it was an important feature for an organisation constructed on commitment, since a positive benefit of it was that the RSC was not daunted by failures. Concomitant with this was a somewhat benign view of their own mistakes, which also had the effect of focusing attention to failure onto the external environment and away from the internal. The sense of power and autonomy was associated with explanations about success being attributed to local endeavour at the expense of the contribution made by circumstance or other groups. At times this amounted to an arrogance about local activity.

The self-image of commitment and being victims served to increase cohesion among members of the RSC, such that a strong, united front could be presented to protagonists. However, most social identities have negative aspects as well: we have already noted an arrogance, which had the effect of isolating the RSC members somewhat, particularly from groups such as the private sector steel workers. Finally, the level of commitment also affected the degree of compromise possible, which was generally rather low. Pragmatic solutions to difficulties were looked on with disfavour and some issues, incapable of immediate resolution, were not abandoned for some time.

This outline of the frames of reference of the RSC members is no more than a sketch, based on a distillation of some of the more salient features of RSC discussions and behaviour. However, the RSC was not a homogeneous group of branch officials. Some members held beliefs and values closer to the above description than others, with a major distinction occurring between ISTC and non-ISTC members. For ISTC members, their frames of reference could be summed up as an essentially simplified view of the world with clear-cut, black and white issues; for example, those who were not wholeheartedly for the strike were seen as being automatically against it. The non-ISTC members, with their greater experience of the wider trade union movement, had a more differentiated view of the strike and the parties involved. They recognised, for example, the internal difficulties of maintaining support for particular moves from the rank and file, or the need to coax support from certain groups through an appeal to their practical and personal interests rather than to the more abstract values of fairness and solidarity. However, the positive aspects of the ISTC members' frames of reference, notably the optimism and commitment, must not be lost sight of. Relative to other strike bodies in South Yorkshire (for example the DSC or CCC), the RSC was in many ways more extreme in its views and identity. This was partly because of their greater isolation from other sources of information, such as union members involved in the national affairs of ISTC.

CHAPTER EIGHT

Debate and decision: inside the strike committee

We will now describe how the RSC functioned, through an examination firstly of the processes internal to the RSC and then of those underlying the RSC's relations with other South Yorkshire strike bodies which claimed the authority to exert control over organisational activities. We concentrate on the discussions and debate which took place in the RSC and where appropriate the decision-making which did or did not take place, since these provide a useful focus for understanding key organisational processes of integration and control.

Decisions internal to the RSC

Decision-making is one means by which organisations attempt to gain control over their environments. However, a superficial glance at the RSC meetings would suggest that very few decisions were being made.

The description we have given of a strike meeting (Chapter 7) showed a good deal of discussion but few concrete decisions about action, and this in spite of the fact that the RSC was involved in a wide range of actions, from organising pickets to establishing various support services.

There are two possible explanations for this apparent absence of decision-making on and by the RSC. Firstly, decisions were being taken at other levels in the organisation. For example, we have already described how picket marshals and their cells exercised considerable discretion in making decisions about the day-to-day running of the picket lines. Other strike and trade union bodies, for example the CCC, the DSC and to a lesser extent the Rotherham Joint Committee, were also making decisions during the strike. Later in the chapter we shall examine how responsibility for decisions was allocated between different strike bodies.

Secondly, decisions in organisations are often harder to identify as events than as *processes,* involving the gradual development over time of constraints and expectations. Decisions 'emerge' or are determined almost by default over quite long time periods. The gradual nature of decision-making which converges on a consensus makes it difficult to observe and identify a clearly delineated choice point which could be described as a decision. Furthermore, the decision-making may be subject to continuing adjustment as the circumstances surrounding the issue change or develop, such that a final decision is in any case sometimes not possible.

The process of decision-making may itself depend on the *type* of decision being made. Decisions over the allocation of resources may be handled differently from decisions requiring individual or collective commitment to action. Or decision processes may vary in terms of their salience in achieving the organisation's major goals, or their consequences for the organisation. We found it useful, therefore, to divide the decision types within the RSC into three categories, although the RSC members themselves did not employ this classification. These were strategic, tactical and administrative decisions. The categorisation is necessarily arbitrary since although a distinction can be made between strategy and tactics based on notions such as goals and sub-goals, or means and ends, it is widely recognised that the notion of goal is problematic within organisation theory because it is difficult to define *a priori*.

Strategic decisions
Strategic decisions related to the setting of the fundamental objectives of the strike organisation. Prior to the strike the Rotherham Joint Committee and the embryonic RSC had had no doubts as to what would be the basic goal of the local organisation: it was to stop steel movement. This had been articulated at the first RJC strike preparation meeting and recurred in later discussions. Any tactics would be adopted insofar as they were instrumental in meeting this aim, and all local resources would be thrown behind it.

Although this objective was interpreted differently by strikers and trade union sympathisers the RSC members were clear in their own minds: stopping steel movement involved paralysing *any* use or movement of steel, and this, inevitably, included its use by the private sector. A corollary was that the private sector should be drawn into the strike, a goal which the RJC had voiced at its first strike preparation meeting of 16 December. The first RSC meeting (13 December) had asked the EC member to propose at the EC that 'a national strike should include the private sector'. The RSC's strategy was at variance with that of the national ISTC organisation where steel movement stoppage was much more qualified, and secondary to negotiations.

As preventing steel movement was essentially the *mission* of the organisation it was accessible to neither doubt nor scrutiny. The consensus over strategy was so widespread and so crucial to the existence of the organisation that a decision between alternative strategies was never evident. The RSC's sense of local power also prevented evaluation of the strategy's appropriateness. Failures to stem the flow of steel were attributed to insufficient resources being directed towards the goal rather than any deficiency in the goal itself. There were after all almost 300 steel producers, users and stockholders in the Rotherham area, over 500 stockholders in Birmingham alone and thousands of steel users and hauliers around the country. Yet with these potential targets and with imported steel pouring into the country at unregistered ports on every coast and even, it was rumoured, being landed at Heathrow airport, the value of the strategy was not raised within the RSC. Instead, efforts were made to increase the resources or their effectiveness, as for example in the numerous attempts to encourage more pickets through appeal at mass meetings or later through threat of sanctions, or the attempts to increase their effectiveness via cell 24.

Even evaluation of the strategy's success was limited, based simply on whether lorries loaded with steel had left a particular plant or not. Successful picketing of an engineering plant, where steel could perhaps be worked on for several months before it became a finished product, was of equal value to stopping more short-term production uses of steel, as in the manufacture of tin cans. Thus, *quantity* of steel stopped was initially the most important criterion, with a focus on larger plants. The priorities of target choice were evident in the committee where little information was presented about the type of steel being produced or used by the plant, only (sometimes) its output in terms of tonnes or lorry-loads. The conflict with the local engineering unions over the definition of 'finished product' in the first two weeks of February might have occupied less time had the RSC reflected on its low value in pressurising BSC given its lengthy processing time (see Chapter 9).

After the widespread return of the private sector in mid-January, when it became glaringly obvious to the RSC that steel movement could not possibly be completely contained, there was some development in strategy evaluation. The RSC had a new interest in using its resources to block essential material supplies for steel-making such as lime or in preventing particular types of steel movement, notably from car plants in the last month. There was a tacit acceptance that certain other targets could not be prevented from working.

Tactical decisions
Tactical decisions concerned choices about *how* the organisational goals were to be carried out, and in this case how steel movement could be prevented. This could be achieved through the two processes of picketing and establishing trade union agreements. Although of lesser importance there was also the threat of the removal of safety cover and the selective use of dispensations.

The centrality of picketing

The major tactic favoured by the RSC as a whole was picketing, which absorbed more time and attention within the Committee than any other topic. Its central significance was illustrated by the opening sentence of a document distributed to pickets by the Strike Co-ordinator in the first few days:

> The heart and soul of the strike is the picket. An effective strike means effective picketing — hard, consistent, well directed picketing. *It does not matter how good everything else is. If the picket is weak and disorganised the strike will fall apart.*

The ISTC members were particularly enthusiastic about picketing, seeing it as the corner-stone of the strike, and it tended to overwhelm consideration of other tactics. The alternative method of stopping steel movement, through establishing agreements with unions inside plants so that they would not touch 'blacked' steel, was raised a number of times by non-ISTC representatives, but did not gain much of a hearing. For example, at the RSC meeting on 23 January, both Joe S. and Tony L., the NCCC representatives, noted that stopping steel movement in the Birmingham area would be difficult to achieve through picketing, given the large number of private sector plants. They argued that 'picketing should become almost redundant if we use the existing trade union organisation' and would be 'more effective than police and pickets'. They advocated the use of more articulate pickets who could be persuasive in encouraging sympathy action from the private sector rather than browbeating firms into closure through the use of picket 'heavies'. This plea was politely listened to but passed over without discussion and the next day the RSC held a closed session for 1 ½ hours with key 'heavy brigade' pickets, instructing them on the use of sabotage and guerrilla tactics to close down plants in Birmingham.

On other occasions the two NCCC representatives again asked the RSC meetings to consider a wider set of alternatives than simply picketing. Tony L. at the 23 January meeting argued that when the private sector joined the dispute, they should be invited onto the RSC, but his suggestion received no reply and he did not pursue it. The optimism of the ISTC members gave them a sense that victory was close at hand and consequently little attention was paid to the private sector. Later, on 1 February the NCCC members again suggested that plans be laid in anticipation of the private sector rejoining the strike after a successful House of Lords appeal. As with many of the non-ISTC suggestions however, the discussion in the RSC moved on to the next topic with only a brief nod of assent to the ideas raised, but with no discussion. Similarly, on 11 February the NCCC member, Tony L., was critical of the failure of the RSC to anticipate the drift back to work of the private sector (Hadfields' strikers had just announced their decision to return that day). Tony L. pointed out that he had been consistently urging the RSC to think about this eventuality over a week ago. The response from one of the RSC members was that this was 'unfortunate' but that 'we have to learn by making mistakes'. A week later, on 19 February, Tony L. was again urging action on the private sector, warning especially of the need to take action about Firth Brown, a large Sheffield firm. But the mood of the meeting was despondent and fatalistic, epitomised in the Chairman's statement that the message 'can't be got across to the private sector since our communication system excludes them'. This seemed to set the limit to how far Tony L. could push the matter and the discussion passed on to considering *post-strike* relations between public and private sectors.

In arguing for attention to be paid to tactics other than picketing, it was clear that the NCCC members were at a disadvantage due to their particular union affiliation: in an ISTC-dominated RSC, the views of a non-ISTC member very often carried less weight than those of an ISTC member. The NCCC members seemed to recognise their marginality within the Committee by tending to present proposals in a highly tentative manner, a style quite inconsistent with their recognised trade union experience and seniority. However, the lack of attention paid to NCCC proposals occurred only in those situations where they advocated the substitution of another activity for picketing.

As picketing was favoured above all other strike tactics considerable attention was paid to collecting information about targets, discussing the details of particular ventures, planning campaigns in new fields, and discussing the pros and cons of the use of particular methods of picketing. Picketing came up at every single RSC meeting and was usually the major focus. As a consequence the information actively solicited by the RSC was dominated by potential targets and the mechanics of matching the supply of pickets to demand. The RSC requested the presence of additional people, typically strikers, at a large number of meetings to provide specific or specialist information on targets. After providing the information, these visitors would leave the RSC. The report-backs also indicated the overwhelming interest in picketing. No RSC meeting ever concluded before several exchanges of information about steel movement and picketing had taken place. Frequently, such information was simply jotted down without discussion by a few of the RSC members, particularly by the Secretary and by the non-ISTC members who could relay the news to their own strike committees or other groups, if they thought it sufficiently important.

The RSC soon acquired a reputation for being one of the most militant of all the strike committees; its militancy can be seen to lie principally in its belief that picketing should be pursued without restraint. The private sector had been picketed from the first day of the strike and geographical limits were unheeded as the RSC dispatched flying picket groups to ports and towns around the country. Only on 30 January when the Divisional Strike Committee allocated regions to its constituent strike committees, confirming the RSC presence in Dover and Birmingham, was the RSC obliged to withdraw from other regions. The RSC also made it clear, for example at its 24 January meeting, that it was prepared to countenance illegal tactics if these were necessary to win the strike.

Picket cells and picket morale
The strong commitment to picketing gave the RSC members an optimism which made it difficult for them to believe it could fail. The concern with action, with the excitement and tension of events in the external task environment, meant that the RSC did not, in the first few weeks of the strike, pay much attention to assessment or control of the internal environment, in terms of the presence of motivated and able pickets.

Although news of picket dissatisfaction reached the RSC from informal contacts and Picket Control the information raised little anxiety for some time. For example, from mid-January Picket Control regularly informed the RSC that some local picket cells were experiencing problems of recruitment and deployment. RSC meetings indicated a widespread confidence that the need for local cells would diminish with the imminent entry of the private sector into the dispute, so that serious attention did not have to be paid to cell deterioration, and the matter was only briefly discussed as a temporary problem.

Further warnings from Picket Control of local cell breakdown continued during February although discussions in the RSC were brief. The RSC advocated tighter control to improve the cell system: somehow greater pressure should be applied to the picket marshals who would transmit it to cell members (though how was unspecified). Alternatively, a suggestion was made that more information should be given to local pickets about the progress of the strike locally, in order to develop motivation. Both the GMWU and the TGWU representatives put forward concrete suggestions for the improvement of the picketing system, based on measures their own strike committees had taken to improve picket morale and effectiveness (including moving cells between different targets in order to give them a change). However, none of these suggestions was accorded more than five minutes' attention; they were not widely discussed. The decline in picket behaviour, while regrettable, did not merit further consideration from the RSC.

One reason for the lack of attention to picket morale was that the signals of its decline came from ISTC staff members (Picket Control). In a committee strongly dominated by manual ISTC branch officials non-manual and non-ISTC members were at a disadvantage in getting their message across (as we have seen in regard to suggestions by NCCC members about alternatives to picketing). Additionally, the RSC members experienced a great sense of constraint in that change in the organisational structure was viewed as possibly more harmful than beneficial. 'It's too late to change the system now but in future strikes we should organise things [the picket cells] differently' (Chairman, 8 February). But most significant of all, perhaps, picket morale and cell breakdown in the first half of the strike received little attention because they were topics viewed by the RSC as less *relevant* since they fell outside the all-important external task environment. Picket morale was not yet seen to be of direct or compelling importance in the fight to win the strike.

Even when picket behaviour was acknowledged to be problematic — in the slough of despondency created by issues such as the fire at the strike office, after the failure of national negotiations, and even more so in relation to the drift back to work of the private sector — the RSC did not engage in a major analysis of the possible causes and cures of deterioration of morale and organisation. Although the subdued meeting on 26 February included a long discussion of the state of the cells, which was in fact the first item on the agenda, the 40 minute discussion was inconclusive. Although the RSC agreed that information about the state of each cell and its target should be collected in a systematic manner in reports, with a view to possibly reorganising or modifying the picket cell system, support for this was not wholehearted and it was left to Picket Control, who were most keen to collect such information in any case, to institute this procedure.

The information collected was in fact brief and ambiguous. At one picket marshals' meeting, when asked to give details of their cells' performance, marshals' comments were no more detailed than 'good' or 'doing OK'. Norms about the manner of presentation were rapidly established, each picket marshal's report following this cursory style. The actual quality of information, so systematically solicited, was therefore very poor. The results of such enquiries were not, however, publicised at the RSC meetings.

Response to criticism

Picketing was so central to the RSC's supremacy and self-image that criticism of picketing was difficult to incorporate or discuss. Criticism of the preoccupation with picketing had been voiced, with varying severity, by a number of sources. The NCCC members had tactfully suggested development of trade union links as an alternative to picketing. There had been a number of occasions when picket marshals had demanded to see the RSC in order to indicate their dissatisfaction with the organisation of local or flying picketing. Senior trade unionists from Sheffield engineering firms had strongly criticised the RSC (3 March) for failing to take heed of their recommendations about picketing targets. The RSC remained impervious to such comments, however well-intentioned the communication. For example on 22 February the GMWU member, in the report-back session, commented that he knew a striker who wanted to picket but who had been unable to join a cell, and that recruitment information was difficult to obtain. Although this raised the wider issue of picket recruitment about which some RSC members, especially Picket Control, had been expressing concern, the response from one RSC member was the fatalistic comment that 'the cells haven't worked 100 per cent' which terminated the issue. The criticism of CSEU officials about the failure to picket certain firms was parried by the Strike Co-ordinator, Secretary and a member of Picket Control who argued that the extent of picketing was much greater than the CSEU officials suggested and in any case it was not the responsibility of the RSC since the targets were under the control of the Sheffield Strike Committee. The matter was then dropped.

When on 5 March six bus marshals burst into the RSC meeting to give their suggestions for improvements in the flying picket system, they also laid the charge that the RSC spent too much time in meetings and were out of touch with pickets. The Secretary pointed out somewhat defensively the difficulties of getting reasonable information from picket marshals, and the problems of liaising with full-time officials. After their departure, the RSC turned back immediately to the interrupted report-backs, with no further discussion of the bus marshals' comments.

Further tactical decisions
The lack of attention paid to exploiting trade union links has already been noted, and it persisted throughout the strike, despite attempts by the two NCCC representatives to encourage planning and action on this matter.

Safety cover and dispensations were tactical issues debated by the RSC. The threat to remove safety cover was first raised on 28 January, although it remained an important issue through the early part of February. Removing safety cover, with possible damage to plant and the subsequent delay of the return to work, was a risky and strike-escalating move and it appealed to many RSC members, given their militant outlook. Yet the issue was highly contentious, causing heated debate and extensive discussion within the RSC, with a number of different views being expressed on its wisdom and feasibility. The dissensus occurred not simply between the members of different unions but, unusually, within the ISTC ranks. The tactics chosen by the RSC, then, were not characterised by complete uniformity about their value. The treatment of NCCC proposals over safety cover contrasted sharply with the RSC's reactions to their other proposals for prosecuting the strike. Joe S. argued that threats to withdraw safety cover would be more effective even than picketing (although he was suggesting these activities should be used additively, not as alternatives). He was listened to and a number of points were taken up and discussed. This topic illustrates the point that inattention to the NCCC proposals on other topics was not entirely due to the source of the message (though that played its part) but was also due to the message characteristics. The NCCC's proposals here were perceived to be directly relevant to winning the strike, unlike those of developing inter-union links.

Dispensations were also part of the range of tactics considered by the RSC, although a subsidiary part, since they occupied relatively little time in the Committee, were handled mainly by a DSC member, and provoked little discussion beyond the pros and cons of a particular application. The RSC recognised that the provision of dispensations gave them a certain degree of power over BSC and other employers but that dispensations only have limited usefulness since 'if you withdraw dispensations you lose some of your bargaining power' (Secretary, 23 January). It was agreed that 'withdrawing dispensations needs to be saved for the major aspects of the strike' (ISTC member, 23 January).

Before leaving the area of tactical decision-making, we should note that the RSC also attempted to influence other groups within the strike organisation by using proposals or recommendations. The most conspicuous example was the unanimous resolution by the ISTC members on 12 February to send a telegram to the Executive Council asking it to examine the conduct of the General Secretary during the strike, and to move a vote of no confidence in the General Secretary, as the RSC had done. Although the RSC had no formal authority to pass resolutions this was clearly seen as an effective way of exerting influence. On 22 February, the ISTC members agreed to convey a resolution to the RJC reminding them of their commitment to examine and consider issues related to the return to work. Given that all the ISTC members of the RSC went to the RJC and could have urged this matter if they had wanted to, it is clear that the use of a formal communication gave extra weight to the proposal. On 12 March, the RSC also tried to influence the national negotiations (the only occasion on which it did) by agreeing to send a telegram to the CNC arguing that 'morale has never been higher' and urging it to settle for no less than 20%, with no strings.

Administrative decisions

Under this heading are all the decisions made by the RSC which simply kept the organisation functioning. They were the decisions concerned with strike maintenance, being predominantly concerned with the internal environment. In this category come the decisions over changing solicitors, establishing rules as to how the hardship fund should be distributed, deciding how much and by what means pickets would be paid, how fuel would be distributed to local picket cells and how much of a picket marshal's telephone bill should be paid. These decisions about the day-to-day running of the strike organisation took up a considerable amount of the RSC's attention and time. As much time was spent on such matters as on the RSC's primary concern with picketing. As the strike progressed time spent on administrative decisions was shortened somewhat through the delegation of certain tasks to individuals or groups.

Extended discussion, often over more than one meeting, occurred where issues were perceived as establishing precedents and hence leading to policies. The time and attention spent on such issues can be partly seen as establishing rules, which aided in the regulation of the internal environment and, in theory at least, prevented the RSC from being submerged by repetitive decisions. Some rules, however, served an additional purpose. This sub-group of administrative decisions we call equity decisions. In these cases, the RSC considered alternative decision choices with an emphasis on minimising injustices to strikers. When alternative choices were considered this was generally with a view to what possible anomalies might arise and how they might be avoided. Decisions were modified as unanticipated injustices and problems came to light. For example, in deciding how to reimburse picket marshals for the increased size of their phone bill, the RSC changed its 7 March decision three times in the following week, changing the basis on which payment should be paid so that it would not be 'unfair' to certain types of marshal. On this issue, opinion was informally canvassed outside the RSC: the RSC was at pains, as with a number of equity decisions, to demonstrate that their choice was made with wide consultation. Similarly, in deciding to recall the Dover picket (25 February) the choice was made partly in relation to overall picketing strategy but more importantly there was an implicit recognition of the need for equity in picketing experiences. The Dover assignment was widely regarded as a 'soft option' compared with some local picketing, because of the easy task of token picketing, the expenses, and the hospitality of local Kent mining families. The Chairman commented that 'it can't be right to spend more than one week at Dover'. The principle of equity was carried even further in the proposal (which was rejected as impractical) that ex-Dover pickets should be obliged to work the unpopular night and weekend shifts for a couple of weeks after their return.

The sensitivity of the RSC to rule-making and more importantly, equity, can be seen as functional in reducing or preventing intra-organisational conflict. In this way, the decisions had an ideological or political significance, aiding the process of maintaining commitment and cohesion. The permeable membership boundaries of the RSC membership previously commented on (Chapter 7), further facilitated the acceptance of equity decisions since all interests were potentially aired through the RSC.

Typically, equity decisions took much longer to resolve at the RSC than most other types of decision, and the time devoted to them was sometimes disproportionate to their influence on the strike outcome. For example, on 4 March, the RSC devoted an hour to deciding how to choose the three bus-loads of strikers who would travel to London for a TUC rally against public expenditure cuts on 9 March. The matter had to be deferred since the RSC could not agree on the correct basis for representation. In contrast, the RSC that same day discussed possible means of opposing the BSC's proposed ballot, but the latter discussion was considerably shorter.

Decision type and discussion

The process of gathering and using information reveals a lot about RSC decision-making. According to rational and bureaucratic models of decision-making, information relevant to potential decision alternatives is gathered and evaluated, leading to a decision choice based on which alternative meets certain goal-based criteria. On the other hand, in political models of decision-making, information provides a legitimating function for action taken or about to be taken.

Information was used by the RSC in different ways according to the type of decision. Administrative decisions, concerned with the continuance of the strike organisation and the equitable distribution of resources amongst its members, involved detailed decision-making using information to direct choice. To make these choices, the RSC gathered and evaluated information on the likely outcomes of the various decision choices available. Decisions were frequently reversed or revised when new information came to light and when criticisms were made. In many ways then, the administrative decisions fitted the pattern of rational decision-making with a (relatively) orderly progression through stages of information collection, evaluation of possible alternative decision choices, followed by an evaluation of the action itself with, in some cases, subsequent modification. Such decision-making, facilitated by the open boundaries of RSC membership, could be useful in generating commitment to and acceptance of a decision, although we have already noted that, evaluated simply in terms of efficiency, the procedure had severe limitations since it, on occasions, consumed RSC time out of proportion to its value. Of all the topics discussed by the RSC those which engendered the greatest dissensus were one-off, highly contentious tactical decisions (such as the removal of safety cover) and also those which were involved in rule-making and equity (although the latter discussions, while extended and complex, were less heated). The range of alternatives considered by the RSC over equity decisions and the variety of opinions contrasts with the convergent decision-making and ideological consensus about the more serious tactical and strategic decisions

Strategic and tactical decisions required an entirely different use of information. Commitment to the strategy of stopping all steel movement, and to the involvement of the private sector, had been decided by Rotherham branch officials in their strike preparation meetings and remained fixed throughout the strike. Commitment to the strategy was a fundamental *raison d'être* for the organisation and it was inconceivable that its value should be questioned. To a lesser extent, the tactics adopted were similarly amenable to little scrutiny or doubt. This explains the apparent interest in positive, and lack of interest in negative, information and the failure to change direction when new information became available, to analyse problems, and to evaluate outcomes and respond to criticism. Information provided a justification for action, and the decision-making which occurred can be characterised as essentially political, designed to develop commitment.

We should note, however, the functional value of this method of decision-making. An organisation operating in a hostile environment may experience strong pressures to remain consistent to its expressed policies. Externally, deviation may be viewed as a sign of weakness, and flexibility as indecisiveness. Internal pressures may exist in that changes in strategy can be confusing to organisation members, may weaken commitment and can disrupt established routines (or the leadership may fear this will happen). For example, within the RSC there were fears expressed by Picket Control that a radical change in the local cell structure would be seriously disruptive, increasing drop-out rates and lowering effectiveness and morale. Within the RSC itself, the use of information to confirm decisions already taken and to indicate the difficulties faced by the strikers, gave the RSC members an opportunity to reaffirm their commitment and to share and reinforce their understandings of their social reality.

Contested and shared authority

We turn now to examine the decisions which were either shared or contested between the RSC and the other strike bodies in South Yorkshire which claimed decision-making responsibility. The processes of negotiating decision-making control were illustrative of the relationship between the strike bodies, and in particular indicate the basis for the authority exerted by the strike leaders in South Yorkshire.

The RSC was not the only decision-making body within the Division. The complex structure described in Chapter 4 developed as the strike was seen locally to be more serious than had at first been anticipated, and several committees had an impact on the decisions claimed by the RSC. The Divisional Strike Committee had been established to 'co-ordinate' picketing and other activities across the four local strike organisations in South Yorkshire and Humberside. The Central Co-ordinating Committee (CCC), had been established on 14 January, after all the unions had formally entered the strike, to foster multi-union co-ordination. The Rotherham Joint Committee, an ISTC body with delegates from most branches, continued to meet throughout the strike and raised matters of concern to ISTC members. The collection of committees, with their varied functions, led one strike activist to comment that the strikers had managed to create more committees than BSC.

At a superficial level, the complex committee structure had the characteristics of a bureaucracy, with a clear and consensually agreed hierarchy of committees each with apparently clear areas of authority. The DSC would co-ordinate activities, though the four local strike committees would act with full autonomy on local issues. The CCC would handle decisions involving multi-union initiatives. Members of the RSC had been included in the informal discussions leading to the establishment of the DSC and CCC and had fully supported the need for such co-ordinating mechanisms.

In practice, however, there was considerable ambiguity about communications and authority, although this was not intended, and was not perceived for several weeks. A major source of ambiguity was the original division of labour between the committes, and the problematic nature of the concept of co-ordination (noted in Chapter 4).

The ambiguity surrounding the division of tasks and decision-making responsibility was exacerbated by the membership of the committees, since communication, and hence clarification of expectations and existing structures, was impeded by the small or non-existent overlap in membership. For example, until 12 February the RSC sent only its Chairman to the DSC meetings (although from then on four to five delegates). In the case of the CCC, the RSC initially was even worse off: the CCC had two ISTC delegates from the Division and these happened to be DSC members with no direct representation from the RSC. Furthermore, delegates could change on an irregular basis, according to their involvement in other strike duties, and so information exchange was impeded by a lack of continuity in attendance.

The lack of clarity over the division of tasks and of membership can be seen in a number of examples. The most notable confusion over responsibility occurred at the RSC meeting on 25 January in the discussion about flying pickets. The GMWU member queried a detail of the CCC's instruction to supply 50 short-term flying pickets daily to the ISTC strike office. The ISTC members had not even heard of the CCC picket request, the TGWU representative had only heard a rumour, and the NCCC members had received different instructions about supplying pickets. No-one in the room was able to state who the pickets were expected to report to, who was responsible for them, or who was arranging their transport. Wider questions were raised: in particular, who passed information from the CCC to the RSC? And for that matter, who passed information from the DSC to the RSC? It appeared that information only passed informally between such bodies, which meant that information was transmitted irregularly and unevenly among RSC members. Although the Strike Co-ordinator was called into the meeting to shed light on these questions, he was able to provide no more than suggestions as to how communications could be improved. An RSC member, Mike W., suggested that there should be daily reports from both the CCC and the DSC, and it was agreed that the Strike Co-ordinator would provide reports from the latter, although since the procedure relied on one busy individual, it later atrophied. There was no-one to liaise with the CCC. Although a clearer information flow was planned, the issue of authority still remained unresolved. Joe S., the NCCC member, posed the dilemma most starkly: was his first allegiance to the CCC or the RSC? Was the RSC subservient to the CCC? There was no clear answer to this. The Strike Co-ordinator commented that the CCC was not functioning very well and also its role was unclear. To solve the immediate, and acute, problems of flying picket co-ordination the RSC decided to arrange for an ISTC member of the CCC (from Stockbridge), the Strike Co-ordinator (representing the DSC), and the RSC Chairman to meet daily to exchange information on flying picket destinations. Again, this decision was dependent on particular individuals being present in the strike office at a particular time.

An additional source of ambiguity was that the committee structure was not stable — or its various functions fixed. The DSC had been established just before the strike started, when it became clear that more concerted strike effort would be required, and its role changed over time. The CCC had arisen out of liaison initiatives by the local (non-striking) engineering unions as much as by the strike activists. Set up on 14 January its effective demise occurred on 7 February, when only two people turned up for a meeting. The unofficial National Strike Committee did not get off the ground until 25 February, at a meeting in a Sheffield hotel called by Corby and Rotherham for Divisional ISTC representatives. Its first steps were tentative and it never really developed a major strike role, although it did attempt co-ordination activities above Divisional level, over, for example, picketing expenses. The changes in roles of certain of these committees will be described in the detailed discussions of certain decision topics within the South Yorkshire strike organisation.

It can be seen, then, that the nexus of committees in South Yorkshire had certain stable bureaucratic features but that these co-existed with an ambiguity of structure, task and membership. We will explore the consequences of these features for the functioning of the South Yorkshire organisation through the examination of two decision topics of crucial importance to the strikers: picketing, and safety cover. Through these we can explore the authority relationships and tensions between the strike bodies, although we will retain our focus on the RSC.

Decision topic 1: picketing

Competing claims as to responsibility for decisions about flying picketing developed from the RSC, the DSC and the CCC. There was no dispute about local picketing cells since that was localised action (within Rotherham's territory) and had quickly become relatively stable and predictable, so that no other strike body had tried to influence RSC decisions in that area. In contrast, flying picketing provided considerable potential for conflict for a number of reasons. We have seen how, as the strike progressed, there was an increasing emphasis on flying picketing. Its importance and centrality as a tactic, not just to the RSC but to other strike bodies, meant that conflict was more likely than if it had been a peripheral issue. In addition, flying picketing was an activity which was constantly changing, for example in geographical location and target choice, and so was difficult to co-ordinate through the establishment of procedural rules. Each occasion had to be dealt with as a separate decision. Rotherham had immediate responsibility for organising the recruitment and welfare of flying pickets but control over their deployment was claimed, at various times, by the DSC because of its 'co-ordinating' function and by the CCC because of multi-union involvement.

Conflict was most clearly expressed in the relationship between the CCC and RSC. Within the first three weeks of the strike, the CCC had become involved in selecting targets for flying picketing and encouraging the participation of the various local strike organisations. The RSC recognised the legitimacy of the CCC's inclusion of flying picketing within its sphere of influence and initially felt that its authority over RSC flying pickets was desirable since it was a more senior strike body with more senior and experienced members. The RSC recognised their dependence on the CCC since it had resources unavailable to the RSC: experienced labour leaders in Sheffield and the ability to mobilise a greater number of multi-union pickets — 'we need them because they are multi-union' (RSC member, 28 January). Yet despite the hierarchical relationship, which was broadly accepted by the RSC, and the sense of dependence, the RSC was always ambivalent about the CCC because of their own desire to retain autonomy and be 'self-reliant'. It began to contest the CCC's authority in the early weeks of the strike.

Trouble had been brewing since the CCC had started organising flying pickets. At its meeting of 23 January the RSC discussed the flying picket trip to a steel stockholder in Blackburn the previous day, organised by the CCC, which, said the Chairman, had been 'a total disaster'. The Chairman catalogued a succession of complaints. The picket, it was said, had been badly managed, in that there had been no-one to meet the flying pickets off the bus, no food was provided, and pickets were unsure who was in charge or what exactly they were supposed to do. Furthermore, the picket had not even been effective since, although the plant had been closed, lorries had gone in and out only half an hour after the pickets had left. The Secretary's view was that 'the co-ordinating people are too far from the situation' and consequently they were making decisions while being unaware of the problems. By contrast, the RSC felt itself to be a powerful and effective organiser of pickets. Tony L., the NCCC member, commented that 'we have the biggest impact in the Division, so *we* need to extend flyers', although his NCCC colleague, Joe S., advised that it would be impossible to supervise the CCC and that 'we must learn to delegate'. The RSC's sense of their strength led one member to suggest that the RSC should make recommendations to the CCC on appropriate targets. In other words, the CCC should be a much more consultative rather than executive body. Other RSC members wanted an even harder line, demanding that the RSC should keep the CCC fully informed of problems and 'if they are not prepared to do what we want, they should relinquish control'.

On 25 January the RSC was again in deep discussion of the CCC's shortcomings, expressing scepticism about the CCC's abilities to choose targets and organise an attack. Their apparently poor organisational skills were underlined by the confusion over the different instructions given to different union pickets to assemble at the ISTC office daily.

On Monday, 28 January, the CCC was again in disfavour. The Secretary gave details of what he felt was another 'mistake': an operation the location of whose target was so secret that the bus departure had been delayed while the bus marshals tracked down a member of the CCC who knew where they were meant to be going! The picket marshals had given the CCC member 'a lot of stick' for it. Almost without exception the RSC members at the meeting chipped in with criticism or raised questions as to whether the CCC possessed sufficient expertise to mount operations. They had 'brilliant ideas' but they were 'all in the air' and 'they're too far removed from the action'. The RSC expressed some of its resentment through their concern for their own pickets, arguing that 'we cannot subject our best marshals to this kind of treatment' because 'it was unfair to them'. They felt they needed to protect their own organisation from indiscriminate abuse by the CCC. The Chairman expressed a general feeling when he commented that 'they see it as a military operation . . . they are the staff and we are just troops'. The RSC's sense of autonomy also surfaced in stronger proposals than previously: instead of talking of consultation at this stage they were talking of full control with the RSC being allowed to pick targets, perhaps from a short-list prepared by the CCC. The Secretary proposed that the CCC be given 'one more chance' and if they failed then to 'leave them to their own devices' by 'withdrawing our organisation and our manpower'. The proposal to become fully autonomous had been raised several times earlier in the meeting, so that one further act of co-operation was seen to be fair.

The RSC on 29 January again brought up the topic of the CCC's control of flying pickets. The picket at Leeds the previous night had been 'a waste of time' since the plant was closed for the night anyway. The NCCC members were particularly fed up since mistakes by the CCC were being blamed by pickets on the local strike organisation. One RSC member argued that the RSC should take a hard line, with the RSC having priority over the CCC in the use of pickets. (In other words, co-operation would continue, with the RSC leading, rather than contributing to, the picketing.) The Chairman argued that the CCC should be made to accept that the responsibility for targets would move to the RSC, and that 'other groups should be told what we expect of them'.

The two NCCC members, in co-operative fashion, suggested a meeting with the CCC to 'thrash out the relationship', but the ISTC members strongly resisted this, arguing that the CCC 'treated the RSC with disdain' and that they would not listen anyway. However, the Secretary and Chairman were persuaded by the co-operative view and the Chairman left the meeting to see two of the CCC members who were at the time in the same building. He came back to report that he had got two different and conflicting responses, one CCC member saying that pickets could not be used by the RSC for their own purposes and the other overruling the first, suggesting that the RSC could do what it wanted.

The RSC in this way contested the authority of the CCC and eventually won its independence, although demands made by the CCC declined in any case, partly because the CCC was not functioning very effectively as a committee over a number of issues. There was disillusionment with the powers and resources of the CCC and the failure of co-operation, not just with the RSC, meant that it effectively ceased functioning in early February. The potential for conflict declined because the RSC began increasingly to concentrate on organising their own forces for long-distance flying picketing at coastal ports, or in response to requests for pickets in such places as Birmingham, Lincolnshire, and a number of ports.

In this case of conflict with the CCC it was clear that while the RSC accepted the formal authority of the CCC — that was never in question — the RSC felt that the appropriate rationale for decision-making was not authority but rather *expertise*. The RSC believed in their own expertise; they felt that their past success was due to their autonomous actions and that only when they had co-operated with the other groups had affairs been mismanaged. RSC members believed they had proved their competence and power within the first two weeks of the strike, but by contrast the CCC had shown itself to be singularly incompetent and lacking in expertise. They felt they were being fair in giving the CCC further opportunities to improve their organisation of flying picketing ventures. If they had been successful, it is highly likely that the RSC would have accepted their control over flying picketing. We must point out that the RSC's view of events was partial: while critical of the mistakes of the CCC they were, as we have seen earlier, relatively insensitive to the criticisms levelled at them from within their own organisation: by picket marshals, non-ISTC members and others. The RSC had also made mistakes in choosing targets, and their dislike of being treated 'like troops' was at variance with their desire to deploy their own pickets in this manner. The RSC in effect were operating something of a double standard, labelling their own conduct in positive ways while viewing that of the CCC more negatively. This would be at least partially anticipated on the basis of theories of group identification and categorisation. The claim by the RSC that it deployed pickets more effectively was essentially a rationalisation in response to loss of autonomy and organisational control. The RSC attempted to regain control over their own resources and decisions by contesting the authority of the CCC to make flying picket decisions. Using their own political power, derived from the considerable number and effectiveness of Rotherham pickets, the RSC won back for themselves the choice of targets and deployment of pickets, although mutual co-operation was not ruled out, as the consideration of DSC requests indicated.

With the gradual demise of the CCC, the DSC gained in importance in launching picketing forays. However, the DSC treated the RSC with considerably more caution. The DSC was careful to *request* the presence of RSC pickets, and to let the RSC be responsible for the implementation of the choice. For example, on 31 Janaury the RSC Chairman reported that the DSC had asked them if they would provide pickets for some demonstrations planned for early February. Although the RSC accepted the higher authority of the DSC in general and on specific topics in particular, they did not relinquish control over the deployment of pickets; they rejected the DSC request on the grounds that 'we have too many other things to do' (Chairman), although it was agreed that off-duty individuals could make their own decisions. Later on, the DSC again demonstrated its persuasive rather than directive mode of influence over the RSC. On 5 February at the RSC the Chairman reported that the DSC was planning a picket of a Midlands car plant for which they had requested around one hundred Rotherham pickets. The RSC felt it was unable to make a decision without further details of the DSC proposal since 'we will suffer the aggro if the project goes wrong'. A senior DSC member was brought into the meeting and revealed some of the details he would have preferred to keep confidential, in order to gain the support and commitment of the RSC.

In the second half of the strike the conflict over control of pickets died away. The RSC retained full, uncontested control of resources and choice of targets. In the conflict with the CCC and the accommodation of the DSC we see persuasion, negotiation, compromise, and sanctions being employed as important methods of influence. The organisation moved more to a political than a bureaucratic model of decision-making over such decisions.

Decision topic 2: safety cover

The topic of safety cover provides an interesting example of a situation where the RSC disagreed with the decisions of higher bodies (as with picketing) but in this case it did not contest them.

The RSC meeting on 28 January was opened by the Chairman who brought up an important item arising from the last CCC meeting. The CCC had decided that, as a consequence of the Denning judgment, the arrest of any member of the CCC would lead to the immediate withdrawal of all safety cover on fuel and boiler plants. The RSC, suggested the Chairman, needed to discuss and ratify this decision. A large number of the RSC members were unhappy about this. One ISTC member angrily commented that 'safety is being covered at the moment not for the sake of BSC but for ourselves when we go back to work' and that 'in any case, it won't have any influence on Denning'. His sentiment was echoed by other members. It was felt that if safety cover was withdrawn, plant could be seriously damaged, delaying a return to work. A South Yorkshire general strike was proposed as an alternative but it was bitterly recognised that the steel unions would get little support. One RSC member mentioned that some strikers had been talking of withdrawing from the CCC and wondered whether ISTC should be sending delegates at all. However, there was agreement when the same member went on to say that 'we can't ignore the call, because the CCC is higher than us'. He felt that 'all we can do is accept their decision but with reservations'. The RSC as a whole assented to these comments. The Chairman added that 'it was a spontaneous decision and it's probably a wrong measure' but that 'nothing can be done about it now', although the RSC agreed to express their misgivings to the CCC. Unusually, the RSC made no effort to contest the decision even though there were strong feelings about its inappropriateness.

Although the idea of using safety cover withdrawal as retaliation was dropped with the reversal of the Denning judgment on 1 February its use as a tactical weapon persisted. At the meeting of the Rotherham Joint Committee on 3 February the matter was raised and extensively discussed. While having benefits in terms of showing the national unions, the private sector and the media that the strikers were serious, such a decision was perilous given the potential damage to machinery and the consequent threat to jobs. The RSC was asked to discuss the matter at its meeting on Monday, 4 February. At this meeting members were divided and the discussion grew heated. Several individuals shifted their position as the arguments were aired, and the meeting became somewhat more cautious. It was noted that, according to procedure, the RSC could only make a recommendation to the DSC, which as the higher strike body would have to decide. The RSC's final recommendation, after much debate, was vague: that the DSC should 'consider the matter very carefully'. Later that day the DSC decided to remove safety cover as soon as possible, which was in line with the recommendation made by the CCC also. The RSC was asked to implement the decision and although many RSC members at the 5 February meeting were clearly disturbed by the decision it was not contested.

As it turned out, the proposals about withdrawing safety cover were later dropped after an ISTC national directive (18 March), so that the RSC was not put in a position of having to act on its commitment to the CCC and DSC decision.

The issue of safety cover is interesting because, as with flying pickets, the RSC was far from convinced of the wisdom of the choices made by higher committees, yet unlike the former case the decisions over safety were not contested. What contingencies determined whether the RSC accepted an unpopular decision or contested it? While there may have been several influences, two factors seem particularly important. In regard to safety cover, the decision had far-reaching consequences not simply for the strike itself but for the resumption of work afterwards. The RSC were conscious of their having been invested with the responsibility for running the local strike organisation, but safety cover went beyond the bounds of their influence. It was a *union* matter, not purely a strike matter. For this reason, it would appear, the Rotherham Joint Committee was brought into the discussions for the first time, while previously its strike role had been simply to ratify RSC decisions. The referral of the issue to the DSC is also in line with this influence and guidance: on the DSC sat the more senior Rotherham branch officials. A second factor was the seriousness of the matter and the risk attaching to the decision: it was one which could have grave and deleterious consequences. The RSC would have been in an invidious position had it claimed control of such a decision: better by far to make a recommendation, thereby spreading the burden of responsibility.

The sharing of responsibility in serious matters is also apparent in some decisions over dispensations. While the RSC had initially disputed the authority of the CCC and DSC to make decisions over dispensation requests, difficult decisions were shared, with the DSC in particular. For example, on 21 February the RSC heard that a small workshop firm wanted a dispensation because it was faced with possible bankruptcy. Although a number of the RSC members expressed sympathy with the firm's plight, and some, including the Secretary, wished to give it, the Chairman and others argued that it should be refused since 'it would set a precedent, and we must be consistent'. The Chairman noted, however, that the RSC could only recommend dispensations: the DSC had to make the final decision. It was uncharacteristic of the RSC to pass on a dispensation request rather than attempt to make the decision themselves, and was indicative of the desire to share responsibility for difficult or unpleasant decisions. Dispensation requests, like the removal of safety cover, were often shared by the South Yorkshire strike bodies, conforming to the formal authority structures established locally.

CHAPTER NINE

Unity is strength: inter-union relations

The complexity of the strike organisation has been described and analysed already, but a further level of complexity is revealed when we consider the participant unions. There are three sets of factors which must be taken into account if we are to fully understand the shifting relations between the various participants. Firstly, we must consider the *structure* of the strike organisation, and its relation to existing union organisations. We have already shown that the strike organisation functioned (at different times) both as an administrative bureaucracy, with clear lines of authority and communications and an agreed division of labour, and as a political system characterised by co-operation and competition based on the power and interests of different groups actively 'negotiating' the order of the strike organisation. Within this multi-faceted organisation could be identified two further sets of structures: pre-existing union structures — such as branch and shop-steward committees, district and regional committees; and new specific structures created by the non-ISTC unions to prosecute the strike and organise their own members. All these structures are described in detail below.

Secondly, inter-union relations were also regulated by the multiple identifications of the strike participants, and by the ways in which they categorised their social world. Members of non-ISTC unions on the RSC, for instance, belonged to several groups which competed for their loyalty and commitment: the RSC; their own union strike committees; their own union branch or district committees, and their own unions' executives. Each of these overlapping groups provided different frames of reference within which to evaluate options and decisions, and as such could represent different economic and political interests. The management of these multiple group memberships could be difficult for the individuals concerned, but was also a problem for the local strike leaders in their efforts to construct an integrated and effective strike organisation. Thirdly, we also need to consider the personal relations between the members of different unions, since individuals do not relate to each other simply as representatives of wider groups and interests.

Within this rather loose framework of organisational structures, inter-group relations, and personal relations, this chapter has three objectives: to analyse relations between the different unions involved (directly or indirectly) in the strike and the factors which influenced them; to explain why certain issues gave rise to conflict within the strike organisation and others did not; and to draw attention to the tensions within the organisation which arose from the desire of local ISTC leaders both to co-operate with other unions and to dominate the strike organisation. The term 'conflict' will be used here to refer to those instances when differences in goals or interests were backed up by the threat or deployment of sanctions by the competing parties.

The following section briefly describes the unions involved in the strike, and the ways in which they came to occupy their seats on the RSC. The chapter continues with an account of co-operation and conflict in the RSC as revealed on a number of key issues. The relations between the local ISTC and SIMA, the private sector steelworkers and the local AUEW are then examined in turn. SIMA, the private steel sector and the AUEW all occupied the position of potential allies (and by the same token, potential enemies) of the strikers, and constitute the three union groups external to the strike organisation to whom the strikers most frequently related.

The state of the unions

In December 1979, the Rotherham Works of BSC employed about 10,000 people, of whom almost 6,000 belonged to ISTC, approximately 1,000 to NCCC and 1,000 to the GMWU. In addition there were several hundred TGWU members and approximately 100 URTU members, whilst of the non-striking unions, several hundreds belonged to each of ASTMS and APEX, and 1,100 to SIMA. Total BSC employment in Rotherham and Sheffield in December 1979 was a little over 23,000, and a further 20,000 workers were employed in the private steel-making and steel processing sector (the largest concentration of private steel works in the UK).

The National Craftsmens Co-ordinating Committee (NCCC) is organised both nationally and locally. Its national executive consists almost entirely of full-time officials from its 11 constituent unions, of which by far the largest is the AUEW, with just over 50% of its total membership. The NCCC is organised locally with South Yorkshire as one area, and several local delegate conferences were held in Sheffield throughout the strike. Its largest member union, the AUEW, is also one of the largest and most influential unions in the Sheffield and Rotherham area. Most AUEW members are organised in geographical branches, and elect delegates to the powerful 40 member District Committee, the next tier in the AUEW structure, which co-ordinates the work of its constituent branches. The Secretary of the AUEW District Committee met frequently with the RSC, as we shall see below. The local AUEW was also the largest member of the Yorkshire region of the Confederation of Shipbuilding and Engineering Unions (CSEU), whose weekly meetings were attended by as many as 300 engineering shop stewards.

As noted in Chapter 4, delegates from some of these other unions had been invited onto the RSC *before* the strike began, and *before* any of these unions had declared their official support for a strike. NCCC members attended early meetings of Rotherham Joint Committee, and there were informal discussions between local ISTC leaders and members of the other steel unions on the question of their support for the strike. Certainly NCCC, TGWU, URTU and GMWU members all refused to cross the local ISTC picket lines from 2 January. Most of the members of these unions invited onto the RSC were known personally to senior members of the 'informal elite' which emerged to prepare the strike organisation at the end of December 1979. The GMWU representative was the Chairman of the largest GMWU steel branch in the area, with 600 members, and belonged to the same works department as the Chairman of the RSC. One of the two NCCC representatives was the only lay-member of the Executive of the NCCC, whilst the second representative was well known to the newly-elected Vice-Chairman of the Rotherham Joint Committee. One of the URTU representatives was a local branch chairman, and again a close contact of the RSC Chairman. He in turn brought along his Branch Secretary to the RSC. The non-ISTC unionist who was the least well-known among the ISTC members of the strike committee was the TGWU representative, a fact that may have influenced their subsequent relationship on the RSC. The rationale for the different numbers of non-ISTC representatives is unclear, (it was certainly not a function of their actual memberships in the steel works) but it partly reflects the permeable boundary of the RSC.

The Divisional Strike Committee was a little slower to invite delegates from other unions: the GMWU and NUB started to attend the Committee on 17 January; the NCCC on 23 January; and private sector ISTC members on 29 January. There is no clear rationale for this sequence, nor for the fact that the TGWU and URTU were neither invited to join, nor attended, meetings of the DSC.

Although somewhat haphazard in their initial relations with other unions, the local ISTC leaders did nevertheless succeed in constructing multi-union strike committees at works and divisional levels very rapidly (compared with other parts of the country), and later in the strike invited representatives from other unions on to the unofficial National Strike Committee. All of these unions (apart from URTU) also maintained their own strike committees which met regularly, though not daily. As an NCCC representative at Scunthorpe said, 'we were not prepared to integrate fully with ISTC, and wanted to keep our own committees for communications with our members about social security and so on'. These committees also controlled the distribution of union strike pay.

Inter-union relations on the strike committees: co-operation, conflict and control

ISTC is the largest, and the only *industrial* union in the steel industry and its (traditional) attitude to the other steel unions was expressed by an official outside South Yorkshire, who said after the strike, 'I don't know what the other unions did during the strike. . . . As far as we (ISTC) are concerned it doesn't matter — our boys are the ones who stop the plant.'

Despite this national background, inter-union relations on the RSC were remarkably cordial. Interviewed after the strike, Tony L. of the NCCC referred to the 'considerable *esprit de corps*' on the RSC, and indeed there were no more than three or four occasions when discussion became acrimonious. For the most part, discussions were business-like, information was freely exchanged (unless it involved internal union affairs), and there was a considerable degree of trust and openness between the members of different unions. The co-operative relations between the unions were most clearly evident at the time of the Denning judgment in the fourth week of the strike. ISTC pickets complied with the law and removed themselves from the plants named in the injunction, but were, by agreement, replaced immediately by pickets from NCCC. In the eighth week of the strike, the RSC decided (against NCCC opposition) to increase the rate per mile paid for petrol expenses to pickets using their cars in the course of the strike, but financial hardship for NCCC was avoided by a decision of the ISTC majority on the committee to subsidise their fellow unionists (an act, incidentally, in breach of ISTC rules).

Inter-union co-operation was also the product of an emergent division of labour, especially on the RSC. URTU representatives were extremely knowledgeable about the local haulage industry (by contrast with ISTC) and their contributions concerning it were highly valued. By confining their contributions to this, and rarely participating in major tactical debates, the URTU members adopted a specialist role on the RSC which was conducive to co-operation. Co-operation was also a product of 'restraint' on the part of non-ISTC unions and their acceptance of ISTC control of the strike and the strike committees. The Chairman of the Scunthorpe Strike Committee described how ISTC branch officers were appointed to the leading positions on the committee, and added that the other 'unions accepted this'.

Conflict on the RSC was much more evident between ISTC and Tom G. (TGWU). Although haulage drivers, in general, were repeatedly criticised for crossing picket lines, and their unions (TGWU and URTU) were castigated for failing to issue *instructions* to their members on respecting picket lines, much of this criticism was, in practice, directed at Tom G. This was partly because ISTC members of the RSC perceived the TGWU as a powerful union, but also because Tom G. was not as well-known to them before the strike, and some of his contributions led to clashes on the RSC over major tactical and strategic issues.

Finance

A further index of co-operation between the unions can be gauged by looking at the issue of finance, where the *potential* for conflict was considerable. Numerous donations were sent by individuals and groups, either to the ISTC strike headquarters in Rotherham, or to the RSC, or the DSC and on both of these committees ISTC was in a comfortable majority. Under its rules ISTC is not permitted to 'transfer' any of this money to other unions, and indeed there were complaints on the DSC (from NCCC members) about ISTC's control over finance. All the unions paid travel expenses incurred by local pickets, and small sums (a few pounds per day) to flying pickets, and all complained about inadequate funding from their own head offices. Finance was undoubtedly a very scarce resource, but conflicts over finance were minimal, for a number of reasons.

After just one week of the strike the DSC produced guidelines regulating distribution of money: funds from organisations, e.g. trade unions, trades councils, companies, had to be channelled through the DSC, but money taken elsewhere, e.g. in pubs or at special functions, could be retained by the unions conducting the collection. This system appears to have been adhered to. Coupled with this formal set of rules was a degree of flexibility on the part of the ISTC majority on the DSC, who occasionally transferred funds (levied by the DSC from local strike committees) to other unions when substantial requests were made. Thirdly, each union in Rotherham and Scunthorpe ran its own hardship funds and treasuries, and some, such as NCCC, were very effective in raising money through weekly levies of £5 on their non-steel members still in work.

Strike tactics

The second potentially divisive major issue, discussed frequently by the RSC, was strike tactics, and in particular, the role of picketing. For the ISTC members of the RSC picketing was the basic function of the strike organisation and the most effective method of ensuring the strikers' victory (see Chapter 8). In the early days of the strike, pickets were despatched to a large number of local steel and engineering plants, but because of ISTC's isolation from the labour movement formal or informal networks of communications were rarely used to establish prior contact with unions inside these plants. Indeed in the earliest days of the strike the first notice many local stewards received about the RSC's requests for support was the physical presence of pickets at their own gates and angry complaints from their members who had to cross ISTC picket lines in order to get to work.

It was differences in inter-group perceptions and frames of reference which predisposed ISTC and NCCC members to place their differing emphases on picketing and negotiations respectively, but notwithstanding the greater strike experience of NCCC, picketing was not to be dislodged so easily from its position of pre-eminence and on 1 February the RSC was faced with a direct conflict over the issue.

A local AUEW convenor was anxious for steel to be moved into his plant from the firm's stockist in order to avoid layoffs and had received the support of the local AUEW. Trade union unity suggested that the AUEW be granted this request; maintenance of local (mainly ISTC) picket morale and the organisation's stated goal of 'no steel movement' suggested that the movement of steel across the picket lines should be prevented. The need to mobilise the power of the local AUEW (and CSEU) persuaded a minority of ISTC members that they should concede the AUEW request, a view not shared by the ISTC majority who implicitly placed their own pickets' morale and their own organisation's goal above trade union unity. Interestingly, Tom G. (TGWU) (who rarely figured as a major protagonist in such 'disputes') argued against the AUEW (and with the ISTC) on the grounds that a firm instruction from Transport House (headquarters of the TGWU) to its own drivers *not* to cross picket lines would never emerge if the RSC was seen to be endorsing steel movement under AUEW pressure. The issue was resolved in favour of picket morale.

Despite *some* conflict over finance and strike tactics, (and the centrality of picketing within the RSC-ISTC frame of reference), these were issues that were most frequently discussed in a friendly and co-operative way. In bargaining terms, they were far more commonly the subject of integrative as distinct from distributive bargaining (Walton & McKersie, 1965), and so too were many other detailed aspects of strike organisation, such as the procurement of physical resources, e.g. coke. Why were these topics the subject of relatively conflict-free decision-making, whereas others, to be discussed shortly, were the focus of major conflicts? Part of the answer lies in the nature of the topics themselves, and those discussed so far — finance, tactics, strike resources — have a number of features in common. Firstly, they were *on-going* rather than *discrete,* or *one-off* decisions. Finance was continually being raised, and physical resources were continually in need of replacement. Secondly, they were *restricted* in their range of implications to the strike period. Once the strike was over unions would revert to their normal methods of raising and distributing finance. Thirdly, *shared* interests outweighed conflicting interests: the strengthening of picket lines promoted the strike as one in which *all* unions were engaged. In other words, it was tactical and administrative decisions which were more likely to engender co-operation between unions.

By contrast, topics which became *issues* and sources of conflict were more likely to involve *one-off* decisions with *far-reaching implications* for the different and *conflicting interests of* the different unions involved, i.e. they were more likely to involve strategic decisions. The clearest examples in these categories were the Central Co-ordinating Committee (third and fourth weeks of the strike) and the proposed removal of safety cover (fifth week of the strike). Both issues were discussed within a relatively short time-span — one or two weeks — whilst topics generating less conflict were likely to span much longer periods.

Central Co-ordinating Committee

The creation of the CCC was a means for co-ordinating the activities of the main steel unions in the strike, with two representatives from each of the ISTC, NCCC, TGWU and GMWU (although other members of these unions attended as 'observers'). As a co-ordinating body, the CCC was of course, unusual in that it was the *only* local strike body in which ISTC was in a minority, a position that was highly discrepant with its dominant relationship with other unions in bargaining and on other strike bodies. The fact that such a body was created at all is surprising, and suggests that ISTC and the other unions held quite different interpretations (administrative and political respectively) of 'co-ordination'. From the outset then both the composition and the goals of the CCC were conducive to inter-union conflict, and ISTC's attitude to the other unions was clearly revealed just before, and shortly after, the CCC's creation.

On 14 January, when the CCC was established, the ISTC leaders of the RSC agreed to work for the appointment of one of their nominees as chairman 'in order to retain ISTC direction over the dispute in the South Yorkshire area'. (DSC minutes, 14 January 1980). On 23 January, the RSC chairman observed that the CCC (meaning its ISTC members) was 'pig sick' of the TGWU and GMWU, and maligned the poor calibre of their delegates. ISTC and NCCC, he continued, had sent very senior representatives, but the other two unions had not, thereby indicating their low estimation of the CCC's significance. And he implied that the CCC could be disbanded because of the TGWU and GMWU. This attack provoked an angry response from Ted R. (GMWU) — indeed it was one of the sharpest inter-union exchanges on the RSC.

It was quickly controlled by conciliatory gestures by several ISTC members, clearly anxious to preserve good inter-union relations, who excluded Ted R. from their criticism of the GMWU. In fact, as the subsequent discussion revealed, it was ISTC that was most hostile to the CCC, and ISTC members strongly criticised a mass picket which it had 'badly organised' on the previous day. Over the next few days they suggested that picketing should be under the full control of the RSC, not the CCC, clearly indicating ISTC dissatisfaction with a body which it was unable to control. Not surprisingly ISTC members of the RSC showed no great desire to reform the CCC, and a proposal by the NCCC to arrange a formal, joint meeting to thrash out relations between it and the RSC was spurned by them on 29 January (although a few informal meetings did take place — without success).

The struggle for control of the CCC was also reflected symbolically in conflict over its location. Its foundation meeting on 14 January was held in the local headquarters of the AUEW, in Sheffield, some miles from the strike headquarters. This venue (and by implication AUEW's symbolic control) was successfully challenged one week later when the CCC was moved to the ISTC strike headquarters in Rotherham, but by 6 February it was back again in Sheffield.

Over the period late January/early February the line pushed by

ISTC, and increasingly (if reluctantly) accepted by the other unions on the RSC was to ignore the CCC and act as if it did not exist. It is surprising that the vehemence with which the CCC was attacked did not result in more inter-union conflict within the RSC. The explanation for this relative lack of conflict is twofold: firstly, all union members on the RSC distanced themselves from their counterparts on the CCC (except for ISTC, neither of whose CCC members sat on the RSC). In the dispute between the RSC and the CCC they identified with the RSC (and sometimes with their own union) rather than with the CCC. The NCCC members favoured 'reform' of the CCC (since they were also members of the AUEW, whose local leaders were strongly committed to the CCC), but none the less shared the ISTC's criticism of its incompetence in the organisation of picketing; Ted R. (GMWU) noted that his counterparts on the CCC were not from Rotherham and were therefore unfamiliar with the local area; whilst Tom G. (TGWU) made no effort at all to defend his CCC counterparts from criticism. Secondly, insofar as the RSC members identified with the RSC and were therefore committed to its decisions the conflict between the committees reinforced this identification.

What was at issue in the dispute over the role (and location) of the CCC was ISTC control over the strike and over other unions. If the CCC had been vested with extensive powers of co-ordination by the RSC and DSC, it would have been extremely difficult for the ISTC majority on the RSC to continue undermining the CCC. In view of the differences between ISTC and NCCC over strike tactics, the power and authority of the multi-union CCC was a divisive issue, with far-reaching implications for the tactics and strategy of the strike.

Safety cover

The second issue which generated inter-union conflict was the proposed removal of all safety cover from BSC plants. The strike by BSC employees was not total since the unions had agreed beforehand that some security and safety staffs would be allowed to continue working. For example, safety cover was needed to maintain furnace walls which, if unheated for more than 72 hours, are liable to collapse, and relining is both expensive and time-consuming. It was the costs to BSC of withdrawing safety cover which made it an increasingly attractive option for the RSC as the strike approached its sixth week. It did though have quite different implications for craft and production workers: withdrawal of safety cover would mean overtime and bonus earnings for NCCC's maintenance workers on the return to work, but a fallback to basic or guaranteed week rates for many ISTC production workers, whilst they awaited the repair of the furnaces and other damaged machinery. Therefore whilst NCCC might have been expected to favour withdrawal of safety cover it seemed certain that production workers (ISTC and TGWU) would be sharply divided.

When the decision was taken on 4 February by the CCC and DSC to remove safety cover (see Chapter 8), it was defended by the ISTC Chairman of the RSC, ostensibly on the grounds that it had been 'passed down' from higher bodies, namely the CCC and the DSC. This appeal to the authority of a third party was important in minimising inter-union conflict on the RSC, since the TGWU and GMWU were both strongly opposed to the decision. The clearest indication of the strength of their opposition was the political attempts of both unions to thwart what they regarded as an extreme, and possibly dangerous measure. In the debate on safety cover the ISTC Chairman of the RSC argued that the chain of command ran from the CCC through the DSC to the RSC and the other union strike committees. Presumably, within this conception, other unions' strike committees were subordinate to this chain of command, a view that was actively contested by both the GMWU and the TGWU representatives. GMWU wrote to the RSC (a *very* rare event in the strike) on 6 February stating that their own strike committee had refused to endorse the RSC's acceptance of the safety cover decision. The TGWU argued that withdrawal of safety cover was such a major development that only a national lay delegate conference had the authority to take such a decision.

This opposition was effective in persuading the hard-liners among the ISTC to back down, and avoid conflict over an issue which was highly divisive. This was the only occasion on which the TGWU and GMWU representatives actively mobilised their own strike committees against those of the ISTC. But their success was not simply the result of the exercise of power, because there were signs that ISTC commitment to the withdrawal of safety cover was less than wholehearted. The initial decision caused considerable concern but was defended by ISTC partly because it had emanated from a 'higher body', yet this body — the CCC — had been the subject of repeated criticism and denunciation by the ISTC over the previous two weeks!

*   *   *   *   *

Within the RSC there emerged a considerable degree of co-operation between the unions, and a commitment by them to the decisions of the RSC. Only the decision to remove safety cover temporarily broke this unity, although other one-off decisions with extensive ramifications, e.g. support for the Central Co-ordinating Committee, threatened to do so. The relations within the RSC were very different however from its relations with external bodies, and it is to these that we now turn, beginning with SIMA, and looking in turn at the ISTC private sector steel-workers, and the local AUEW and CSEU.

SIMA: the functional enemy

Relations between ISTC and SIMA had been hostile for many years, partly because they had been in competition for the recruitment of steel managers. In addition, ISTC had successfully opposed several applications from SIMA to affiliate to the TUC, on the grounds that it was not fully independent of management. SIMA, in common with the other white-collar unions, APEX and ASTMS, did not officially participate in the strike, and its members (in common with those of APEX, but by contrast with many in ASTMS) crossed picket lines throughout the strike. It was also claimed on the RSC that SIMA members carried out ISTC duties once at work; that they were being paid extra for doing so; and that they stood to gain (indirectly) from the settlement finally reached since their own pay rises were usually tied to those gained by ISTC.

Throughout the strike SIMA served as a negative reference group for the RSC, and hostility to SIMA served to reinforce the values and cohesion of the RSC. Occasionally SIMA functioned as a scapegoat in the wake of problems with the strike. When several more militant members of SIMA sent a cheque for £130 to the RSC, the DSC Treasurer, with the full support of the RSC, returned it, saying they would not accept money from a body they refused to recognise. In discussions on the return to work the RSC Chairman declared it was morally wrong for SIMA to cover for ISTC during the strike, but it would be perfectly acceptable for ISTC to take over SIMA jobs, since 'SIMA was not a union'.

The clearest indication of ISTC hostility to SIMA emerged at the RSC on 23 January in a discussion on 'the Brinsworth pavilion'. The pavilion was a sports and social club, jointly run by the unions, but mainly by SIMA. Many RSC members initially felt the club should be left open for the benefit of strikers, but throughout the strike the club continued serving meals to SIMA members. The fact that 'their' club was being used in this way, whilst ISTC members were 'out in the cold, on picket lines' infuriated ISTC members on the RSC, who discussed what they should do (if anything) for one hour until Joe S. (NCCC) suggested there was really far more pressing business. Judged in relation to the strike's formal objectives, this was undoubtedly true, but for the ISTC members, most of whom were in a major strike for the first time, there was an important symbolic issue of group identity. The pursuit of aggressive secondary picketing served *inter alia* to promote the RSC as one of the most militant areas of the steel strike, and the repeated denunciations of SIMA were part of a process of identity maintenance. For the NCCC members, by contrast, their greater strike experience, and less frequent contact with SIMA, rendered such processes superfluous and diversionary.

In the wake of the closure by mass picketing of Hadfields on 14 February, the RSC despatched a delegation to the local BSC management demanding that SIMA should no longer be recognised by them, and that all managers should join ISTC. This extension of strike hostilities against SIMA in the aftermath of a local victory, contrasted sharply with the debate over SIMA held less than a week later. By 21 February, the mass picket at Sheerness had failed, and Hadfields was returning to work, and in this context the calls for action against SIMA signified a displacement of strike forces arising from failure, not an extension resulting from success. Unable to break private sector resistance to striking, the RSC (and especially its ISTC members) again turned their anger against SIMA, overriding the objections of NCCC that this was a diversion from the main struggle, and organised on 22 February a demonstration-cum-picket of SIMA (and non-union white-collar) workers at the local BSC offices.

Although SIMA undoubtedly did some damage to the strike by continuing to work, it is hard to believe this was significant, especially when compared with the actual production and distribution of steel by the private sector. The significance of SIMA was symbolic rather than material: they served as a reference group permitting the local ISTC to shape its own identity as a militant strike leadership, and as a scapegoat for the anger and hostility of ISTC in the wake of the failure of mass picketing. As such they were a functional aid to the strikers' sense of purpose and determination.

The private sector steel workers: in, but not of, the union

As noted already, the bargaining structure in the steel industry divided the public and private sector plants, and the latter were themselves divided into three separate bargaining units. Local union structures were also non-overlapping, with public and private sector ISTC branches sending delegates to separate joint committees.

In the month before the strike, when non-ISTC representatives were assiduously recruited onto the RSC, no invitation was issued to private sector steel workers (although the matter was discussed at the RJC). The question of their representation was raised by NCCC members at the RSC on 23 January, but provoked no comment, for or against. The DSC invited private sector delegates on 28 January (but the one regular attender dropped out after 22 February). RSC members were not completely unaware of the problems of mobilising the private sector, and their meeting on 14 January showed an appreciation of the different responses to a strike call that were likely to emerge, with Hadfields singled out as a potential 'problem' (i.e. a plant reluctant to strike). Equally, the ISTC Executive was aware of differences of interest between the sectors. But in practice, ISTC members of the RSC operated on the whole with very fixed categorisations of private sector workers. Central to their frame of reference was the assumption that private sector workers would identify their interests with those of steelworkers as a whole, or ISTC members as a whole, and fully support the BSC workers' strike, and this assumption was continually reiterated in the early weeks of the strike.

On 22 January, a discussion on picketing confidently anticipated the demise of local pickets, 'once the private sector is out'; in a discussion on 28 January (the private sector had been called out from 27 January) it was asserted 'now that the private sector is out, they will take some getting back'; and on 6 February (in the fifth week of the strike) the RSC Chairman confidently dismissed press and television reports of an imminent return to work by Hadfields, the biggest local private plant. This confidence was consistent with the RSC's general reluctance to countenance unpleasant information. Five days later, Hadfields' workers voted at mass meetings to return to work in order to protect their jobs. A similar degree of faith was evident in relation to the large local engineering and steel processing firm, Firth Brown. At the DSC on 19 February, a return to work by Firth Brown was said by RSC members to be 'unlikely', although NCCC members had warned of the possibility earlier in the day at the RSC. Both the Chairman and Secretary of the RSC were rather apologetic in this discussion, claiming BSC workers had no links with the private sector, and that no ground work had been done with the private sector (both of which were true). One week later Firth Brown returned to work (fearful of threats to their jobs) and by 3 March (after eight weeks of the strike) almost the whole of the private sector had done likewise.

The RSC response to developments in the private sector took several forms, of which mass picketing (see Chapter 6) was the first. Following its short-lived success at Hadfields, it was agreed (on 15 February) that

EC members would tour local private firms and persuade them to stay out on strike, or return on strike, and that if they refused to comply, mass pickets would be used as an alternative form of persuasion. After the failure of mass picketing, the ISTC members of the RSC continued their posture of 'punitive militancy': if the private sector workers would not support their fellow ISTC members, then they should be expelled from the union, as indeed were the 600 workers at Sheerness Steel works, in the South of England. A similar posture was adopted by the DSC who despatched a telegram to the ISTC Executive on 3 March calling for the expulsion of union lay officers who returned to work.

But what explanations did the RSC offer for the failure of some ISTC members to support an ISTC strike? Sheerness steelworkers were described, at an exhaustive post-mortem on the day after the unsuccessful mass picket, as 'insular', and 'close to management'. They were also dependent on Sheerness steel — it was the only large employer in the area — earned high wages, and had little commitment to ISTC which only two years previously had failed to offer *them* support in a local dispute. This complex explanation contrasted with the simplistic accounts offered for the behaviour of the much-despised Hadfields. The plant convenor was described by the RSC Chairman as 'parochial' (meaning he was concerned only with his own members at Hadfields), and at the RSC on 13 February a form of conspiracy theory was invoked, in the suggestion that the return to work took place with the 'connivance' of Bill Sirs and Derek Norton, Hadfields' Managing Director. (Sirs, in fact, recommended that the DSC should grant a dispensation to work to Hadfields, but later admitted this was a tactical mistake.) In short, the local ISTC *assumed* an identity of interests between the private and public sector workers, and when the latter failed to meet these expectations, RSC's ISTC leadership responded mainly with 'punitive militancy' — mass picketing and exclusion from the union. The private sector workers passed in a very short space of time from being imminent allies to actual enemies. As the largest (though by no means the only) local private steel firm, Hadfields came to represent symbolically the private steel sector as a whole and bore the brunt of the 'February offensive' of mass pickets.

AUEW and CSEU: solidarity and self-interest

Relations between craft and production workers within the steel industry have always contained considerable elements of conflict. National and local officials of ISTC have often perceived craft workers as elitist, the craft side of the industry as 'overmanned', and the craft unions as politically ambitious within the industry (perceptions which were partly mirrored in craftworkers' views of ISTC).

Relations with the non-striking, local AUEW were hampered by lack of contact between the unions before the strike, and by the political difficulties facing AUEW officials and stewards in the course of it. On the one hand many of their local leaders were anxious to support the steelworkers, but they also had to consider the interests of their own 28,000 Sheffield and Rotherham members and the effects of an engineering strike at a time of economic recession. At the same time they perceived the local ISTC leaders as inexperienced in strike action, and if engineering workers were to be involved in the strike, engineering (i.e. AUEW and CSEU) leaders wanted some influence: hence the struggles over the role and location of the multi-union CCC. The local ISTC was also seen as reluctant to co-operate with others: a local AUEW full-time offical claimed that NCCC members had only been invited onto the RSC as a result of engineering union pressure.

The first recorded formal meeting between CSEU stewards and ISTC strike leaders was on 9 January (the second week of the strike), when the stewards agreed to monitor steel movement and consumption, provided ISTC would remove pickets from their (CSEU) plants. Though it was anxious to co-operate with the local AUEW and CSEU leaders, ISTC also had its own priorities, and the 18 January DSC meeting backed the ISTC Executive call for a mass picket of a local firm '. . . despite the possibility of antagonising Confederation Convenors.' By the following week, the local CSEU had agreed that token pickets could be placed on their plants, and that any steel crossing these lines would not be unloaded. For the RSC even this gesture of support was seen as inadequate, and at its 28 January meeting, more militant members accused the CSEU, and particularly its leader (who was also Secretary of the powerful AUEW District Committee) of '. . . making sure that *their* people were not affected by the strike'.

By 15 February (the sixth week of the strike) the CSEU had agreed to supply the steel strike committees with its own list of steel-using plants. Pickets placed on these plants would then result in the blacking of any steel moving across the lines. This decision by the CSEU reflected both its lack of trust in the ability of the steel strike committees effectively to organise local picketing, and its desire to retain control over picketing targets. Its lack of faith in the committees seemed to be borne out when Tony L. (NCCC) reported to the 21 February meeting of the RSC that a neighbouring strike committee had so far placed pickets on only three of the 13 targets supplied by the CSEU/AUEW.

By this stage of the strike, a number of private steel and engineering plants were returning to work, and the CSEU policy of blacking any steel that crossed picket lines was coming under increasing strain. Some local engineering stewards were anxious about their jobs, whilst others were concerned about lay-offs and earnings. The local CSEU/AUEW leadership faced a potential split in its own ranks, based on such calculations of self-interest, and fuelled by suspicions that ISTC might not reciprocate support in the event of a local engineering dispute. At the 3 March RSC, the CSEU/AUEW leaders came to the meeting and sharply criticised ISTC picket organisation, complaining that many plants were still without pickets, and it was therefore (presumably) ISTC's responsibility if AUEW support was not forthcoming. ISTC reaction to these charges was highly defensive (see Chapter 8).

The following week witnessed the last major interaction between the two groups. The Executive of the TGWU finally issued an *instruction* (and not just a recommendation) to its members not to cross ISTC picket lines, and on 10 March the local CSEU duly followed suit, as a result of which there was a rapid shutdown of local engineering plants as their workers refused to cross picket lines. It was understood amongst local CSEU/AUEW leaders that engineering workers throughout the country would be adopting a similar position, but by Friday 14 March a national stoppage had clearly failed to materialise. At their weekly meeting the CSEU stewards voted overwhelmingly to call off their own action (and return to the status quo of blacking steel) but justified themselves by saying they could not support ISTC because of its 'infantile' behaviour (a demonstration-cum-picket at Hadfields two days earlier). This action, and in particular the justification given, was interpreted as might be expected within the low-trust relationship which had developed between the strikers and their fellow workers in engineering. The ISTC Strike Co-ordinator described the CSEU solidarity strike as a 'political manoeuvre' called in anticipation of the imminent end of the steel strike, to which the local CSEU leaders could then claim to have made a significant contribution. These conflicts did not however jeopardise relations within the RSC, between NCCC and ISTC. The former continually advocated the importance of maintaining CSEU support, but did not participate in or convey CSEU/AUEW criticism of the ISTC, except occasionally, and then in very mild form.

From the outset of the strike the RSC placed considerable demands on local members of AUEW and CSEU, and any reluctance to co-operate fully was interpreted as lack of *commitment* to the strike resulting from a concern with their own self-interest. This perception of their subsequent actions was both cause and effect of the low-trust relationship which developed between the unions. Lack of trust was compounded by political factors: the leader of the CSEU and Secretary of the AUEW District Committee was an extremely influential, veteran member of the local labour movement, and had no intention of participating in a strike in which he and his colleagues did not exert considerable influence. This 'struggle' for control of the strike was conducted indirectly, through various issues (picketing targets, CCC) and further reinforced the low-trust nature of the relationship between the unions.

CHAPTER TEN

The return to work

RSC preparations for the return to work

'If people can return with their heads held high then that makes a lot of difference in terms of their dealing with problems later on and their relations with management.'

As usual, it was an NCCC representative, in this case Joe S., who, speaking at the 22 February meeting, pinpointed the strategy which the RSC should adopt in its return to work preparations. All RSC members recognised that the manner in which the return to work was conducted, and the morale of the strikers, would be crucial in determining post-strike events and would have strong implications for union power.

The strike organisation had been established as a temporary body: at some stage arrangements would have to be made for the transfer of decisions and activities back to the pre-existing trade union organisations, which would manage the resumption of union-management relations. Demobilisation is an important strike process, to which Hiller (1928) draws attention. Active and elaborate preparations for the return to work occurred well before the end of the strike as strikers anticipated its final stages. It is significant to note that locally the strike was not typified by a gradual slowing down of the pace of activity: the RSC had the same number of buses for flying pickets out on the very last morning as in earlier stages of the strike.

The return to work was discussed at three RSC meetings during February (on the 8th, 22nd and 26th). Previously, the return to work had been discussed only in relation to particular courses of strike action (for example, withdrawal of safety cover) but these meetings were directly focused on it: how it should be conducted and how solidarity could be maintained. The February discussions were all initiated, through report-backs, by individuals who were keen to see a consistent policy: two staff officials from Picket Control, whose members had a lot of job contact with SIMA, and a manual branch official who had strong views about 'cowboy' lorry drivers and whose branch had already discussed return-to-work proposals by early February. Mike W., the manual branch official, set an elaborate plan with eight proposals before the RSC, which discussed in outline some possible problems of implementation.

The return to work was not discussed further until the last two weeks of the strike. From 17 March it was raised every day and on the 27th a whole RSC meeting was devoted to it. As in the earlier discussions, these prominently featured Mike W. and the two staff members. While the major content of meetings in the last fortnight was still concerned with steel leakage and picketing, considerable attention was also given to national level events (the progress of the negotiations) and the return to work. In this time attendance, by both core and periphery, grew in proportion to the anxiety about the final settlement.

In substantive terms, discussion centred on the eight major points made in the proposals by Mike W. on 8 February. He had argued that following the return to work there should be: action against scabs; the operation of a blacklist of transport firms; no overtime; the creation of new multi-union bodies (including the preservation of the RSC); a strike fund to be levied and controlled at local level; branch action against individuals who had not picketed; and the maintenance of the status quo on working conditions (i.e. no co-operation with any management attempts to implement some of the 'strings' of the proposed settlement).

A further clause asked for the reinstatement of all previous employees, (principally directed towards the BSC management's sacking of two union lay officials prior to the strike, although this became less important later as the officials' circumstances changed). Three of the proposals, those for action against scabs, non-pickets and 'cowboy' lorry drivers, concerned the meting out of retribution towards strikers or potential sympathisers from whom greater help had been anticipated. This could also be seen as functional in maintaining intra-group solidarity by emphasising the differences between strikers and non-strikers.

The emotional issue of blacking was extensively discussed. At the 27 March meeting, ISTC members were in favour of using the blacklist to punish those who had crossed picket lines, although they recognised potential problems of enforcement, given management's view of the blacklist as illegitimate and given the national ISTC office's lack of direction on the matter. Accepting these difficulties Joe S., the NCCC member, tried to change the RSC's perspective from one of retribution to one of challenging managerial prerogative by ensuring that in future only transport firms employing union labour should be allowed on site. This would be a more constructive approach, he argued, since it would prevent similar problems in any future strike and also would avoid a transport shortage on the return to work. However, since the blacking sub-committee had already drawn up the blacklist and circulated it to other strike committees, the attempt to modify its purpose was unsuccessful.

Action resisting management control was integral to the proposals, partly through the clause about SIMA but also in the call for a ban on overtime and the maintenance of the status quo on working conditions. Joe S. was cautious about this, warning of the danger of advocating unenforceable positions, such as the overtime ban when there would be rank and file pressure for extra hours.

The strike bodies, temporary though they were, had generated unprecedented feelings of union power, enthusiasm and solidarity. The desire not to lose this momentum led to proposals for establishing new multi-union bodies and the setting up of a strike fund based on a regular local levy. In these ways both management and the national ISTC organisation could be more effectively challenged and local autonomy further developed. The constitutionalism underlying these discussions should be noted. Although the idea of continuing the RSC after the strike was supported, this was not intended as a challenge but as a *supplement* to the existing trade union organisation. In fact, the Rotherham Joint Committee was seen to be a more appropriate forum even for some of the the return-to-work deliberations, such as an extensive discussion concerning action against SIMA. The Chairman pointed out that continuing the RSC would raise constitutional problems and that no-one wished to maintain an illegitimate body.

Underlying these discussions certain themes may be identified which were to be significant in the behaviour of the strikers after the return to work. First, there was an unarticulated tension between the desire for collective, solidaristic action and the long-standing ISTC tradition of branch autonomy. A number of RSC members spoke of the need for collective action: that indeed was a primary reason for the extensive discussion of Mike W.'s proposals. Attempts had been made by the RSC to push collective action further by taking items such as the blacklist to the unofficial National Strike Committee. There had been dismay and frustration at the failure of the ISTC national office to adopt any of the suggestions about returning to work, or to issue national directives (e.g. over blacking). On the other hand, it was recognised that individual branch discretion was paramount, and that collective action could not be imposed by such bodies as the RSC or RJC, although clearly wide debate might help to foster support from individual branch officials. Yet, while the RSC was generally in favour of co-ordinated action by branches, it did not always act in accordance with those beliefs. At the end of the 27 March meeting a document was circulated, for information only, detailing the recommendations from the Stocksbridge Strike Committee for the return to work. There was no discussion about how the proposals might impinge on Rotherham's decisions or vice versa. This may have been a realistic view given the supremacy of branch autonomy but was somewhat unexpected in view of the expressed desire for collective action.

Secondly, the frames of reference of RSC members, in particular their sense of power and of the moral rectitude of their position, encouraged an idealistic rather than pragmatic approach to considering the implementation of the proposals. The discussions about the blacklist and action against SIMA indicated that RSC members felt they would be able to impose stringent conditions, but there was also evidence of an unwillingness among several members to consider the counter-productive features of full implementation of decisions. For example, Joe S. had already warned of a severe transport shortage if the blacklist was implemented and similarly strong action against SIMA could be self-defeating in areas of high SIMA density because production would then be halted or severely hindered. It was the non-ISTC members who urged a more pragmatic approach to issues, based on a recognition of the need for rank and file support and of what was feasible rather than ideal.

The regularity and detail of RSC discussions on the return to work in the final two weeks of the strike contrasted strongly with the concerns and behaviour of the DSC, which continued to focus on steel movement and picketing even on the day when the national unions had accepted the settlement. The only reference in the DSC minutes to the return to work was when the RSC delegates gave a brief resumé of their extended discussion at their 27 March meeting. This information failed to provoke comment or discussion at the DSC that day, despite the imminence of the return to work. The extent of collective action was clearly circumscribed.

The final days

In the closing few days of the strike, with the Committee of Inquiry under way and the NCCC, TGWU and GMWU unreservedly committed to accepting its findings, the mood of the RSC became fatalistic. The outcome of 'their' strike was now in the hands of the three-man Inquiry and following that would be in those of the national negotiators and EC members. In contrast to their former autonomy and power there was now little the RSC could do to influence the outcome of the strike, save to mechanically keep up the pressure of picketing. They had sent a telegram, which had been endorsed by the DSC, to the General Secretary on 24 March urging that he shelve the Committee of Inquiry until 'the efforts of the dock strike are realised', but this had not had the desired effect. In addition, the RSC was threatened by the lack of solidarity between the unions at national level, which could undermine the highly-valued local solidarity. On Monday, 31 March it seemed likely that the ISTC, which had refused to be bound by the Inquiry, might instruct its members to return to work later than the other unions. The possibility of a discrepancy in the return date was viewed on the RSC with the gravest concern since they believed it would weaken solidarity just at the time when it was most badly needed. To have to return to work piece-meal would constitute a defeat and signal to management the strikers' ineffectualness and lack of cohesion. To avoid this situation, both the ISTC and NCCC made gestures of solidarity towards each other. The RSC Secretary suggested that ISTC should return with the craftsmen, even if that meant defying the EC's instructions (31 March). The response to this suggestion was mixed, with one ISTC member pointing out that acting on their own initiative was exactly what the Hadfields ISTC members had done when they returned to work earlier in the strike! At the RSC meeting the following day, Joe S. announced that the local NCCC had decided to return on the same day as ISTC. In the event, such solidaristic action was not called for, but it is interesting to note that local ties were still more important at this stage than national affiliations.

The last RSC meeting

On the afternoon of Monday, 1 April, the two EC members rang from London to give the news: the offer had been accepted by the CNC with voting of 41 to 27, and the ISTC/NUB joint EC had called off the strike. It was no surprise, since such a decision had come to be seen as inevitable over the previous few days. An emergency meeting of the RJC was called for 8 p.m. that evening to discuss the mechanics of the return to work, to examine several of the proposals a little further and to choose six representatives for the forthcoming meetings with local senior management. The other non-ISTC members of the RSC were present despite the RJC being an ISTC body, and two NCCC and one URTU member were also co-opted to meet management.

The final RSC meeting on 2 April was fairly jovial and slightly disorderly. Although the Chairman was at the meeting, the chair was taken by an NCCC member who had previously only attended DSC meetings. The new chairman symbolised the multi-union solidarity. The meeting was large, with 22 members, including two regular DSC members. It ran through the return to work proposals, concentrating on the blacklist, although overtime, SIMA action and job losses were also discussed. It was recognised by everyone that despite the support for the general proposals, the details would have to be left to branches.

A problem was raised as to what action should be taken if the rumour were confirmed that Port Talbot steelworkers might stay on strike, in order to continue the fight over job losses and closures. What should Rotherham workers do if they were faced by Welsh pickets? One ISTC member was firmly in favour of crossing their picket lines since the national strike had been called over wages and was now settled: if the Port Talbot steelworkers wanted to stay out that was their business. This view was strongly attacked by a number of ISTC members because it was seen to be a further example of the traditional ISTC non-solidarity, and also because the strikers had just spent 13 weeks urging other trade unionists to respect *their* picket lines. The matter was not decided at the RSC though, since the NCCC chairman proposed the issue be put to all the strikers at a mass meeting to be held in the town that afternoon. In fact, many members of the RSC commented that they would not cross a Welsh picket line even if their members did. As it turned out, the allegiance of the RSC members to trade union principles was not put to the test.

Reactions to the settlement

The immediate reactions of RSC members to the result of the Committee of Inquiry were most clearly evident in the Divisional Strike Committee meeting on 31 March, just after the Inquiry findings had been announced, although the strike had not yet been called off by ISTC and NUB. There was an air of inevitability about the strike's termination, especially since the other unions were committed to accepting the Inquiry outcome. The DSC meeting that afternoon provided the first opportunity for strike activists to air their feelings about the settlement and the impending return to work. Consequently RSC member attendance was higher than usual with eight present compared with the late strike average of four or five. All four strike committees had more representatives than usual, resulting in a total of 26 present (18 was the average March figure).

The meeting began with no hint of any new developments in the strike. The Scunthorpe Chairman adhered to the formal agenda and

the meeting began with reports from the four areas about steel movement, picketing and dispensations. One of the EC members then
shifted the meeting towards the issue which people were reluctant to
initiate discussion on although passionately interested in: the ending of
the strike. He asked for guidance for the EC meeting the following day.
Once the issue of the settlement had been raised, there was a flood of
comments as speaker after speaker criticised the way negotiations had
been handled and the terms of reference of the Inquiry. Attacks were
particularly directed at the national leadership of ISTC although criticism also embraced the non-ISTC unions at national level. An
impassioned speech by one hard-line Rotherham official was sympath-
etically received. He argued strongly for rejection of the Inquiry
findings, saying they were 'totally unacceptable' and that he was 'not
interested in realism'. He would 'sooner reject the offer and stay out on
strike than accept such a rotten offer'. Other branch officials echoed his
sentiments. Yet the meeting was dividing into those who wished to
reject the settlement (although with no proposals for how the strike
could be continued) and those who could see no alternative but to
return, however dissatisfied they felt. The full-time officials were
cautious, pointing out that it would be difficult to stay out and that they
personally were bound to follow national directives.

The strong feelings of bitterness, disappointment and defeat co-
existed with a sense of inevitability despite the calls for unilateral action
by South Yorkshire. The local strike leaders wished to distance themselves from the ending of the strike. Hiller (1928) noted that the process
of distancing from national events in the face of imminent defeat is
functional in fostering local solidarity. The attribution of failure to the
national level of the unions, the reluctance to broach the subject of the
ending of the strike and the avoidance of instructions to the EC
members (despite several requests from them to do so) are all indicative
of the desire to maintain distance from the final outcome of the strike.
This can also be seen in the voting which took place at the end of the
meeting. The Rotherham branch official who had so eloquently
attacked the strike outcome moved a resolution that the Inquiry
findings should be rejected. Overriding the Chairman's procedural
objections that the resolution had not been discussed by the area strike
committees, a vote was taken (ISTC only) with 12 to 4 accepting the
resolution. The final vote was symbolic since it could not be a mandate
and there was no discussion of its implications for action. The
Chairman then closed the meeting. He had established the practice that
the DSC meeting should last one hour only, and this occasion was not
going to be an exception.

The reactions of the rank and file showed a similar high level of dissatisfaction, the multi-union mass meeting held in Clifton Park, Rotherham, on the final day of the strike (2 April) also being marked by passionate speech-making which laid the blame for the strike defeat firmly on the national leadership. Although a number of the branch officials who spoke urged the continuance of action, the mood of the meeting was one of resigned bitterness and defeat.

More systematic data were derived from the questionnaires given to a number of branches after the strike. The responses, given three to nine weeks after the strike (with no change in expressed attitude as the strike receded in time) are shown in Table 10.1. The majority of the respondents expressed dissatisfaction with the settlement (59%). When the results are broken down by job, differences are marked. Almost half (49%) of the manual workers were very dissatisfied, compared with 14% of clerical and 13% of supervisory employees.

Table 10.1 How satisifed are you with the settlement that was eventually agreed?

	%
Very satisfied	3.6
Fairly satisfied	33.0
Not sure	4.7
Fairly dissatisfied	23.8
Very dissatisfied	35.0
Total	100 (N = 535)

It is interesting to note that expectations of the settlement had shifted during the strike, since in the post-strike survey 57.9% of the respondents reported that on 2 January they had expected a 15% or less settlement (see Appendix). We might assume that if expectations had remained stable then a greater proportion of the strikers should have been satisfied with the settlement. The discrepancy can be explained by an increase in expectations over time, perhaps brought about by the RSC's '20% — and no strings' slogan.

The strike after the strike

The foregoing account indicates that feelings were running high at the end of the strike, and that while the outcome was seen overall as a defeat, the attribution of failure to the national leadership meant that the RSC and other activists continued to see themselves as powerful and competent. The determination to avoid defeat at local level focused on the blacklist, underlying which lay the issue of managerial control at the workplace. If the unions were able to get management to accept the blacklist, this would be an important victory, significantly extending the scope of workplace bargaining and rolling back unilateral management control.

Normal working was to be resumed on Thursday, 3 April, commencing with the 6 a.m. shift. But the resumption of work was far from smooth, with Rotherham again making the headlines that day with a second, unofficial strike. Every person who had been on the 13-week strike was out again.

The 'strike after the strike' was precipitated by a blacklisted lorry which drove on to the Aldwarke site around 10.30 a.m. The weigh-bridgeman refused to sign it in, and local management instructed the driver to proceed to the unloading bay without a weigh-in. Discussion between the general manager and the senior ISTC branch official (who was also the EC member) at Aldwarke turned to argument over the general principles of blacking, and this case in particular. The manager refused to recognise the blacklist as a legitimate topic for negotiation. The branch official, accompanied by several ex-RSC branch officials from nearby departments, went to instruct his members not to unload the lorry. Management threatened action against the loaders and the senior branch official agreed to put the case into procedure. At this point, three more blacked lorries arrived and because he refused to weigh them in, the weighbridgeman was suspended. By this time, the telephone grapevine had already primed all the ex-RSC members on both sites, so they were ready to call out their own branch members when the stoppage was signalled. Several branch officials reported an immediate walk out of their members after the situation had been briefly explained to them. Within an hour, the stoppage at Rotherham from all unions was complete and, later on, the night shifts at Sheffield and Stocksbridge joined the dispute. The next day began with what was now a familiar experience for many people: a picket on the gates of BSC. Large numbers of strikers milled about on each plant entrance, preventing management from going to work.

The speed and force of this reaction testify to the strong feelings about the end of the 'main strike' and to support for the idea of enforcing the blacklist. However, many people were clearly worried about the prospect of another possibly lengthy strike. There would be pressure on the ex-RSC branch officials to reach an agreement with management.

On the day of the dispute, a meeting had been arranged with a senior

BSC industrial relations manager to discuss general issues about the transition back to work, but the stoppage gave the meeting a new focus. Management continued on principle to refuse to discuss blacking and although the meeting lasted several hours it broke up without making any progress. A second meeting, convened for the next day, again lasted several hours but with little apparent movement on either side. The trade union side found itself powerless to enforce its own views. It had been hoped that the dramatic and complete show of strength in the stoppage would shock management into submission, but management had unexpectedly held its position. The trade union officials felt constrained to adopt a procedural position which saved face; it was agreed that a Working Party be set up to report a fortnight later. The terms of reference were to examine hauliers' contracts, with a view to encouraging union-only labour on site in the future, rather than to discuss blacking, which was still totally unacceptable to management. During the fortnight, the status quo would apply, which meant that managerial discretion over lorries would be accepted, since this had been the procedure prior to the national strike. The Working Party consisted of half a dozen managers and a similar number of trade unionists, drawn principally from the blacking sub-committee. Its recommendation was that in future hauliers should employ union drivers only. The RJC, at its next meeting, accepted the Working Party report. The battle for control over blacking had effectively been lost. The full blacking list had been proving problematic in any case since it threatened a severe materials shortage if implemented, so the RJC had been discussing a reduction of this list to a much smaller, 'very black' list.

Although the unions could not induce management to accept the blacklist, some direct, localised blacking was carried out informally, with the tacit collusion of some departmental managers. For several weeks, some lorries of 'very black' firms were kept waiting by ISTC loaders: in one area five or six hours' delay was common, and one haulier complained that his lorry had been held up for 17½ hours. Other lorries were badly loaded, so that the job had to be done again, causing 'unavoidable' delay. As a consequence, certain firms withdrew from their contracts with BSC and the ISTC officials congratulated themselves that at least part of their objective had been achieved, by restricting action only to some of the worst offenders.

The issue of blacked lorries remained sensitive for some time, however, with incidents resulting in stoppages through April and May. On 25 April, a stoppage occurred in one department after a blacked lorry drove on site. The incident provides an interesting example of the post-strike tensions between collective action and individual branch autonomy. The ISTC branch official who called the stoppage was Mike W., who had fervently supported the need for and desirability of collective post-strike action in RSC discussions. However, the stoppage was over a lorry which was not on the tacit 'very black' list of the RJC; Mike W. was holding to the original policy, thereby disturbing the collectively agreed stance encouraged by the RJC. ISTC branch officials indicated to Mike W. that they did not basically approve of the position he was taking, and the matter went into procedure.

The aftermath

'Treated with contempt — never again.' (South Yorkshire strike poster.)
'We shocked even ourselves. Nobody would ever have thought we would last 14 weeks. The unity shone through, which we never had before but which we intend to keep.' (Comment from steelworker on post-strike questionnaire.)

We turn now to consider what, if any, were the effects of the strike on the participants, their institutions and their interactions in the workplace. The question is of particular significance in situations where, as in the steel strike, workers have been engaged in a major industrial dispute for the first time in their lives. One could anticipate attitudinal and behavioural change since being on strike can mean being involved in novel activities, encountering new people, learning different arguments and counter-arguments. Essentially, it can be an educative process. If the strike is felt to have been won, a new-found sense of power in collective action may be generated which can be used in the future to challenge opponents. Alternatively, there could be little change if the experience was *so* radically different and novel that it was not perceived to be relevant to normal working life. If the strike ended in defeat, then the participants may view the whole experience as painful, wasteful and best forgotten. The question to address then, is what kinds of changes occurred for the steelworkers, and how permanent were they? Few case studies have attempted to assess the degree of change in the post-strike period, and certainly in the present case it is a difficult task to undertake, since there were profound changes taking place in the steel industry at the same time which may have had more far-reaching implications than the strike itself. We will consider the wider context in a following section but here we try to assess the effect of the strike, in the clear recognition that a strike does not simply end, with no longer-term impact on the individuals, their unions or their relations with management.

Individual change

The feelings of the ex-strikers about their first experience of a major strike remained strong for several months. Reactions were mixed. On the one hand, there was a great pride in the fact that the steelworkers had been out on strike for 13 weeks and there had not been a single black-leg in the ranks; pride in having taken a stand and fought in a way which had surprised large sections of society.

It may also be said that for some steelworkers, particularly the younger ones who had been flying pickets, the experience of the strike had been rich and novel. The excitement of picketing, visiting new parts of the country, meeting new people, staying away from home, was a far cry from the predictability of working in a steel plant or rolling mill. Rather like war veterans, some ex-pickets grew nostalgic about their involvement in the strike. Yet we can see that the nostalgia simply emphasised how much life had returned to its usual rhythm.

On the negative side, it should not be forgotten that the strike had involved hardship and struggle for many, with over 2,000 in Rotherham claiming from the hardship fund, and over £1,000 loss in pay for each steelworker during the strike. A number of strikers felt that the second half of the strike had been a waste of time since it had resulted only in a further 1.1% pay increase.

The negative feelings about the circumstances and outcome of the strike were vividly recorded in the comments written at the end of the post-strike questionnaire, in the open section for 'any further comments'. Firstly, the strength of feeling about the strike was indicated by the large number (43%, N = 231) of the sample who chose to add comments, often detailed and passionate. Of 408 comments (some respondents wrote about more than one aspect of the strike) all were negative save nine. The largest group of comments was critical of parties to the strike (N = 316) and was as follows (see Table 10.2 overleaf):

Table 10.2 Questionnaire comments

Criticism of:	
National union leadership	132
Government	62
BSC management	39
Other unions (including ISTC private sector)	35
Media	18
Police	15
Local leadership	15
Total	316

These opinions, though lacking scientific reliability, do give a useful general indication of the feeling on the shop-floor following the return to work. The largest number of criticisms was directed at the national leadership's timing and organisation of the strike, handling of negotiations and failure to award strike pay. The part played by the government in the strike was also attacked. Surprisingly, perhaps, BSC management received far less criticism. It is interesting that more blame or criticism was attached to the strikers' own side (the national leadership) than to the parties seen to be opponents in the dispute: the government and BSC management. This can be seen as another manifestation of distancing to help maintain unity at local level. Related to this point, criticism of the local leadership was low and self-criticism non-existent. It is common, in situations of failure or defeat, for groups and individuals to attribute blame to sources external to themselves, and that appeared to be happening in the explanations and beliefs about the steel strike outcome. In this way dissonance about an unsatisfactory outcome is reduced since the strikers do not have to feel responsible for the strike failure.

Similar external attributions about the failure of the strike were evident in the discussions which occurred at post-strike meetings. At the meeting in May of the South Yorkshire strike committees, held at a local college near Sheffield, the discussion kept returning to the failures of other groups to give support to the efforts of the local strike committees. Similarly, at the November 1980 one-day ISTC Annual Delegate Conference, there was considerable criticism of the TGWU and the private sector steelworkers in particular for their activities during the strike, although criticism of the leadership, in the presence of the full EC, was muted.

How far did the experience of the strike create longer-term changes, for example in political consciousness and behaviour? In the question-naire, we examined attitudinal militancy by asking whether respondents felt that the strike had changed their attitudes towards industrial relations in the steel industry. The responses were as follows:

Table 10.3 Do you think the experience of being on strike has changed your attitudes to industrial relations in the steel industry?

It has made me:	%
Much more militant	40.1
A little more militant	37.1
Had no effect	20.2
A little less militant	1.1
Much less militant	1.5
Total	100 (N = 534)

Over three-quarters of the sample (77%) felt that the strike had made them much more militant.

However, a self-report of increased militancy may not be trans-formed into militant behaviour. Indeed, several steelworkers reported that they would be much more wary about striking in the future, despite feeling that their attitudes to management had hardened. Branch officials also reported the reaction of some of their members who simply wanted to forget the strike completely and get back to work and, especially, to get some overtime in order to make up for lost wages. They did not refer to the strike events or settlement in their conversations at work.

On the other hand, amongst a large number of strikers the strike had generated a greater awareness and cynicism about the political under-currents of the strike and in particular the government interest in the outcome. Many felt that the defeat over pay would simply be the first in a line of defeats over job loss, contraction and privatisation, (a feeling justified by later events). Prior to the strike few steelworkers had given much thought to the state of the steel industry, and for some subsequently there was evidence of a more analytical mode of thought. For a few the strike proved a political training ground, where members who had previously been politically inactive and irregularly attended union meetings, subsequently got into the mainstream of union activities through local committee elections. One of these was elected onto the EC within 18 months.

In the short term, then, feelings about the strike were strong but mixed; disappointment co-existed with pride. However, the attribution of blame to external sources points to the overall sense of defeat. A number of branch officials described their constituents a couple of months after the strike as 'subdued'. Longer-term reactions were varied, ranging from those who wished to forget the strike as soon as possible to those who developed confidence and commitment to the union as a result of their strike experiences, although these were, perhaps, in a minority. The sense of defeat, and the prospect of further defeat to come, meant that overall, individual change was less than might have occurred following a perceived victory. The increased political awareness in these circumstances reinforced people's feelings of their lack of power.

Union change

The experience of the strike had pointed up two issues for local activists: firstly their own sense of collective power locally, and secondly the deficiencies of the national organisation of ISTC, whose structures and decision-making were seen to constrain local initiatives. The frustration with the national organisation crystallised into personal antagonism directed at the figure of the General Secretary and at what was viewed as the archaic and authoritarian decision-making structures of the EC. These feelings were concentrated on the issues of the calling and ending of the strike, the decision not to award strike pay, and the limitations on local disciplinary action against inactive strikers because of their right of appeal to the EC. The RSC members expressed the feeling that they lacked control or influence within their own union, which contrasted with the contribution they had made during the strike. The objectives though not the tactics of the Reform Group (the pressure group which had striven to democratise the union in earlier years) were rekindled in new interests and concerns of the RJC.

Discussion at RJC meetings in the couple of months following the strike focused on the need to increase local autonomy and curb the powers of the EC and General Secretary. The RJC, in fact, started to meet twice instead of once a month, and, for the first time, had agenda and finance sub-committees. Attention was directed towards establishing autonomy for the local organisation through an independent financial base. A levy of branches, as suggested in the RSC return-to-work discussions was established (although this still required, of course, individual branch approval) and quickly amassed quite a fund, despite being contrary to ISTC rules. However, the local levy was short-lived since the London office of ISTC instituted an audit of union funds, ostensibly because of its concern over the legal bills amassed during the strike; in Rotherham however, the investigation was seen simply as a pretext for a wider examination of local funds, including the new levy. Full-time and senior branch officials were interrogated and this generated considerable hostility amongst the steelworkers including the traditionally more moderate staff branches. Militants and moderates alike expressed the sentiment that, at a time of heavy job loss and widespread short-time working, the national office should be engaged in combative activities against management rather than against its own members.

Local meetings were initiated by the RJC to learn from the strike and to plan strategy for union change. The post-mortem on the strike was called by the ex-Strike Co-ordinator who arranged a one-day meeting at a local college in May. All the South Yorkshire strike committees were invited, and chairs laid out for the anticipated 100 attenders. On the day, only 10 ex-strikers and one NUM branch official turned up, of whom four were from Rotherham. Prominent RSC members were absent, possibly working the lucrative Sunday overtime available in some branches. The discussion focused on the blame to be apportioned in the strike, and consequently less attention was paid to the lessons to be learned.

However, RJC meetings organised in order to plan union change were more successful. The RJC set up 'teach-ins' at a local college to examine and discuss the rule-book. Much attention was directed towards the complex rules governing EC elections. Later, after meeting with other Divisional joint committees to 'carve up' EC seats, a local branch official (the Secretary of the old RSC) achieved nomination for the EC and eventual election, causing jubilation among Rotherham ISTC activists. Later, a second South Yorkshire branch official was elected onto the EC.

Attempts to create national level change through the Conference were also under way from a variety of ISTC branches. At the 1981 ISTC Annual Delegate Conference held in Bournemouth, there were several motions concerned with internal constitutional change. Although the motions were filibustered or defeated, the process of change had begun and at the 1982 conference a motion was carried transforming conference from a consultative to a policy-making body. A new enthusiasm was also evident in the wider sphere of the labour movement, with debates in 1981, for example, on the future of the Labour Party and nuclear disarmament, heralding a change in the pre-occupations of the union.

At local level, several branches toyed with the idea of applying sanctions to non-pickets, partly as retributive justice and also in preparation for more effective industrial action in the future. A number of methods were contemplated and discussed including demotion in the strict job seniority system, refusing to allocate overtime to non-pickets, and even, in two branches, the suggestion that non-pickets should be placed at the bottom of the voluntary redundancy list, i.e. they should be denied the opportunity to volunteer. These suggestions were dropped however, because of difficulties of implementation and their potentially divisive effects. Branches varied in the level of membership involvement and where this was low, as in some staff branches, sanctions would have been very difficult to implement. There was also the question of priorities in the administration of punishment for non-pickets, since they had at least gone out on strike and stayed out. Many Rotherham branch officials felt that any sanctions should be directed primarily towards the private sector steelworkers who had crossed picket lines or disobeyed EC directions.

There was a local determination to maintain the recently-developed inter-union co-operation, although in this, as during the strike, the local ISTC members exhibited a familiar mixture of solidarity and chauvinism. In the return-to-work discussions at the RSC, it had been proposed that the joint consultation body and the Trade Union Delegate Section Council be replaced with the newly-elected Joint Representatives Committee which was to meet about once a month to make recommendations affecting the unions jointly, although branch and union autonomy would still be paramount. The JRC was also to be used to meet management to negotiate the local value-added bonus scheme. This was implemented, though assessments of the value of the JRC varied greatly among branch officials and six months after the strike it was only meeting intermittently. One problem was that old partisan allegiances still persisted because the ISTC, as previously, still formed a large majority. There was also a considerable overlap in membership between the new JRC and the ISTC Rotherham Joint Committee, so that meetings of the latter had the effect of being ISTC caucus meetings, at least in the view of the non-ISTC JRC members. Additionally, the GMWU lost representation on the new body because in the eyes of certain ISTC branch officials it was not a 'significant' or 'substantial' union. One ISTC branch official, while aware of the dissatisfaction with ISTC influence, commented that 'other unions resent the ISTC domination on the JRC but we did better than other unions in the strike so that criticism is rather hollow'.

National level changes also occurred in the ISTC following the strike. The union's dull but glossy journal *Man and Metal* was replaced by *Steelworker's Banner* (later the title was changed to *ISTC Banner*), produced in the popular newspaper style developed for the strike and with an editorial policy more critical of BSC. A further publication was *New Deal for Steel,* a closely argued 180-page book rejecting the notion that BSC was uncompetitive due to poor employment practices, and instead locating the cause for poor performance in government policies on prices, interest rates and energy costs. *New Deal for Steel* was distributed to a number of MPs and other interested parties. While there was considerable press coverage, there was no associated union campaign, despite local efforts in South Yorkshire to hold meetings to discuss the book.

At national level, inter-union links were strengthened through the Triple Alliance forged between the ISTC, NUR and NUM, in recognition of their common interests as public sector industrial unions whose declining fortunes were linked. Talks of a union amalgamation between ISTC and the NUB, in response to declining membership, occurred although action on the matter has not been taken.

There was, then, a strong desire for internal ISTC change, channelled into efforts to democratise the union and to create greater opportunities for local joint committee autonomy, in spite of the external attributions made about the causes of the strike failure by the local RSC members. Efforts for change were not commensurate with outcome in that the national level of the organisation resisted challenges to its authority and control, but undoubtedly some internal change had been set in motion.

Change in union-management relations
Kelly and Nicholson (1980) describe strikes as having substantive, procedural and climate outcomes, which feed back into the complex set of relationships between union and management. In terms of climate, initially, relations with management at departmental level were either non-existent or strained. Some shift and departmental managers who were SIMA members were 'sent to Coventry', and in one case, steelworkers asked for their money back from a retirement collection when they discovered the proposed recipient was in SIMA. In some departments contact with SIMA could not be avoided if production was to commence, but was restricted to purely formal communication. The strength of shopfloor feeling caused a number of section managers to be wary and conciliatory in their treatment of the ex-strikers, which gave the steelworkers an initial, euphoric sense of power.

In the short term, union-management relations were bitter and feelings ran high for several months, but at the same time there were factors conducive to a normalisation of relations, under production pressures and as the strike receded in importance in people's minds.

Additionally, shortly after the strike it was announced that SIMA was to amalgamate with the staff section of the EEPTU. Many of the South Yorkshire craftsmen were chagrined by the news, since they would now be linked in trade union brotherhood with the group to whom such a short time before they had been implacably opposed. The sense of defeat for the unions over the strike made it difficult to sustain antagonistic attitudes towards management, although clearly the level of trust and collaboration had decreased. Feelings over blacking receded over time and some branch officials reported that their members were 'not that bothered' about it a couple of months after the strike.

Procedural changes also exacerbated the strained relations between the parties. The complete withdrawal on the union side from joint consultation meant that management and unions only faced each other across the bargaining table, effectively narrowing their perceptions of each other. This had serious consequences, when local negotiations ran into difficulties, as one manager claimed, because each side was less able to judge the seriousness of the other's position.

Negotiations in the immediate post-strike period centred on the local bonus payments which had been included in the national agreement. The 'strings' were complex but in South Yorkshire the bonus was to be made quarterly on a 'value added' basis calculated on the difference between production and sales costs per tonne of steel. A 4½ % bonus was guaranteed if an 'enabling' agreement was signed locally by 1 July, although further department-based negotiations would be necessary later if the bonus was to be increased. The 'enabling' agreement was negotiated by the multi-union JRC, leaving branches and departments to negotiate how the scheme should be implemented in detail. The JRC members felt constrained to accept the scheme since local productivity improvements had been written into the national agreement and since they did not wish to deprive their members of additional financial reward. A number of ISTC officials argued that the enabling agreement was only a commitment 'to talk' at departmental level, with extra money guaranteed without any cost to the union. However, although resistance to management's proposals over job loss was claimed by union leaders to be high, the signed agreement meant that the struggle was located at departmental level, with the consequence that weaker branches would just have to fare as best they could. Most branch officials claimed that there would be only 'a few' jobs lost in their own department, but figures on job loss in Rotherham in 1980 (detailed below, p. 164) belie this optimism and indicate the traditional difficulty ISTC experienced in fighting job loss, particularly when solidaristic action was replaced by branch autonomy. Union performance in the negotiations over both blacking and the local bonus payments suggests that the defeat over the wage claim was carried over into work-place relations with management.

The wider context: post-strike developments

It is important to be aware of some of the wider, contextual factors which have shaped industrial relations in the steel industry in the post-strike period, although we will avoid an extended discussion because other commentators have addressed this topic (for example Bryer *et al* 1982, Upham 1983, Warren 1981). The impact of the strike itself in the short term could be seen in the new-found sense of power and optimism among the union activists, and their initiatives in challenging centralised union authority and management power, although this was rapidly eroded by the restructuring in the industry which subsequently began to take place.

Towards the latter part of the strike, there had been strong rumours that the Chairman of BSC, Charles Villiers, would be replaced on the expiry of his contract. Shortly afterwards, Sir Keith Joseph, Industry Minister, announced his choice: for a large 'transfer fee', paid to his US employer and himself, Ian McGregor was to become head of BSC. For many steelworkers the announcement foretold mass redundancies and privatisation, although more optimistic commentators felt that the new man might generate an aggressive marketing strategy for BSC which would win back lost customers and gain new ones.

In December 1980, the new Chairman unveiled a scheme to revitalise BSC: the 'McGregor Plan' called for massive restructuring of the industry and an unspecified job loss, although with at least 25,000 redundancies in iron- and steel-making. Union consultation was avoided and instead BSC organised a ballot, conducted on 16 January 1981, seeking approval for the plan. 65% of the work-force voted, with 78% approving the scheme. The ISTC opposed the plan from its inception because of its vagueness and, to strengthen its opposition, conducted its own ballot of members three days later. 15,525 voted against the Plan compared with 11,558 who approved it. The ISTC was the only union to maintain strong opposition to the Plan.

Although the McGregor Plan initially talked of 25,000 redundancies, later press leaks mentioned a further 19,000, and still there was no assurance that this would be the end of the sacrifices needed to keep BSC viable. There was speculation that the undisclosed parts of the McGregor Plan envisaged a final total of 90,000 BSC employees, with only 75,000 of those in iron- and steel-making. By 1982 even this looked optimistic.

National plans had their impact on Rotherham and redundancies increased. In 1974 amongst manual workers there had been 29 voluntary and compulsory redundancies; in 1979 it was 53. However, in 1980 there were 637 redundancies. Amongst staff, redundancy was also high: nine in 1974, 17 in 1979 and 100 in 1980. In total, then, almost 9% of the Rotherham workforce left in 1980. The process accelerated in 1981, with approximately 1,500 redundancies in the first nine months of the year.

Some job loss in Rotherham was the result of technological development, planned long in advance of the strike or the recession. For example a new continuous casting plant at Templeborough created 500 redundancies. Decisions to restructure the industry created other redundancies. The closure of two furnaces at Templeborough Electric Melting Shop was a blow to management and unions alike. It was only in the early '70s that the melting shop had gained a reputation throughout the steel industry for high quality and productivity. As with Corby and Consett, it was clear that a good production record and good profits were no guarantee of survival.

For those whose jobs were secure, short-time working was the order of the day for over six months after the strike, experienced by all industrial grade workers, save in one or two departments. Consequently, one branch official estimated, real wages were actually 20% down on 1979 and people were finding it difficult to recover from the personal financial difficulties caused by the strike.

Some commentators blamed the strike for damaged production records and lost markets, but by November 1981 BSC had virtually recovered its market share. The market itself however, for both public and private sectors, was shrinking, since the steel industry was particularly vulnerable to the deepening economic recession which hit virtually all sectors of industry. Private sector firms were in grave trouble. Government intervention and policies, particularly over energy costs, the strong pound, and high interest rates, were seen to be key influences on the industry in a study by Sheffield City Council (1981) and similar analyses came from the CBI, TUC, individual steel unions and private sector unions and management. The Iron and Steel Act (1980) was passed, paving the way for denationalisation. Subsequently, in July 1981, a merger took place between two BSC plants and GKN, forming Allied Steel and Wire, and other mergers have been planned.

The economic and political influences on the steel industry over the past two years have had a marked effect on the attitudes and behaviour of the ex-strikers. The recession, with job loss and short-time working, has done much to erode the confidence and enthusiasm noticeable in the immediate post-strike period. Fighting the extensive job loss and closures has been difficult, and sapping of the energy and motivation of ISTC branch officials. Additionally, in Rotherham, in ISTC and other unions, senior and experienced branch officials have been lost through redundancy schemes, which has had a serious effect on union organisation. Whatever the changes effected by the strike, they have been overlaid by the wider events occurring in the industry.

Who won the strike?

The question is sometimes posed as to who won the steel strike, a difficult but not futile question to answer. The time perspective adopted is important, as are the issues and parties involved.

Taking first the *union* side, and focusing on ISTC, to what extent can the latter be seen as the victor? The strike was certainly successful in terms of improving the national wage offer from 2% to 11%. The unions also resisted management plans to shift collective bargaining completely from national to local level. While not wholly successful, given the 4½% to be negotiated locally, it was an improvement on the original BSC proposal. The resistance to managerial pressures during the strike fostered an unprecedented feeling of power and confidence; ISTC showed its mettle and there was a new-found sense of pride and enthusiasm in the union, which in Rotherham was directed towards internal change. The strike also encouraged a better relationship between the unions, however delicate and precarious, since at national level all unions agreed to negotiate with management jointly (while remaining independent over decisions on action), although ISTC's concern to be the dominant union continues to cause friction at times.

In the longer term, the gains are more doubtful. The steel unions have been unable to resist industrial restructuring and the consequent job loss. ISTC, in particular, has suffered a dramatic decrease in numbers. The job losses have also weakened ISTC's position relative to other unions in the steel industry and more widely within the TUC.

The weak position of the unions is visible in their collective bargaining performance following the strike. The 1981 wage round ended in July with ISTC accepting, after a conference vote, the management offer of a 7½% pay rise from August (i.e. only around 3% average across the year), and a delay to the introduction of the 39 hour week.

On the *management* side, gains and losses have also occurred, so to talk in simple terms of victory or defeat is inappropriate. There were gains in terms of procedural changes in collective bargaining, since a move was initiated, even if it did not go as far as some managers wished, for pay rises to be based on local productivity rather than national cost-of-living increases. In this way, labour costs were reduced, and the corporation's 'image' with government was improved, an important factor if cash limits were to be relaxed. Management also gained from the small but significant moves toward joint union bargaining which, although attempted in previous years, had never been successful. Further gains relate to the smoother transition to a smaller workforce and changed working practices, especially between craft and production workers, though it is arguable that these could have occurred without the strike.

However, the handling of the negotiations lost management a great deal of credibility. One Rotherham manager complained that previously he had been proud to work for BSC, but now hardly dared mention who his employer was. The recession, too, was in many ways as demoralising and frustrating for management as for unions. Struggling to keep expenditure within tight cash limits, management have been hampered by the lower domestic demand for steel, the difficulties in boosting exports, and fluctuations in interest and exchange rates.

The steel strike, however, consisted of more than two protagonists: many political commentators have pointed to the direct interest of the Conservative *government* in the strike outcome. This administration had come to power in May 1979 with a strong commitment to reduce inflation through monetary control and to the operation of market pressures in moderating wage claims. The steel strike was advantageous to the government in setting a low ceiling which other unions might be expected to observe, especially in the public sector.

More crucial for a government pledged to reform trade unions was the issue of union power. While the strike was in progress, the Employment Act (1980) was being steered through Parliament. Although the legislation was prompted and justified predominantly by the strikes of the 'winter of discontent' (1978-9), the steel strike fuelled public discussions about picketing. The TV coverage of large pickets, seemingly like political demonstrations, gave support to the view that trade unions were too powerful. Furthermore, the notorious Denning judgment ruled that the steel strike was not a trade dispute but a political strike and thus could not be afforded the protection of the law. Although reversed at appeal a few days later, the point had been made. The definition of a trade dispute became a matter of significance in the first and second Employment Bills (1980 and 1982). The steel strike, then, was a useful background against which the government could gain legitimacy for its legal measures. In many ways the government, more than either unions or management, were the winners of the strike.

CHAPTER ELEVEN

The steel strike: a theoretical overview

In Chapter 1 we argued that our research related to three hitherto fairly discrete bodies of thought, on strikes, unions, and complex organisations — and that ideas from the last of these, organisation theory, could be used to supply an integrated framework for our case description and its theoretical implications. Accordingly, this final interpretive chapter will relate some of the key findings to the two themes in organisation theory we described in Chapter 1. First, we shall use ideas from the functionalist systems paradigm to evaluate how features of strike organisation were related to its 'performance' in handling internal and external uncertainty. Secondly, we shall invoke a political/cultural perspective to give an account of how the strike organisation developed over time and to explain the emergent properties of the behaviour and interactions of organisational members.

Strike organisation, function and effectiveness

A strike organisation is a fighting organisation. Its 'mission' is to win a struggle, and its design and functioning are effective if they achieve the goal of victory. This is the simple and unambiguous account that most strike participants would give to explain the behaviour of the strike organisation, but it is one that demands answers to some further questions: 1. what is the boundary of the fighting organisation? 2. who is the opponent and for what objectives? 3. how did the organisation attain its structural design? 4. what functions have to be fulfilled for the organisation to achieve its goals? Let us consider these questions in turn.

Organisational boundaries

First, if we are to think of organisations as systems and analyse their effectiveness, we need to decide what elements we are going to count as being inside the system. All the BSC strikers? All the strike organisations of South Yorkshire? The Rotherham Strike Committee? For most of our narrative the RSC has been the focal point, though we have also included other local organisations (DSC, CCC) in our considerations. In short, where you draw the boundary depends upon where you stand, but this is not an arbitrary decision, for its location determines the answers to our other three questions. In this discussion we shall be talking about the RSC strike organisation as being the system. An important corollary of this is that the environment with which it had to interact, whether with intent to subdue or co-operate, included other levels of the union hierarchy, other unions, and organisations separate from the primary 'enemy'. Another dimension of the environment of these strike bodies is *internal:* the membership they organise but who do not directly participate in their decision-making. These environments constitute sources of uncertainty which the strike organisations must contend with in order to advance towards their objective of winning the strike. To shut down the steelworks requires, for example, one, that the activities initiated are legitimated by the parent union organisation; two, that assistance is obtained from other organisations; and three, that control is exercised over the activities of members. In our narrative it is apparent that the RSC spent most of its time managing its relationships with people other than the 'enemy' (the BSC top management and the government): groups such as the CCC, DSC, the local police, picket marshals, the media, committees of other unions, private steelmakers, people requesting dispensations, and so on.

Organisational goals
Does this definition of boundaries cast doubt on the assumption that the strike organisation's goal was to win the strike? It does not in so far as these activities and interactions can be seen as goals subordinate to winning the strike, though we may admit that the notion of 'winning' is a lot less clear-cut than union rhetoric might lead us to believe. What counts as winning? — getting 20% with no strings? reversing government policy on steel cutbacks? preventing all movement of steel in the UK? keeping the BSC plants closed for as long as the union decrees? The first two of these goals are final outcomes, under the aegis of the national organisation and thus beyond the control of the South Yorkshire strike organisation, whilst the latter two are more clearly local operational goals assumed to help achieve those final outcomes. So the strike organisation's primary goals were not so much fighting and winning against BSC and the government as maintaining solid strike action to prevent the production and movement of steel. The primary goal of stopping steel production in the public sector was largely

unproblematic. This was effectively achieved by the mass withdrawal of labour from BSC plants, since the employer did not attempt to contest this by encouraging strike-breaking. The main goal of the strike organisation therefore became the prevention of steel movement, from stockholders, importers and manufacturers of finished products, that is, activities concentrated in the private sector. Various methods were considered and employed to achieve this goal, though from the outset the most favoured means was the one over which the strike organisation had most control: picketing.

Looking more closely at it we can see that the strike organisation had very mixed success in this goal. The movement of steel and steel products, between firms and through the importation of steel at major ports of entry, continued throughout the strike and despite the large numbers of pickets and volume of effort deployed on the task. Continual awareness of this problem was a major source of pressure on the RSC — so much so that their strategy perceptibly changed to one of 'hitting key plants' rather than stopping all steel movement. Towards the end of the strike mass pickets had turned into 'mass demonstrations'. What does this show? As we shall be arguing it shows that picketing became progressively more a symbolic than a purely functional activity, whose purpose was to maintain the motivation and direction of strike participation and to communicate strength of feeling and intent in the wider domain of the public propaganda war.

A characteristic of the strike organisation's goals and functions was, as we have seen, interaction with various groups of differing sympathy and interest. The environmental uncertainty that confronted the organisation was produced by these groups. It is apparent that the organisation was not in the powerless position of merely trying to react to an environment over which it had low or negligible control, like some small business trying to manage its markets. On the contrary it exhibited what has been called 'linked interdependence' (Thompson, 1967) of a kind that meant the organisation played a part in the creation of its own environment. Moreover, given its inability to achieve success in its primary goals, many of these relationships assumed symbolic as much as functional importance. Two prominent examples are relationships with the police, and relations with SIMA.

Relations with the police were initially low key, for picketing of BSC plants did not arouse the issue of legality. Far from it, for as we have seen, a not unnatural fraternal spirit often typified the casual interactions of the pickets and police who both somewhat aimlessly patrolled the same uneventful space. Cordiality also characterised relations between the RSC and senior officers when they periodically met. In both these cases the functional logic is apparent: both parties had an interest in rendering each other's behaviour co-operative and predictable. However, at the same time there was a powerful set of opposite forces, born of ideological needs. Rumours of phone taps and police espionage were rife, and 'fraternising' was actively discouraged, especially as the strike tactics became more militant (mass pickets) and strikers more often began to fall foul of the law.

There was less ambivalence and more symbolic significance in relations with the reviled SIMA, for this union was actually a poor target as a substantive threat to the strike. The accusation of 'strike-breakers' and 'scabs' was partly undeserved, since SIMA members did not engage in the direct production of steel. They crossed picket lines for the purpose of plant maintenance, though this *was* work normally carried out by the striking union members. The issue of the Brinsworth Pavilion club canteen facilities raised their visibility as a symbolic enemy; a role to which they were well suited by virtue of their status as past protagonists in union rivalry, and as management representatives. The fact (revealed by our interview programme) that most of the middle management whom SIMA represented were probably sympathetic to the strikers' cause and antagonistic to their own senior management was evaded, for this was incompatible with the demands of their ideological orientation. The sending back of the £130 donation neatly symbolises this rejection of inconsistent information.

Organisational design

Let us now turn to consider the characteristics of the organisational design and how it functioned. First, it is apparent that it had a number of origins. It owed a great deal to prior union structures, and to prior traditions and union folklore about how to run a strike. At the same time there were emergent properties to the organisation, and a 'negotiated' order to the way its institutions and practices developed, as indeed one might expect in a totally novel structure. The ascendancy of the RSC and the early disappearance of two 'junior' strike committees (Aldwarke and Templeborough) illustrate this organic quality. Yet once it was established the organisational framework proved remarkably resistant to change, though *how* it was used did vary over time.

These points are borne out in the case of picket organisation. The choice of geographically based picket cells in preference to branch-based cells was an interesting victory for novelty and presumed tactical superiority over tradition and central union control; it was advocated by their advisers whose received wisdom was based on memories of the miners' strike of 1971-2. The decision, in hindsight, proved to be highly significant and indirectly enhanced the domination of informal power arrangements. On the picket lines the arrangement created power and autonomy for picket marshals and Picket Control, the 'new' functionaries associated with this structure. Within the wider strike organisation geographical cells favoured the leadership role of the RSC. The alternative of branch-based cells would have reinforced the union-based elements of the strike organisation and the established union hierarchy, traditions of branch 'autonomy' notwithstanding, for the system of branch organisation is the mainstay of ISTC's pattern of hierarchical control. Equally instructive is the failure of the briefly mooted move to change to a system of branch organisation when picket 'morale' (i.e. picket *control*) became an issue, later in the strike. The organisational design had become embedded by practice and by interest, i.e. any presumed tactical advantages of change were insubstantial compared to the weight of inertia in established practice, or compared to the many voices with an active stake in the system as presently constituted.

From organisation theory one is directed away from the formal mechanisms of bureaucracy towards analysis of the work that they do, for organisational designs are inevitably 'incomplete', i.e. they are incapable of specifying the details of precisely *how* they are to be operated by people, and hence owe much more to evolving patterns of action and interaction. For organisations to achieve effective management of environmental uncertainty they need to have two counterbalancing sets of capabilities: to reduce, screen out, control or integrate uncertainty, and to increase, diversify, and innovatively adapt to and match uncertainty and complexity. These are often considered under the two headings of integration and differentiation, though here we shall look at them more closely through a more precise identification of system functions: production, leadership, regulation, maintenance, intelligence, and innovation.

Organisational functions

Production refers to the deployment of energy for the organisation's primary task. This we have already discussed above, arguing that the equivalent of production here was picketing, and although the union was never really in danger of failing to get substantial numbers of strikers out on picket duty, complete success in this task was beyond their resource capability. The second system function is the *leadership* or executive function, which denotes the organisation's directing and co-ordinating functions, usually centralised in some legitimate or hierarchical authority. This function was ambiguously divided among various parts of the strike organisation. Whilst DSC and CCC had some legitimacy in this role and did on occasions fulfil the function, it was the RSC that took most responsibility. It did so largely on the basis of initiative and primacy, as the body first in field with the formulation of strategy and the execution of tactics. Its ability to do this was inspired by its ideological cohesion, and the initially successful performance of these functions at an early stage created a *de facto* legitimacy for its leadership role. The nature of the ideological basis for this power is the focus of the second part of this chapter, but here we should reflect a little on its functional basis. The RSC's initiative was manifest in a number of events and processes. First, by taking the major responsibility for the 'appointment' of picket marshals, and by making their selection upon subjective criteria ('leadership qualities'), the RSC gave itself a lasting source of legitimate authority, if not formally. Second, the RSC developed expertise and a reputation for its legitimate authority before, historically, the DSC had time to 'co-ordinate' it. The growing autonomy of the RSC as an executive was symbolised by the reduction of the overlap between the two bodies early in the strike, when RSC members with joint membership of the DSC withdrew from the latter body. The RSC further strengthened its position at an early stage, undermining the traditional union hierarchy of control by encouraging full time officials to continue to fulfil their 'normal duties'. In consequence four of the six Divisional full time officials did have a highly restricted low-power function in the strike, concerned almost exclusively with day-to-day activities (e.g. welfare and hardship).

At the same time the RSC was not an undifferentiated source of 'executive' power, for three reasons. One was that within its ranks was an inner circle, the core of influential members, who in the terminology of political analysis might be termed a 'dominant coalition'. The second was that the RSC maintained fluid and permeable boundaries, which, as we have argued, constituted a source of legitimation. Third, lacking a statutory legitimacy within the union machine the RSC's power was actually quite fragile and open to challenge. Even if its position as a co-ordinating and directing leadership was never seriously threatened, the insecurity of its power base was revealed on the few occasions where it backed off from the challenge of unco-operative pickets. This amounted to a fundamental ambiguity in its leadership and was reflected in the way its decision-making character changed over time; what could be termed a shift in the balance of attention from the external to the internal environment.

Third is the function of *regulation* or control. This was formally constituted in a chain of command from the RSC to Picket Co-ordinators, thence to Picket Marshals, down to the operation of picket cells. This chain of command also served as a channel for upward communication, which we shall consider under the heading of intelligence functions. However, in the crucial area of downward control the dominant metaphor used by the actors (and to be found in most commentaries on strikes), was the military one. Certainly this might seem to be appropriate to the idea of pickets as a fighting force in a hostile environment, and it does superficially fit the way 'targets' were initially selected and allocated to cells. However, as picketing in many situations stabilised, the choice of targets in others became controversial, and the commitment of pickets to the centrally directed militant policy became less unanimous, the military analogy can be seen to have more rhetorical than functional significance. From being unproblematic the issue of regulation became critical, symbolised by the repeated assertion that pickets were 'volunteers' and not 'conscripts' and could not be instructed to conform with centrally directed policies, *a fortiori* because they were not in receipt of strike pay. It was this crisis which raised the proposal in RSC that cells should be reorganised on branch lines, for it was apparent that unions other than ISTC, relying upon more traditional power structures, felt little compunction and experienced less difficulty about *instructing* their members. In fact, the more appropriate metaphor for picket regulation is that of employment. Picket marshals organised their cells like small work organisations, evolving shift systems that in many cases were a direct carry-over from relationships in production; systems in keeping with the uneventful tedium of their day-to-day tasks. The term 'absenteeism' was even used in the RSC's discussions of the problem of picket morale. However, even the employment analogy should not be taken too far, for strikers' duties were not constrained by the compulsive quality of contractual obligations in employment, although at times the resemblance was strong. Only the flying pickets and others in the front line of conflict truly fit the military model in image and action, and even here the metaphor breaks down in crucial respects, principally in the lack of disciplined and unquestioning obedience to hierarchical authority. In the more normal situation of 'stabilised' pickets the problem of regulation was heightened by the variation in how intermediate levels of authority, Picket Marshals and Co-ordinators, perceived their roles, and in some cases directly and indirectly successfully challenged the right of central strike committees to regulate their practice.

This amounted to a growing crisis of control, whose inner dynamic is most clearly visible in the dilemma over pay for pickets. The debates on this issue were partly about equity and democracy, but they were also an uncomfortable near-recognition of the fact that far from being a volunteer *army,* pickets were a *workforce* of variable motivation and reliability who might need the sanction of rewards and punishments to induce an adequate performance on their job.

Fourth, *maintenance* functions were fundamentally less problematic though particular issues did absorb a lot of time and energy. Stabilised picket cells looked after themselves on a day-to-day basis, though often in relative isolation (a factor that contributed to their 'fraternisation' with police and other 'enemies'). Picket Control and other intermediaries ensured that pickets were adequately resourced, and flying pickets received compensation for travel costs. More generally there was also the relatively straightforward disposition of hardship funds to strikers' families as well as welfare and legal support services, administered through the formal union hierarchies of full-time officials and representative committees. None of these matters constituted serious challenges to the decision-making apparatus, but they did impose a major burden upon it in administrative terms. The need for limited resources to be distributed equitably amongst those qualifying for support was an issue that could not be speedily and efficiently managed by the administrative system. The reason for this was that it was an issue of symbolic or moral significance, disguised as a functional maintenance problem. The fundamentally political/moral order of the strike organisation prevented the problem of equity from being treated solely as a bureaucratic issue; thus it absorbed time and effort inefficiently, and disproportionately to its low functional centrality and importance.

Fifth was *intelligence,* or the need for the organisation to have an adequate representation of its internal and external environments. We shall defer consideration of information flow *outwards* to these bodies until later in the discussion, since this is more appropriately viewed as constituting organisational action, both task and symbolic. Here we concentrate on *incoming* information available to the central strike organisations. For the day-to-day running of the strike the normal peace-time methods of branch meetings were inadequate due to irregular and erratic attendance, and because under the strike structure they lacked a formal role in prosecuting the strike. The regular meetings of picket marshals were a far more significant source of feedback on day-to-day strike events, and it was through this source that the regulation crisis became evident to the leadership. Information about the wider local environment was provided by the innovation of 'reconnaissance squads' and by the more haphazard process of informal contacts with people requesting dispensations and with other occasional visitors to the strike headquarters. RSC's intelligence about other union bodies was provided by the regular reporting of its members who had dual membership of other bodies, principally the DSC and the EC. But to identify the sources and channels is to present only half of the picture, for equally crucial was the final decoding and evaluation of information at its destination. This proved to be another critical problem area in RSC functioning. Operating in a spirit of militancy, the RSC's hostile anticipation of negative propaganda is understandable, and to a degree justifiable in so far as a media war was being waged between the proponents of different viewpoints. This led to the RSC developing a tendency to evaluate information in terms of its *source,* in precedence to its *content.* Externally, union sources were preferred to non-union, and internally ISTC voices were listened to with greater attention than non-ISTC, even when those other voices (such as NCCC members of RSC) had greater experience of the area in question and had been proven right in prior prognostications. The dynamic underlying this, as we shall be considering, was the RSC's need to protect itself against dissonant information and loss of leadership, and the consequence was that the RSC developed a selective and highly distorted image of the environment it was attempting to control. The crises of control, and the wasteful absorption of energies on peripheral concerns such as the SIMA canteen-use issue, stem largely from the increasing deficiencies in the quality of intelligence and its appreciation. The problems of information veridicality were also complicated by the need for security in a climate of external threat — the dangers of police and employers anticipating the strikers' more radical and controversial tactics. This had the effect of constricting information flow to the point where it led to dysfunctional breakdowns of internal communication and distorted the content of messages.

Sixth and finally is the system function of *innovation.* The whole structure had various novel elements that had been designed for its unfamiliar task, but the term innovation here refers to the organisation's capacity to adapt its structures to meet the demands of change as the strike progressed. The ability of the organisation to adapt to day-to-day variations in environmental challenges is largely attributable to its character as a 'loosely coupled system' (Weick, 1979, quoting Glassman, 1973). By this is meant the relatively low overlap between sub-systems, or the lack of overarching rules and procedures that bind sub-systems together, which has the effect of absorbing or containing rather than amplifying the variations that confront the total system. Picket cells can be seen as loosely-coupled sub-systems, aiding the rapid adaptive evolution of varied picketing tactics and choice of targets. Another way of looking at this is to say that it helped achieve a 'requisite variety' of response, i.e. a felicitous matching of response complexity with the complexity of environmental demands and changes. As we have seen, this response flexibility was also served by the pragmatic change in the way committees were used as the strike developed. More particular innovations to aid adjustment in different operational areas were the use of reconnaissance squads to find out about private sector steel movements, and the development of cell 24, with its roving commission to raise the effectiveness of slackening picket cells. The latter example nicely demonstrates how the opposing functions of increasing and dampening down complexity can complement one another, for cell 24 was a structural innovation aimed at enhancing centrally regulated control.

The analysis we have undertaken here points towards other kinds of analysis. First, we have emphasised throughout how the relationship between structure and performance changed over time, and one way of extending this analysis would be to illustrate how there were functional changes at key historical junctures such as the Denning judgment and the first mass picket, but we shall not be pursuing this analysis here. Second, it is apparent that although there is overlap and interaction between the different sub-system functions we have discussed, they are unequal in significance, taking as a criterion for significance the amount of time and energy deployed on them. In the language of open-systems theory it could be said that there were 'leading' sub-system functions which dominated the others; the leading ones in this case were firstly regulation, secondly leadership, and thirdly intelligence. The narrative account we have set out in this book is largely taken up with these three areas and the attendant crises of legitimation, power, and communication. Functional analysis can take us no further in the analysis of these issues, such are the limitations of its assumptions. Therefore, at this juncture we shall need to turn to a quite different conception of organisational activity: construing the strike organisation as a political system.

The politics of strike organisation

The strike organisation was discussed by its participants and by many outside observers in rationalist terms as a formal bureaucracy comprising rules and procedures for executing certain pre-ordained tasks, whereas in reality its operation was considerably more anarchic, spontaneous, value-laden, conflictual, and symbolic. Why was there this disparity between image and actuality?

Firstly, it is important to understand that it is not uncommon for organisations to have misleading self-imagery. In particular, organisations which are subject to the external control of other organisations or whose legitimacy rests upon the accreditation of some higher body, experience pressure to legitimate their own activities. The formalising of procedures and offices fulfils this need, and the bureaucratic features of the strike organisation and the terms in which it was discussed were similarly responses to the perceived need to demonstrate its legitimacy visibly to other authorities: the national executives of the unions in the strike and other local union bodies. The reality of the political ethos of organisational action, however, was a response to the high uncertainty of the task environment, to which a political style of operation is more suited than the mechanisms of bureaucracy.

In political systems organisational offices are not occupied on the basis of formal criteria or specialist skills but of particular interests seeking to advance the power of their position or their vision of how the wider organisation should function. The effect of this is to transform communication, decision-making, and control from the rationalist model into something quite different, as we shall see. First, though, let us look at some of the aspects of organisational design that indicate its political status. The design itself can be seen as non-neutral and non-rational, in the sense that it was by no means a 'naturally' evolved structure providing optimum task effectiveness — it is evident that strike organisations in other areas, such as Scunthorpe, conducted the strike with quite different formal arrangements. The design was in fact *constructed* by the agreement of different parties or interests to suit their purposes, and how the initial committee structure was formed was of lasting significance to the way the strike was prosecuted in South Yorkshire. The role of informal elite or dominant coalition was seized at an early stage by the militant lay officials on the Rotherham Joint Committee, who perpetuated their recently acquired ascendancy on that body by creating a new body, the RSC, to which their domination could be transferred. Thereafter, the RSC expanded its membership and reinforced its dominant ethos by attracting kindred spirits. The policy of permeable boundaries encouraged the self-selection of sympathetic members, and at the same time valuably enhanced the legitimacy of the RSC as a 'democratic' institution. The RSC's openness thus had the effect of underlining its leadership, whilst helping to diffuse responsibility for decisions and deflect attention away from its internal oligarchical tendencies.

The duplication of function and ambiguous division of responsibility between the RSC and the DSC is another indicator that these two bodies represented different sets of interests rather than clearly separated functions. The RSC's political character is also demonstrated by exception. It is no accident that the one occasion where the RSC appealed to a higher authority to justify a decision was over the only really explosively controversial issue, the removal of safety cover, on which occasion it sheltered behind the 'higher' authority of the CCC.

In theories of rational decision-making the procedure ideally to be followed is: setting objectives → defining the immediate problem and success criteria → listing alternative action strategies → evaluating alternative action strategies → implementing one → evaluating outcomes. In political systems this sequence is often reversed, though rarely with conscious intent or self awareness that this is happening. From stated or unstated objectives commitment is made to actions consistent with them. The problem is then defined in terms that make the desired action the inevitable or best choice. Action is implemented and afterwards success criteria are constructed that are consistent with a favourable evaluation of the actual outcome. Decision-making is self-validating and self-fulfilling.

On the RSC decision-making varied between these two extremes, often according to the type of issue under consideration. For many routinised maintenance issues decision-making approached the ideal of administrative rationality, though as a political system lacking the bureaucratic design of clear rules and division of responsibility, the RSC's handling of these was often less than efficient. A more common and 'natural' mode of decision-making for the RSC was the 'mobilisation of bias' (Bachrach and Baratz, 1970) for or against different outcomes. This was the case when decision outcomes could not be unequivocally evaluated, i.e. when the thrust of decision-making was more symbolic than task-functional. For example, decisions about dispensations were often less material to the outcome of the strike than they were demonstrations of power, magnanimity, and ideological rectitude. In such cases decisions often did not even look like decisions. The analysis of decision-making in political systems is complicated by the prevalence of implicit exclusions from the decisional arena. Neglecting to raise an issue can be a significant decision itself, advancing the cause of some particular set of interests. Decisions were voted upon only four times in the life of the RSC, and the occasion of each of the four votes bears out this analysis. Two were votes of no confidence (one in the ISTC General Secretary, the other in Scunthorpe's strike committee), one was to urge the RJC to hurry up its deliberations on the conditions for the return to work after the strike, and one was a vote of support for the GMWU's withdrawal of canteen staff in the SIMA canteen affair. Only the last could be said to be in any way a substantive decision and indeed this was the only one yielding a close vote — all the others were carried unanimously. But all these four were alike in their status as communicative acts rather than as leading to behavioural outcomes.

Why was there so little voting if, as we have said, this was a predomi-nantly political system? The reason is the power of consensus. In climates of high uncertainty consensus is highly valued. Where speed of reaction is not paramount it is preferable to undertake the painstaking process of building unanimity rather than engage in the divisiveness of voting. In political systems committee chairpersons, for example, often owe their influential position to their ability to construct compromise and agreement over potentially divisive issues. Nor need the process necessarily be so painstaking for, over time, consensus can become more speedily attained with practice and habit. In an organisation like the RSC which has open boundaries, there will be a tendency for the members of consensus-building coalitions to mutually reinforce each other's active participation, with sympathetic additional members drifting into the organisation and potential antagonists being discouraged or alienated. The outcome of this is that consensus becomes more speedily and effectively generated, a tendency that is enhanced by membership commitment to extreme group decisions. What has been called 'groupthink' is established (Janis, 1972). The more radical the character of decision-making, the more closely bound together are internal group interests, a process that is heightened as they increasingly see themselves as being at odds with the interests and opinions of the world outside.

To a degree this is what occurred within the RSC, whose militant self-image (analysed in Chapter 7) and radical decisions tended to be mutually reinforcing, and whose decisions consequently took on some of the character of 'groupthink'. Some of the classic signs of groupthink are avoidance of divergent viewpoints, distorted imagery of the outside world, and increased emphasis upon the post-hoc legitimation and rationalisation of decisions. Manifestations of this process within the RSC could be seen in their scornful attitude toward the possibility of their failure and belief in 'imminent breakthrough' in the private sector. Locked into this belief system, their response to actual failures was to set in motion actions designed to maintain commitment and consensus rather than to change direction. It was in this manner that towards the end of the strike the RSC fixed upon the strategy of mass pickets as forms of 'demonstration' rather than searching for other methods of stopping steel production and movement, though there was some tactical variation in the later selection of 'key' plants.

These developments can be seen as part of a shifting emphasis throughout the strike from the need to maintain *consensus* towards the need to generate *commitment*. Commitment, the motivational counterpart to consensus, was unproblematic in the early days of the strike. The novelty of the situation and the anger of strikers meant that the strike organisation only had to reach consensus about strategies and tactics; behavioural commitment could be taken for granted. But as the long strike settled in, and people became inured to their tasks, the strike came to exhibit the characteristics of normal peace-time union business and increasingly to confront the problem of membership motivation, whilst consensus became less troublesome with the practised accept-ance of general objectives. Peace-time unions are voluntary organisa-tions and consequently must repeatedly face the problem of how to maintain acceptably high levels of membership involvement, whilst lack-ing the expedients open to other types of organisations, such as the ability to recruit new and freshly committed members or recourse to hierarch-ically based control systems of rewards and punishments. Indeed, as we have seen, the problem of picket 'morale' did increasingly lead the strike organisation to search for and consider what control mechanisms could be invoked to maintain commitment. Branch and mass meetings were also used to maintain momentum, and the innovation of the *Steelworkers Banner* was similarly important in this role.

Within the RSC commitment was assured. More at issue was the continuing need for consensus, for as a multi-union body its decisions were always in danger of cutting across the different group interests of its members. As we have seen the ISTC majority on the RSC tended to pay little more than polite attention to the usually equally polite dissent of its non-ISTC minority. The latter members faced a dilemma. On the one hand they shared a behavioural commitment through their active participation in the RSC to a series of relatively 'extreme' decisions, and at the same time they enjoyed the esteem of being identified with the leading body of the strike. On the other hand, as the junior partners of their alliance, they were accorded scant influence over events, while at the same time they were conscious that their union experience was broader than that of most of the RSC's ISTC members and of the fact that the decisions they were called upon to endorse were ones that conflicted with the interests of their fellow trade unionists outside the RSC. The debates about the removal of safety cover and the denigra-tion of the competence of the CCC provided clear examples of this dilemma. Although these occasioned some disquiet among them the non-ISTC minority went against their rational group interest (they and their non-ISTC comrades stood to lose from the outcomes of the decisions) and maintained solidarity with the RSC. This constitutes a powerful demonstration of the overriding power of consensus and commitment in multi-union decision-making bodies. Their relative autonomy and the ideological basis of their action gives them a power as political sub-cultures that can eclipse the influence of other reference groups.

This brings us to the issue of power relations. It was important to the ISTC to 'lead' the strike. This derived partly from its pre-strike status as the largest of the steel unions, and partly from the character of its 'new' local leadership. On the latter point it is significant that the dominant voices on the RSC were ISTC activists, many of whom had been openly critical in the past of the union establishment and its local peace-time leadership. They wanted a more radical union body; thus, their control over the RSC and their relegation of most full-time officers to union maintenance tasks had added political significance. The two notable exceptions to this were full-time officials whose force of personality was sufficient to transgress the circumscription of their role; one being a well-known dissident within the ISTC establishment. However, we should not overidentify the strike leadership with 'personalities', although personal qualities were of some importance. First, it is not that easy to point out individuals as strike leaders — within the RSC inner core there was variation in whose voice seemed to carry most weight. Personal qualities of cognitive and communicative skills obviously did play a part in the character of individual contributions, but more important was the ability to construct shared meaning and this depends upon both the content and the style of communication. The purpose of communication in political systems is sense-making, and this is achieved by expressions, language, and symbolic acts that create shared meaning and the power of consensus. The strike was a culture, in which systems of belief were created by the use of language, expressions of value, rituals, myths and the recounting of epic sagas. There were numerous instances at all levels of the strike organisation of story-telling that had this cultural import, in relation to particular pickets, encounters with the police, reported exchanges with notable individual outsiders and so on. The use of these devices to create or sustain meaning can be seen as fulfilling two vital purposes. First, it provides an interpretation of past events and actions that legitimates past decisions and current positions. Secondly, this interpretive framework also contains implicit advocacy of future actions and choices.

Together, these build the power of consensus.

Special languages are often used in political systems, which can often disguise the real thrust of communicative acts. The terms used are those which are consistent with the dominant ideology. In trade unions the language of democracy is the favoured currency of social exchange with notions such as 'mandate' or 'representation' used as a code to discuss the rights and obligations of individuals. Debates develop into negotiations or contests about who can claim to be employing the true usage of a term or whose ideas represent the real spirit of democracy. The apparent triviality of such debates is misleading, for they are messages in code about whose power and interests will prevail. We have seen how the military analogy was favoured in the strike: a set of usages that implicitly legitimates central authority and control. Another prime example is the term 'morale', used to signify the RSC's anxiety about pickets' deviance from their centrally directed purpose, also fundamentally an issue of control.

In the wider context of the strike, some acts and events can be seen as fundamentally symbolic and as achieving parallel purposes. As we have already argued, conflicts with other bodies and groups, such as SIMA, were of chief significance as identity and ideology reinforcement, and some of the mass pickets had similar value. In effect, the environment that 'fits' the organisation's orientation and capacities is 'enacted' by the organisation.

For this reason it would be wrong to convey the impression that the RSC was functioning in a spirit of isolated self-interest, cut off from the world. It is a measure of its success as a strike institution that it was able to embody and create a sense of purpose among thousands of men and women beyond its committee room's boundaries. This ability to enact the culture through ideology and action is the art of political leadership, which the RSC effectively mastered. Power and leadership in political systems are therefore only matters of personality and skills in so far as those qualities are deployed in the direction of certain cultural themes and values. In the strike the power of these cultural meanings derived from their ability to mobilise collective action and reduce uncertainty, and from their uniqueness, i.e. their irreplaceability by alternative means which would accomplish the same ends. The power of individuals rested upon their grasp of this confluence. However, it would be mistaken to view the transmission of power and influence as all in one direction, from the leadership to the membership. The RSC's legitimate authority was limited, and often its position on issues was partially a response to the grassroots opinion of pickets and other strikers, imported to the RSC by its members, albeit through the filter of selective attention to and biased evaluation of their external informants. But the need to respond can be seen as part of the compulsive force of the democratic ethos in unions.

This brings us back to the dilemmas that we identified in Chapter 1 as confronting all union organisations — the collaboration dilemma and the democracy dilemma — and it is appropriate now briefly to evaluate their significance in the light of our present analysis.

First, it is apparent that the latter dilemma was far more acute than the former, though the high level of consensus in decision-making gave neither much overt expression in debate. That does not mean they were unimportant. The collaboration dilemma was chiefly visible in decisions about picketing, blacking, dispensations and safety cover. In each case action was engaged only after conflicts about how far the severity of long-term outcomes should be considered. Only on the last of these did the RSC duck out of the dilemma: in the other cases a militant approach was pursued, to the limits of practicality and beyond, capturing the spirit of the strike culture but often at the expense of task effectiveness.

The democracy dilemma (the conflict between democracy as an end in itself and as a means to other ends) here was balanced in favour of oligarchy. The RSC did not engage in much heart-searching about its right to direct and control the strike, for the simple reason that so much of its efforts were devoted to establishing the legitimacy of its status and decisions. However, this needs to be qualified in several ways. First, the oligarchical distribution of power, embodied in the RSC's leadership of the strike and the dominance of an active core within the RSC, was the product of a negotiated order without institutional or judicial basis. When the RSC's authority was challenged by the Picket Marshal who expressed his defiance in person to the committee, and by the picket cells which refused to join the later mass pickets, the RSC hastily backed down — in what was tantamount to an admission of the fact that it had no formal legitimate leadership authority in these areas. Second, the democracy dilemma is less problematic when collective action is being engaged by a union. Here the principle of 'negative control' (Nicholson, Ursell and Blyton, 1981) comes into play. This principle embodies the assumption that the interests of democracy are safe so long as the membership signifies its commitment or assent through co-operative action, or through refraining from unco-operative action. Hence, it is an important source of legitimation for leadership to be able to say that democracy is served through members acting as 'volunteers' rather than 'conscripts'. Another telling example was the debate about how pickets should be paid for their efforts. The meagreness of the sums involved serves to emphasise that they were of symbolic rather than instrumental importance. It is significant that concern was expressed that the money should be paid for past behaviour rather than for future performance. Symbolically, this represents a desire to achieve control by rewarding commitment, and a rejection of the employment-like connotations of using a pecuniary incentive to enforce legitimate control, though clearly the latter motive was not unmixed in the RSC's actions. Negative control is thus evident on those occasions where members 'vote with their feet' and decline to conform with leadership directives. However, for negative control to act as an effective restraint upon leadership, leadership must be sensitive to information about membership commitment. As we have seen, the RSC was a lot better at initiating action to maintain commitment than it was at being receptive to feedback about how its directives might be appraised. Finally, one can anticipate certain long-term consequences of these processes, following the ending of the strike. After the turbulence of the period immediately subsequent to settlement of the main strike, workplace and union relations settled down, back to the day-to-day routine of steelmaking, but this has to some extent concealed subtle ways in which the union culture has been permanently altered by the strike experience. These changes lie in the 'unfreezing' and reshaping of power relationships and union ideology rather than more noticeable and overt shifts in strategy and decision-making. But that is another story, and one that must be left to be told by others in the future.

Conclusion

This book has started and ended with theory, but it has not been *about* theory. It has been about a saga, a dramatic interlude that overtook the lives of many workers. People were confronted with new situations over which they had imperfect control, and events and experiences which challenged them to act and understand, which they had to accept or change. The raw material of such events and experiences are not reducible to abstraction and cannot be reproduced on the printed page. That has not been the purpose of this case history, for it has not been our ambition to achieve the impossible art of faithful reproduction. Social reality is too many-sided and abstract for this, and case accounts that attempt to do so can only at best offer journalistic partiality and over-simplification. We have seen our purpose as one of trying to unravel the complexities and meanings of the strike by simultaneous descriptive and analytical narrative. To do this is only possible with the help of ideas, ideas whose value is as tools for uncovering or dissecting social behaviour. These ideas are theories, models, assumptions and methods.

So it was in Chapter 1 that we gave priority to explicating these, and so it is now that in the final chapter we have concluded by returning to them. The major criterion for the value of the kind of analysis we have undertaken is the degree to which it can illuminate, reform or enlarge these tools for understanding. Part of this must be a consideration of how our insights might be built upon by other researchers. It would be presumptuous for us to try to do this in any detail, for much of the value of social and behavioural research lies in the distinctiveness of different scholars' approaches. However, it is not inappropriate to say in very broad and general terms that we are able to conclude optimistically for at least three future research orientations, and that the study of strike processes can help bring a constructive coherence to these three areas and their associated ideas. The areas are those that we reviewed in Chapter 1. First, we conclude that attempting to get to grips with the uniqueness of an individual strike also reveals themes and processes that can be observed in many other strikes, and thus in diverse ways enlarges our understanding of strike causes and outcomes. Second, the research has shown that the perennial dilemmas of union government are not somehow suspended during a strike, but should continue to claim our attention as of the utmost importance to the conduct of strikes. Analysing union behaviour under strike conditions tells us much about the fundamental issues of trade unionism. Third, our organisation theory orientation has led us to questions and conclusions that often elude industrial relations researchers, and our application of these ideas to strikes has led to issues that evade many organisational researchers. In short, we hope that other researchers will feel that the difficulties in pursuing investigations of this kind are well repaid by the benefits of building bridges between the different approaches available.

Finally, we would like to raise the issue of what benefits this kind of research may hold for the people who are caught up in the drama of strikes and must live through their consequences. While it would be foolish to imagine that we could enact some magic that will prevent strikes in the future or neutralise their painfulness, we hope that our contribution may help to make sense of the strike experience, and that this may prove of value to some of those who lived through the strike as well as to those who, like us, wish to observe and understand.

Appendices

Appendix I:
Research methodology

Our research contact with the strikers began in a tentative way through a visit by the authors to the strike office to elicit from key activists information about their perceptions and attitudes towards the strike. Having been welcomed into the strike office by certain members of the RSC, we grew more confident, gathering information partly through 'hanging about' to talk to anyone, picket or strike organiser, who was available for either a snatched conversation or a longer discussion. Gradually, from several days' immersion at the centre of the strike organisation we were able to discern some aspects of its structure and functioning and we began to direct our investigations, informally interviewing key activists and organisers. Such interviews were frequently carried out in the most unfavourable circumstances from a research point of view as they were interrupted by competing claims on the strikers' attention. The interviews with strike committee (RSC) members and others continued throughout the strike, and with increasing familiarity on both sides they became more like conversations between friends.

Entry to the RSC followed a formal request to the committee, where we presented the Chairman with a single page document outlining what we would like to study and how the information would be used. Our status was clearly and firmly that of observers. We sat around the table with the RSC members but did not participate in the discussions. We took extensive notes while the meeting was in progress, noting who spoke, in what circumstances and conveying what message. Using equipment such as tape recorders we felt would be inappropriate, given the sensitive political setting of our study. We found note-taking, in any case, adequate. Notes from meetings and interviews were written up in greater detail within a day or two. For the first two weeks, two of the researchers were full-time in the field, working together and making extensive comparisons of notes and interpretations on leaving the strike office. Later, we took it in turn to attend the strike office each day, missing only a few days in the mid-strike lull.

Observation and interviews were also used when we attended numerous other strike meetings, for example the Divisional Strike Committee, trade union branch meetings, mass meetings, rallies and

Picket Marshals' meetings. We interviewed 20 Picket Marshals two to four weeks after the strike. We also interviewed a small number of local industrial relations and personnel managers of BSC both during and after the strike. Contact with ex-RSC members continued after the strike, and we attended a variety of meetings such as the local post-mortem meeting in May and the 1980 and 1981 Annual Conferences.

These methods were supplemented by the use of documentary material: we obtained a variety of pamphlets, minutes and newspapers (including the weekly *Steelworkers Banner*). Additionally, in our investigation of strike participation and post-strike attitudes we conducted a questionnaire survey of 535 ISTC members after the strike (described separately in Appendix II).

Because our original plans were for a different study of industrial relations in the steel industry, we were not initially equipped with a conceptual framework with which to understand the rich and novel circumstances of the strike. Earlier theoretical work on industrial conflict (Kelly and Nicholson, 1980) proved to be useful but rudimentary (for example, the model pointed to the importance of intra-party bargaining but was not specific as to how it might be analysed) and it did not sufficiently emphasise the organisational features which we felt from our observations were important. The unanticipated nature of the study, combined with the special circumstances of this particular strike, necessitated a grounded theory approach to analysis (Glaser and Strauss, 1967). We developed our analysis through scrutiny of our notes, followed by extensive discussions, followed by a re-examination of the notes, in an iterative manner. This meant that our analysis and interpretation of events changed as we worked with the material, as we attempted to develop a framework which would accommodate the data we had collected.

Appendix II:
The questionnaire survey of Rotherham strikers after the return to work

The questionnaire

POST STRIKE QUESTIONNAIRE   *Confidential*

A Study by Sheffield University Industrial Relations research group.

We hope you can spare a few minutes to complete this questionnaire. We are a small research team with close contact with the steel industry. We have been following the events of the strike by daily attending meetings of the Rotherham Strike Committee. Your branch officials have discussed and approved this questionnaire at a branch meeting. They agree that it could be very useful in understanding how the strike has affected people. This could be important in understanding future industrial relations.

Your answers will be completely confidential and will only be seen by the researchers. It will be impossible to identify individuals in the findings. Your participation in this study is entirely voluntary but, of course, the more people who help, the better and more useful the results will be. You will learn of the conclusions from your local branch officials. If you have any queries about the research, please contact your branch officials or ourselves (address given below). We hope you will find the questionnaire interesting to complete. Please return it in the attached pre-paid envelope.

Jean Hartley
John Kelly
Psychology Unit
University of Sheffield

1. Age? .... years.

2. Sex? male ☐ female ☐

3. What is your job title? ....
....

4. Which branch of the ISTC do you belong to? ....

5.   How long have you been a member of ISTC? _____ years.

6.   During the strike, how many members of your household were

    a) wage earners _____

    b) dependants _____

7.   How many ISTC branch meetings did you attend *last year* (1979)?

_____

8.   How many times in your working life have you been on strike for more than one day before? (tick one box).

Never   ☐

1-2 times   ☐

3-4 times   ☐

More than 4 times ☐

9.   On *average*, how much time did you spend on picketing during the strike in:

    January _____ hours per week (approx).

    February _____

    March _____

10. Were you involved in other strike activities (e.g. driving, office work etc?).

Yes ☐

No   ☐

    If yes, what were they? _____

_____

11. How many branch or mass meetings did you attend during the strike?

_____ (total number).

12. How often were you troubled by serious financial worries during the strike? (tick one box for each month).

	Very Often	Occasionally	Hardly Ever
January	☐	☐	☐
February	☐	☐	☐
March	☐	☐	☐

13. On 2 January 1980, at the start of the strike what % increase in earnings did you think you were likely to get?

.... %

14. On 2 Janaury 1980, how many weeks did you think you would be out on strike?

.... weeks.

15. How satisfied are you with the settlement that was eventually agreed? (tick one box).

very satisfied	fairly satisfied	not sure	fairly dissatisfied	very dissatisfied
☐	☐	☐	☐	☐

16. How strong is your interest in politics? (tick one box).

very strong	fairly strong	fairly weak	very weak
☐	☐	☐	☐

17. How would you describe your own political views? (tick one box).

far left	left	centre left	centre right	right	far right	don't know
☐	☐	☐	☐	☐	☐	☐

18. *Before the strike started* how would you have described union-management relations in your department? (tick one box).

very co-operative	mainly co-operative	mainly antagonistic	very antagonistic
☐	☐	☐	☐

19. Before the strike started how satisfied were you with the quality of management in your department (tick one box).

very satisfied	fairly satisfied	not sure	fairly dissatisfied	very dissatisfied
☐	☐	☐	☐	☐

20. Do you think the experience of being on strike has changed your attitudes to industrial relations in the steel industry? (tick one box).

It has made me:	much more militant	a little more militant	had no effect
	☐	☐	☐

a little less militant	much less militant
☐	☐

21. How reliable did you find each of the following as a means of finding out what was going on in the strike *nationally?* (tick one box for each source).

	news media (t.v., radio, papers).	official union sources (e.g. bulletins, meetings)	informal sources and personal contacts in the industry.
very reliable	☐	☐	☐
fairly reliable	☐	☐	☐
fairly unreliable	☐	☐	☐
very unreliable	☐	☐	☐
not sure	☐	☐	☐

22. If there are other issues or opinions about the strike that have concerned you please use the space below — continue over the page if necessary.

THANK YOU.

Questionnaire distribution

Questionnaires were distributed to public sector members of ISTC at both major steelmaking sites at Rotherham, between 22 April (3 weeks after the end of the strike) and 3 June. The sample was chosen from eight ISTC branches covering a variety of jobs, departments and locations. We approached branch officials of selected branches, and also sent a letter explaining the research. Questionnaires were distributed by three means: through the mail, on the factory shop-floor and in one case at a well-attended branch meeting, the method of distribution chosen being that considered as most appropriate to local branch conditions. Method of distribution was found to be unrelated to results. Stamped, addressed envelopes were provided for the anonymous return of completed questionnaires.

1,610 questionnaires were distributed, and 535 returned, a response rate of 33%. The response rates for manual, clerical and supervisory employees were similar, although there was variation between branches. The respondents represented a variety of jobs and grades, and the proportions of staff employees (30%) and women (7%) were similar to the population of all BSC employees in Rotherham according to personnel records (28% and 9% respectively). Results were not correlated with the time interval between the strike and the completion of the questionnaire.

RESULTS

1. *Age*   Mean = 38.4 years   S.D. = 12.1
2. *Sex*   Male 93%
           Female 7% (All in clerical grades)

3. *Job Grade*

	%
Manual	68.7
Clerical	21.0
Supervisory	10.2
TOTAL	100 (N = 528)

5. *Union involvement*
   How long have you been a member of ISTC?
      mean = 15.2 years   S.D. = 10.6

6. *Other sources of income*
   Data unusable.

7. *Branch meetings 1979*
   How many branch meetings did you attend in 1979?
      mean = 4.6   S.D. = 2.5

8. *Previous strike experience*
   How many times in your working life have you been on strike for more than one day before?

	%
Never	73.0
One or more times	27.0
TOTAL	100 (N = 534)

9. *Interest in politics*
   How strong is your interest in politics?

	%
Very strong interest	10.5
Fairly strong interest	48.6
Fairly weak interest	29.8
Very weak interest	11.1
TOTAL	100 (N = 531)

10. *Political position**
    How would you describe your own political views?

	%
Far left	3.3
Left	22.8
Centre left	34.4
Centre right	17.5
Right	4.4
Far right	0.2
(Don't know)	(17.5)
TOTAL	100 (N = 521)

11. *Departmental union-management relations*
    Before the strike started, how would you have described union-management relations in your department?

	%
Very co-operative	15.6
Mainly co-operative	59.4
Mainly antagonistic	18.2
Very antagonistic	6.8
TOTAL	100 (N = 532)

12. *Views about local management*
    Before the strike started how satisfied were you with the quality of management in your department?

* These findings are similar to those reported in Fosh's (1981) study of Sheffield ISTC union activists.

	%
Very satisfied	5.5
Fairly satisfied	38.7
Not sure	6.6
Fairly dissatisfied	28.8
Very dissatisfied	20.5
TOTAL	100.1 (N = 532)

13. *Expectations of the settlement*

On 2 January 1980, at the start of the strike, what % increase in earnings did you think you were likely to get? (at the end of the strike)

	%
5% or under	6.1
5—10%	16.3
10—15%	35.5
15—20%	41.1
Over 20%	1.0
TOTAL	100 (N = 513)

mean = 14.8% (S.D = 4.4)

14. *Expectations of strike duration*

On 2 January 1980, how many weeks did you think you would be out on strike?

	%
2 weeks or under	15.4
2—4	24.7
4—8	41.8
Over 8 weeks	18.1
TOTAL	100 (N = 526)

mean = 6.2 weeks (S.D = 3.6)

15. *Picketing*

On *average* how much time did you spend on picketing during the strike?

Hours worked per week	*January* %	*February* %	*March* %
0	17.0	20.3	21.0
1—20	24.4	23.2	25.0
21—40	48.9	46.9	45.9
41 and above	9.7	9.7	8.1
TOTAL	100	100	100
	(N = 517)	(N = 518)	(N = 519)
	mean = 23.7	mean = 23.0	mean = 22.6
	S.D = 16.6	S.D = 17.2	S.D = 17.6

16. *Other strike duties*

Were you involved in other strike activities (e.g. driving, office work etc.)?

	%
Yes Worked in strike office	6
Worked in field (picket marshal, despatch rider, supplies driver etc).	13
TOTAL	19 (N = 103)

17. *Strike meetings*

How many branch or mass meetings did you attend during the strike?

	%
0	9
1— 5	40
6—10	25.1
11—15	19.1
Over 15	7.0
TOTAL	100 (N = 525)

18. *Financial situation*

How often were you troubled by serious financial worries during the strike?

	January (%)	*February* (%)	*March* (%)
Very often	24	35	49
Occasionally	30	38	30
Hardly ever	46	27	21
TOTAL	100	100	100
	(N = 523)	(N = 532)	(N = 531)

19. *Information sources during the strike*
    How reliable did you find each of the following as a means of
    finding out what was going on in the strike nationally?

	News media	Official union sources	Informal sources
	(%)	(%)	(%)
Very reliable	7.6	20.0	10.8
Fairly reliable	28.3	54.5	41.8
Fairly unreliable	22.6	10.4	19.8
Very unreliable	38.3	10.2	19.3
Not sure	3.2	4.8	8.3
TOTAL	100	100	100
	(N = 527)	(N = 519)	(N = 509)

20. *Satisfaction with settlement*
    How satisfied are you with the settlement that was eventually
    agreed?

	%
Very satisfied	3.6
Fairly satisfied	33.0
Not sure	4.7
Fairly dissatisfied	23.8
Very dissatisfied	35.0
TOTAL	100 (N = 535)

21. *Attitudinal militancy*
    Do you think the experience of being on strike has changed your
    attitudes to industrial relations in the steel industry?

	%
It has made me:	
Much more militant	40.1
A little more militant	37.1
Had no effect	20.2
A little less militant	1.1
Much less militant	1.5
TOTAL	100 (N = 534)

Table 1   One-Way ANOVA on Job Grade

** = differences significant at 1% level with post hoc t-test
 * = differences significant at 5% level

Questionnaire
Item
No.   *Variable*

No.	Variable	Job Grade					
		manual (N = 363)		clerical (N = 111)		supervisory (N = 54)	
		mean	S.D	mean	S.D	mean	S.D
1	Age	38.50	11.8	35.36	13.0	43.89**	10.5
5	Union involvement	17.28	10.3	7.39**	7.3	16.70	10.9
7	Branch meeting attendance 1979	4.87	3.7	2.95**	3.7	5.34	3.8
13	Expected increase	15.38**	4.5	13.66	4.0	13.41	3.7
14	Expected strike duration	6.32	3.8	5.28	3.0	6.75	3.5
15	Picketing hours:						
	January	28.80**	15.0	10.75	14.4	16.96	14.4
	February	27.47**	15.1	10.63	15.2	19.22	20.8
	March	27.09**	15.8	10.51	15.9	18.37	20.0
17	Strike meetings attended	7.46	5.4	5.22**	5.6	7.72	5.8
21	Attitudinal militancy (low value = militant)	1.78*	0.8	2.07	0.9	1.98	0.8
20	Satisfaction with settlement (low value = satisfaction)	3.84**	1.3	2.85	1.3	2.92	1.2
10	Political position (low value = left, 'don't knows' excluded)	2.87**	0.9	3.10	0.9	3.30**	0.9
9	Interest in politics (low value = strong)	2.44	0.8	2.39	0.7	2.23	0.8
11	Departmental I.R (low value = co-operative)	2.18	0.8	2.14	0.8	2.08	0.6
12	Views of management (low value = satisfaction)	3.25	1.3	3.02**	1.3	3.22	1.2

17		Financial situation: January			Financial situation: March		
troubled:		manual	clerical	superv.	manual	clerical	superv.
very often		107	15	3	202	47	11
occasionally		98	39	19	96	34	27

Questionnaire Item No.	*Variable*			*Job Grade*			
		manual (N = 363)		*clerical (N = 111)*		*supervisory (N = 54)*	
	hardly ever	149	19	32	61	30	16
		$\chi^2 = 23.86$, p = .00			$\chi^2 = 28.87$, p = .00		

Picketing during the strike

During the strike, systematic information about non-pickets was difficult to obtain since these strikers had little contact with the strike organisation. Here, aided by the anonymity of the questionnaire, we can compare non-pickets' characteristics and behaviour with those of pickets. The data are examined in terms of the three occupational groups, among whom systematic differences have been noted in Table 1. The division of the sample into pickets and non-pickets is based on the criterion of activity during January.

Table 2   Pickets and non-pickets according to job (January %)

	Manual	Clerical	Supervisory
Pickets	93.7	51.4	70.2
Non-pickets	6.3	48.6	29.8
TOTAL	100 (N = 349)	100 (N = 109)	100 (N = 57)

Table 3   T-tests comparing manual pickets and non-pickets
** = significant at 1% level
 * = significant at 5% level

	Pickets (N = 327)		Non-pickets (N = 22)			
	mean	S.D	mean	S.D	t	p
Age	37.58	11.3	49.77	11.7	4.87**	
Union involvement	16.53	9.7	26.57	13.2	4.50**	
Strike meetings	7.68	5.4	3.90	4.5	3.14**	
Increase expected	15.50	4.4	13.10	5.3	2.40*	
View of management	3.27	1.3	3.27	1.6	0.02	
Departmental I.R.	2.19	0.8	1.91	0.7	1.65	
Branch meetings 1979	4.96	3.6	3.77	4.1	1.47	

Satisfaction with settlement	3.85	1.3	3.54	1.5	1.06
Strike duration	6.19	3.5	8.03	6.2	1.35
Attitudinal militancy	1.78	0.9	2.00	0.8	1.18
Political position	2.89	0.9	2.78	1.2	0.47
Interest in politics	2.46	0.8	2.36	0.9	0.50

Table 4   T-tests comparing clerical pickets and non-pickets
** = significant at 1% level
 * = significant at 5% level

	Pickets (N = 56)		Non-pickets (N = 53)		
	mean	S.D	mean	S.D	t
Strike meetings	8.32	5.8	2.02	3.0	7.16**
Branch meetings 1979	4.12	4.0	1.62	2.9	3.76**
Attitudinal militancy	2.38	0.9	1.80	0.8	3.48**
Political position	2.84	0.6	3.24	1.1	3.19**
Interest in politics	2.20	0.7	2.57	0.8	2.67**
Union involvement	8.89	8.9	5.94	4.7	2.17*
Satisfaction with settlement	3.11	1.2	2.57	1.3	2.24*
Age	33.27	12.5	38.11	13.2	1.97*
Strike duration	5.87	3.0	4.79	3.0	1.88
View of management	2.89	1.2	3.17	1.4	1.10
Departmental I.R.	2.13	0.7	2.17	0.9	0.32
Increase expected	14.21	3.2	12.97	4.6	1.60

Table 5   T-tests comparing supervisory pickets and non-pickets
** = significant at 1% level
 * = significant at 5% level

	Pickets (N = 40)		Non-pickets (N = 17)		
	mean	S.D	mean	S.D	t
Strike meetings	9.05	5.6	3.09	3.9	3.32**
Strike duration	7.40	3.4	4.42	3.1	2.72**
Attitudinal militancy	1.85	0.8	2.42	0.8	2.22*
Age	41.90	9.1	49.02	13.1	2.14
Union involvement	16.95	9.7	13.08	12.8	1.12
Branch meetings 1979	5.45	3.7	4.64	4.0	0.64
Satisfaction with settlement	2.95	1.1	2.85	1.5	0.29
Increase expected	13.85	3.3	12.04	4.9	1.44
View of management	3.40	1.2	2.83	1.3	1.42
Departmental I.R.	2.10	0.6	2.00	0.9	0.35
Political position	3.22	0.8	3.45	1.1	0.77
Interest in politics	2.26	0.7	2.17	0.9	0.37

Bibliography

ALLEN, V.L. (1954), *Power in Trade Unions*, Longman.

ARNISON, J. (1970), *The Million-Pound Strike*, Lawrence & Wishart.

ARNOT, R.P. (1955), *A History of the Scottish Miners*, Allen & Unwin.

BACHRACH, P. and BARATZ, M.S. (1970), *Power and Poverty: Theory and Practice*, Oxford University Press, New York.

BAIN, G.S. (1970), *The Growth of White-Collar Unionism*, Clarendon Press, Oxford.

BATSTONE, E., BORASTON, I. and FRENKEL, S. (1977), *Shop Stewards in Action*, Blackwell, Oxford.

BATSTONE, E., BORASTON, I. and FRENKEL, S. (1978), *The Social Organisation of Strikes*, Blackwell, Oxford.

BECK, T. (1974), *The Fine Tubes Strike*, Stage One Books.

BEER, S. (1972), *The Brain of the Firm*, Herder & Herder, New York.

BERMAN, P. (1974), *Revolutionary Organization*, D.C. Heath, Lexington.

BOWEN, P. (1976), *Social Control in Industrial Organisations*, Routledge.

BRYER, R.A., BRIGNALL, T.J. and MAUNDERS, A. (1982), *Accounting for British Steel*, Gower Press.

BURNS, T. and STALKER, G.M. (1961), *The Management of Innovation*, Tavistock.

BURRELL, G. and MORGAN, G. (1979), *Sociological Paradigms and Organisational Analysis*, Heinemann.

CHILD, J., LOVERIDGE, R. and WARNER, M. (1973), 'Towards an organisational study of trade unions', *Sociology*, 7, 71-91.

CLEGG, H.A. (1976), *Trade Unionism Under Collective Bargaining*, Blackwell, Oxford.

CLEGG, H.A., KILLICK, A.J. and ADAMS, R. (1961), *Trade Union Officers*, Blackwell, Oxford.

DEPARTMENT OF TRADE AND INDUSTRY (1973), *British Steel Corporation: Ten Year Development Strategy*, Cmnd 5226, HMSO.

DOCHERTY, C. (1983), *Steel and Steelworkers*, Heinemann.

DROMEY, J. and TAYLOR, G. (1978), *Grunwick: The Workers' Story*, Lawrence & Wishart.

DONOVAN, Lord (Chairman) (1968), *Royal Commission on Trade Unions and Employers' Associations,* HMSO.

EDELSTEIN, J.D. and WARNER, M. (1975), *Comparative Union Democracy,* Allen & Unwin.

ETZIONI, A. (1961), *A Comparative Analysis of Complex Organizations,* Free Press, Glencoe, Illinois.

FLANDERS, A. (1970), *Management and Unions,* Faber & Faber.

FOSH, P. (1981), *The Active Trade Unionist,* Cambridge University Press.

FRENCH, J.R. and RAVEN, B. (1959), 'The bases of social power', in D. CARTWRIGHT (ed.), *Studies in Social Power,* Institute for Social Research, University of Michigan, Ann Arbor.

GALBRAITH, J. (1973), *Designing Complex Organizations,* Addison-Wesley, Reading, Mass.

GLASSMAN, P.B. (1973), 'Persistence and loose coupling in living systems', *Behavioral Science, 18,* 83-98.

GOODMAN, J.F.B. and WHITTINGHAM, T.G. (1969), *Shop Stewards in British Industry,* McGraw-Hill, Maidenhead.

GOULDNER, A. (1954), *Wildcat Strike,* Harper & Row, New York.

HEMINGWAY, J. (1978), *Conflict and Democracy: Studies in Trade Union Government,* Clarendon Press, Oxford.

HILLER, E.T. (1969), *The Strike (1928),* Arno Press, New York.

INTERNATIONAL MARXIST GROUP (1980), *Lessons of the Steel Strike and the Fight to Kick out the Tories,* IMG.

IRON AND STEEL ACT (1980), HMSO.

IRON AND STEEL TRADES CONFEDERATION (1979/1980), *Executive Council Minutes,* ISTC.

IRON AND STEEL TRADES CONFEDERATION, *Man and Metal,* 1978, 1979. *Steelworkers Banner,* 1980, 1-14. *ISTC Banner,* 1980/1982, ISTC.

IRON AND STEEL TRADES CONFEDERATION (1980), *New Deal for Steel,* ISTC.

IRON AND STEEL TRADES CONFEDERATION (1976/1977/1978/1979), Annual Conference Reports, ISTC.

JANIS, I. (1972), *Victims of Groupthink,* Houghton Mifflin, Boston.

JOHNSTON, E. (1975), *Industrial Action,* Arrow.

KARSH, B. (1958, *Diary of a Strike,* University of Illinois Press, Urbana, Illinois.

KATZ, D. and KAHN, R.L. (1978), *The Social Psychology of Organizations* (1st edition, 1966), 2nd edition, Wiley, New York.

KELLY, J.E. and NICHOLSON, N. (1980), 'The causation of strikes: A review of the literature and the potential contribution of social psychology', *Human Relations, 33,* 853-883.

LANE, T. and ROBERTS, K. (1971), *Strike at Pilkingtons,* Fontana.

LAWRENCE, P.R. and LORSCH, J. (1967), *Organization and Environment,* Harvard University Press, Cambridge, Mass.

LIPSET, S.M., TROW, M. and COLEMAN, J. (1956), *Union Democracy,* Free Press, Glencoe, Illinois.

LUKES, S. (1974), *Power,* Macmillan.

MARCH, J. and SIMON, H. (1958), *Organizations,* Wiley, New York.

MARSH, A. and GILLIES, J. (1981), 'The incidence of picketing in 1979', *Personnel Review, 10* (2), 16-22.

MARSH, P. (1967), *The Anatomy of a Strike,* Institute for Race Relations.

MATHEWS, J. (1972), *Ford Strike: the workers' story,* Panther.

MERTON, R.K. (1957), *Social Theory and Social Structure,* Free Press, Glencoe, Illinois.

MINTZBERG, H. (1979), *The Structuring of Organizations,* Prentice-Hall, Englewood Cliffs, N.J.

MORAN, J. (1964), *NATSOPA, Seventy Five Years,* NATSOPA.

NICHOLSON, N., URSELL, G. and BLYTON, P. (1981), *The Dynamics of White Collar Unionism,* Academic Press.

OVENDEN, K. (1978), *The Politics of Steel,* Macmillan.

PARSONS, T. (1949), *The Structure of Social Action,* Free Press, Glencoe, Illinois.

PETTIGREW, A. (1979), 'On studying organizational cultures', *Administrative Science Quarterly, 24,* 570-581.

PFEFFER, J. (1981), *Power in Organizations,* Pitman, Marshfield, Mass.

PITT, M. (1978), *The World on our Backs: Kent miners and the 1972 miners strike,* Lawrence & Wishart.

POPE, L. (1942), *Millhands and Preachers,* Yale University Press, New Haven, Conn.

PUGH, D. (ed.) (1971), *Writers and Organisations,* Penguin, Harmondsworth.

ROBERTS, B.C. (1956), *Trade Union Government and Administration in Great Britain,* Bell.

ROSEN, H. and ROSEN, R.A.H. (1955), *The Union Member Speaks,* Prentice-Hall, Englewood Cliffs, N.J.

SALAMAN, G. (1979), *Work Organizations: Resistance and Control,* Longman.

SEIDMAN, J., LONDON, J., KARSH, B. and TAGLIOCOZZO, D.L. (1958), *The Worker Views His Union,* University of Chicago Press, Chicago.

SHEFFIELD CITY COUNCIL (1980), *Sheffield and Rotherham Steel Industry Study,* SCC, Sheffield.

SILVERMAN, D. (1970), *The Theory of Organizations,* Heinemann.

SOCIALIST WORKERS PARTY (1980), *Steelworkers' Power,* SWP.

SOUTH YORKSHIRE POLICE (1980), *The National Steel Strike 1980,* Unpublished Report, South Yorkshire Police, Sheffield.

STRAUSS, A. (1978), *Negotiations,* Jossey-Bass, San Francisco.

STRAUSS, A., SCHATZMAN, L., ERLICH, D., BUCHER, R. and SABSHIN, M. (1963), 'The hospital and its negotiated order', in E. FRIEDSON (ed.), *The Hospital in Modern Society,* Macmillan, New York.

TAJFEL, H. (1978), 'Intergroup Behaviours II: group perspectives', in H. TAJFEL and C. FRASER (eds.), *Introducing Social Psychology,* Penguin, Harmondsworth.

TANNENBAUM, A.S. and KAHN, R.L. (1958), *Participation in Union Locals,* Row, Peterson, Evanston, Illinois.

THOMPSON, J.D. (1967), *Organizations in Action,* McGraw-Hill, New York.

TRADES UNION CONGRESS (1979), *Conduct of Industrial Disputes,* TUC.

UPHAM, M. (1980), 'British Steel: retrospect and prospect', *Industrial Relations Journal, 11,* 5-21.

UPHAM, M. (1983), 'What will happen to steel?', in T. MANWARING and J.E. KELLY (eds.), *For Popular Socialism: The Alternative Economic Strategy and Beyond,* CSE Books.

WALTON, R.E. and McKERSIE, R.B. (1965), *A Behavioral Theory of Labor Negotiations,* McGraw-Hill, New York.

WARREN, J. (1982), 'The restructuring of British Steel, 1980-1981', *Economic Bulletin, 9,* 14-21.

WARNER, W.N. and LOW, J.O. (1947), *The Social System of a Modern Factory,* Yale University Press, New Haven, Conn.

WEICK, K.E. (1979), *The Social Psychology of Organizing* (1st edition, 1969), 3rd edition, Addison-Wesley, Reading, Mass.

WILLMAN, P. (1980), 'Leadership and trade union principles', *Industrial Relations Journal, 11,* 39-49.

YORKSHIRE, HUMBERSIDE STEEL STRIKE COMMITTEE (1980), *Steel Strike,* YHSSC, Sheffield.

Index

A113   0668313 4

HD 5366 .I52 1980 H37

Hartley, Jean.

Steel strike